PENGUIN BOOKS

THE SELF-TAUGHT GARDENER

Sydney Eddison is the author of three books of garden writing and has lectured and taught widely on the subject. Her own garden has been featured in numerous magazines and on television. She lives in Newtown, Connecticut.

The
Self-Taught
Gardener

Lessons from a Country Garden

Sydney Eddison

Illustrations by Steve Buchanan

PENGUIN BOOKS

PENGUIN BOOKS
Published by the Penguin Group
Penguin Putnam Inc., 375 Hudson Street, New York, New York 10014, U.S.A.
Penguin Books Ltd, 27 Wrights Lane, London W8 5TZ, England
Penguin Books Australia Ltd, Ringwood, Victoria, Australia
Penguin Books Canada Ltd, 10 Alcorn Avenue, Toronto, Ontario, Canada M4V 3B2
Penguin Books (N.Z.) Ltd, 182–190 Wairau Road, Auckland 10, New Zealand

Penguin Books Ltd, Registered Offices:
Harmondsworth, Middlesex, England

First published in the United States of America by Viking Penguin,
a division of Penguin Books USA Inc. 1997
Published in Penguin Books 1998

1 3 5 7 9 10 8 6 4 2

ILLUSTRATION CREDITS:
First color photograph insert: page 1 by Mark Kane,
Copyright Taunton Press, Inc.; pages 4, 5, and 6 by Chris Curless,
Copyright Taunton Press, Inc.; page 7 by Sydney Eddison.
Other photographs and all line drawings by Steve Buchanan.

THE LIBRARY OF CONGRESS HAS CATALOGUED THE HARDCOVER AS FOLLOWS:
Eddison, Sydney, date.
The self-taught gardener / by Sydney Eddison.
p.   cm.
Includes index.
ISBN 0-670-86071-9 (hc.)
ISBN 0 14 02.4555 3 (pbk.)
1. Landscape gardening.   2. Flower gardening.   I. Title.
SB473.E33   1997
635.9—dc20   96–36151

Printed in the United States of America
Set in Goudy
Designed by Kathryn Parise

This book is dedicated to the gardeners
for whom it was written, and to
those who made it possible,
especially

Martha and Bill
Lynden and Leigh
Ragna and Tom

Acknowledgments

❧

Ten years ago, the premiere issue of *Fine Gardening* was still a gleam in the eye of its first editor, Roger Holmes. At that time, he and I used to spend a lot of time talking about gardening and what gardeners need and want to know. Roger was an experienced editor and talented woodworker, but relatively new to gardening. Our conversations over the years planted the seeds of this book, and it was Roger who helped me forge the outline.

Fine Gardening also brought me the friendship of Rita and Steve Buchanan. Rita, who followed Roger as the magazine's editor, has helped with scientific questions, and Steve's drawings have doubled the value of the text. It was his idea to make the illustrations look like sketches from the notebooks that played such a vital part in my gardening education.

The present editor, Lee Anne White, has kindly given me permission to use photos of my garden that were first published in *Fine Gardening*. They were taken by other friends on the staff, Chris Curless and former editor Mark Kane. Thank you all.

As for the McKeons, Lynden Miller, and Ragna Goddard, who let me pick their brains and use their gardens, I don't know where to start. I can only say that your kindness has been in a good cause. You have set a shining example and given encouragement to other gardeners. My friend Mary Stambaugh once said, "It's so important, if you are going to be a gardener, to be as generous as you can." Thank you, Mary. And thank you, Peter Wooster, Maureen and Dick

Acknowl-
edgments
*

McLachlan, Diane Campbell, Mike Ruggiero, Betty Ajay, Betty Graubaum, and Jeni Webber.

Words fail me when I think of Gregory Piotrowski's contribution to this and other books I've written. A gardener at the New York Botanical Garden, he has with care and patience corrected botanical nomenclature and caught errors. For this book, he suggested keeping the Latin names that appear in the text to a minimum so that readers could focus on the business of gardening.

Courtney Hodell, my editor, has been wonderful throughout; my agent, Caroline Press, is a treasure; and my spouse is a saint. What more can I say? This has really been the dream team.

Contents

Introduction

✿

In the fall of 1960, the last thing on my mind was gardening. My husband and I were recently married and had just bought an old farmhouse in southwestern Connecticut. When we first saw the house, it was surrounded by a forest on fire with red, yellow, and gold autumn foliage. When we took possession in January, there was a foot of snow on the ground.

After moving in, I remember looking around the unfurnished living room and suddenly feeling a great surge of proprietary excitement. But it did not compare to the thrill I felt when I looked out-of-doors. The black-and-white landscape dropped away to the east and unscrolled upward to the north and west, like a Japanese print.

That winter, we concentrated on the inside of the house, but the instant the snow began to melt, my gaze turned outward. Beyond an unkempt lawn dotted with old maples and decrepit apple trees, forest stretched across what had once been open farmland. Through the leafless undergrowth at the edge of the woods, you could see stone walls and, behind a rampant twiggy hedge, a handsome red barn. It was all ours.

The house, separated from the barn by a few hundred feet, was enveloped in barberry bushes. From the side porch, an uneven fieldstone walk led down to a logging road, which former owners had used as a driveway. On either side of the walk, neglected flower beds showed signs of life, and among the emerging weeds I recognized peony sprouts and clumps of bearded iris.

Nothing arouses the gardening instinct like owning a piece of ground. All winter, we had been building bookcases and scraping years of wax off the beautiful old oak floorboards. What I had in mind was cleaning up the out-of-doors and making it our own, in the same way we were making the house our own. I did not know that the desire to *do* something to the landscape is the first symptom of the gardening bug.

My friends at that time were other schoolteachers, and none were gardeners. Unbelievable as it now seems, sources of information about gardening were few and far between. We had no local garden center, and mail-order nurseries did not automatically fill the mailbox with tempting catalogs. You had to know what you wanted and send away for it.

There were educational programs, if you knew where to look. The nearest for me would have been at the New York Botanical Garden. But it would never have occurred to me to make the two-hour drive to the Bronx. I spent enough time in classrooms during the school year. During vacations, I wanted to play outside. So instead of going to classes, I went in search of a book that would tell me what to do with our landscape.

At the library, books about garden design and gardening occupied half a shelf. The first volume I consulted told me how to double dig a border. Others gave instructions for growing annuals, perennials, and vegetables. But none offered advice on what to do with an overgrown cow pasture. I needed a book that said, "Go out and cut down all those prickly bushes that you hate. In fact, feel free to cut to the ground any straggling shrub that you don't like."

Gardening books should tell you that most common deciduous shrubs recover from this harsh treatment and put forth new growth at the base. They should also define terms like *deciduous*, which is derived from two Latin words— *de*, from, and *cadere*, to fall—and refers to any plant that sheds its leaves in the autumn.

Evergreens, which retain their needles, do not survive drastic pruning, and books should say so. My own feeling is that if something is so ugly that you want to cut it down, it probably won't be missed anyway. Besides, you might prefer to plant something different. I would have welcomed a book that gave me permission to do these things.

A lot of gardening is a matter of common sense, but in order to grow plants you need a little more information. You need to know, for instance, whether your site is sunny or shady. Only a southern exposure guarantees sun all day long, but six hours is considered sunny and provides plenty of light for most sun-loving plants.

Shade is a more complex subject. Obviously, there are degrees of shade, but you don't need to read elaborate descriptions of each. You need to know that plants recommended for partial shade can stand morning sun. Afternoon sun is another story. The heat is more intense and continues to build until early evening. No shade-lover will prosper if it is exposed to several hours of hot afternoon sun. Fortunately, there are a number of exceptionally tolerant plants that put up with either sun or shade.

Most books tell you more than you need to know about more plants than you can ever grow. What you really need are two relatively short lists—one for sun and one for shade—of beautiful, indestructible, readily available plants that can be combined to make an effective year-round garden.

In the chapters entitled Some Easy Perennials for Sun and Some Easy Perennials for Shade, you will meet my choices. There are about a dozen in each category. At the back of the book, there are expanded lists compiled with the aid of several gardening friends, each of whom contributed ten favorites and a few runners-up. To be included in the final list, all the plants had to receive at least three votes, including mine.

Today, gardening is "in." Everyone you meet either has a garden or wants one. Books, courses, nurseries, mail-order firms, and garden centers abound. Computer technology has made it possible to chat with other gardeners on the Internet and bring plant descriptions to the screen. There are even programs that help you design your own garden using three-dimensional images. The amount of information available to would-be gardeners is overwhelming.

My gut feeling is that gardeners really do not need another book or computer program. They need a gardening friend who is a step or two ahead of them. Think of me as that friend. I am here to pass along what I have learned, to applaud your first attempts, and to give you a little guidance as you forge ahead.

First-time homeowners are highly susceptible to the gardening bug. The size of your property doesn't matter. It may be a small city lot or a rural spread. But it's yours, and you want to do something to it. In addition to a gardening friend, you need a road map. The purpose of the map is not to tell you which roads to take but to show you possible routes.

This book is meant for gardeners-in-the-making who find themselves standing at back doors around the country musing upon a course of action. If you think to yourself, "Maybe I should cut down those evergreens blocking the dining room windows," do it, and you will be taking the first step down the garden path. One thing inevitably leads to another. Next, you'll want some flowers for color.

If you feel like digging up a circle in the middle of the lawn and planting marigolds, go right ahead. Every really great gardener starts out this way—by grabbing a spade. Your first garden may not please you, but next year you can change it and try something else.

Maybe a rectilinear bed would look better in relation to the geometry of the house. Put up a picket fence around a square. Put an arbor in the middle of one side. See how it looks. Divide the space within into four beds, and put in annuals, perennials, vegetables, and herbs, or some of each.

If you still don't like the look of the garden, don't worry. You can always move the perennials. For that matter, you can move the fence. Nothing about a garden is written in stone—unless you are talking about installations like driveways, swimming pools, and terraces.

Even seemingly permanent structures need not clutter up your life and garden forever. We gleefully filled in our swimming pool, and a friend of ours made her pool into a beautiful rock garden. Just remember that making changes in so-called hardscape costs money.

As you go about whacking down shrubs and digging the inevitable flower bed, tell yourself that this is *your* property and you can do anything you like to it. If you are feeling insecure, listen to Hanna Rion, who wrote: "When you buy a piece of land, remember—you own all above it; you own that far reach of ether in which the stars drift over your land, the moon as it hangs above your trees, the sun as it passes through your sky-claim; and best of all you possess all the dreams which lie between you and infinity.

"And you own down, down, down to the center of the earth's axis, and this is why owning land gives one such a sense of anchorage and solidity."

To be as joyous as Hanna Rion, you have to be independent. You can't worry about what someone else thinks of what you are doing to your landscape. Say to yourself, "I can make any kind of garden here that I want." There is no one way to make a garden. There are hundreds of ways, all of them right—if they work. And they will work if your plants are healthy and the garden does your heart good.

Pleasure is the only reasonable excuse for making a garden. Unless you

My garden is informally arranged along an imaginary line that runs from the center of the house northward.

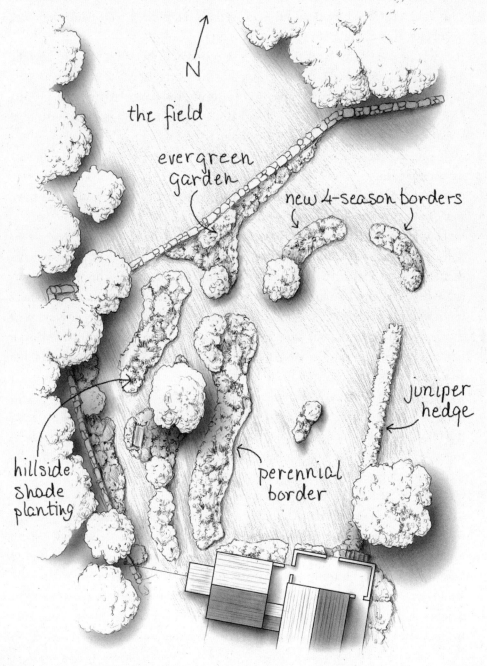

N

the field

evergreen garden

new 4-season borders

juniper hedge

hillside shade planting

perennial border

garden for the fun of it, there's no point in gardening at all. You will soon know whether you like playing with plants and trying to do something with your land. If you enjoy this kind of activity, you are a gardener at heart, and I can help you. At the very least, I can point out my mistakes, and you can avoid them. But you will make others. Making mistakes is an essential part of your education. Remember that gardening is a very forgiving art.

The purpose of this book is to give you courage. That's all it takes to become a self-taught gardener. You have to step in where angels fear to tread. You have to be foolish, stubborn, and adventurous. It also helps to be prepared for surprises—some glorious, some horrible. Most important of all, you have to love the process of gardening, not just the product.

If you embark on garden making in this spirit, I promise that you will have a wonderful garden. It will be yours in a way that has nothing to do with mere ownership. A garden is an ongoing story. It is an autobiography. Gardens have souls, and your garden will have your soul.

Having seen many gardens, I believe with all my heart that the most original, satisfying, and beautiful are those made by the garden owner. I also believe that self-taught gardeners are the happiest gardeners. Advice is fine. So is physical help. But if you do a lot of the work yourself; if you strive to acquire the necessary skills; wrestle with a vision of what you want and the appropriateness of that vision in terms of your land, your strength, and your budget; if you observe minutely and digest the lessons learned by doing, you will have a garden that fits you, your landscape, and your lifestyle.

Gardening is not easy. American gardeners have a lot to contend with in terms of weather. Except for a few favored locations, like the Pacific Northwest, the climate leaves much to be desired. The Middle West features staggering extremes of hot and cold. New England can also be brutal; my English husband describes our Connecticut weather as "uncivilized."

However, if you deplore the climate in your particular area, remember that some plants actually *like* these conditions and are adapted to them. Fortunately, we are rediscovering American native plants. European gardeners have been using and admiring American perennials for years: joe-pye weed, black-eyed Susan, goldenrod, butterfly weed, asters, and others. Wherever you live, look around. See what plants are flourishing along the roads, in wild places, and in neighborhood gardens. Every garden needs tough, dependable plants to carry it through the growing season and, indeed, through the year.

Of course, many discouraging things happen in gardens. Woodchucks eat favorite perennials. Once-handsome ornamental trees succumb to disease, air pollution, and age. Shrubs get hopelessly out of hand or dwindle and die. Some losses are just bad luck; others are the result of negligence, unsuitable plant choices, or sheer stupidity. Sometimes, you can't resist planting something that needs sun in a shady spot in the hope of getting away with it.

Once you have been bitten by the gardening bug, though, you will rise above disappointments. I am here to egg you on. My fondest hope is that this book will be to gardeners what Dr. Benjamin Spock's book has been to generations of parents—a source of comfort and reassurance.

Because my mother was English and a trip to her homeland raised my gardening consciousness, I use the word "garden" in its broad sense. To me, a garden includes: the piece of property with its own unique features and naturally occurring vegetation, plus flowers, shrubs, and trees added for their ornamental value; the house itself with all its man-made comforts and conveniences, such as deck, terrace, garage; and any other outbuildings.

A word about the arrangement of this book. I believe that gardeners learn in an order that has nothing to do with programmatic study and everything to do with the impatient nature of the beast. Therefore, you won't find "site selection" followed by "soil preparation." These topics will be introduced as necessary and in a progression dictated by real-life garden making.

At first, gardeners tend to feel overwhelmed by their land. Compared to the interior of a house, the out-of-doors appears vast, disorganized, and unmanageable. So the early chapters offer tips on reducing vegetative clutter and tackling what *is* manageable.

Because at some point everyone wants flowers, the core of the book deals with making and caring for a flower bed. You don't fall in love with gardening by double digging, you fall in love with the face of a pansy, the color of a daylily, the perfume of a rose. But if you really *want* a beautiful shrub rose, you resign yourself to digging a hole 3 feet wide and 2 feet deep; if you adore daylilies, removing their faded flowers every day is the least you can do in return for their weeks of bloom.

The nitty-gritty of gardening is just the price you have to pay for all the wonderful things that you want to grow. This book explains the techniques of preparing the ground and tending the plants as you go along. You don't have to master a number of steps in sequence. Nobody gardens that way. You learn on the job—by doing. That's half the fun of it.

The advice offered in the chapters that follow comes from the heart and from practical experience, my own and that of friends. You have no idea how generous and eager people have been to help with this book. Many are people who have so much to do that they have to go into hiding in order to grab a few hours in their own gardens. But they want to get other gardeners going.

While some are now professionals, all are passionate home gardeners. And we all began the same way—by digging a hole and putting a plant in it. Our gardens serve as examples. They are real-life gardens at different stages of development, made by self-taught gardeners with varying amounts of outside help, which we will also discuss. So pluck up your courage and join this happy breed.

Part One

Getting Started

❈ ❈

Moral Support

✣

Every gardener I know has, at some period in his or her life, been blessed with a mentor. For one, this benign, encouraging figure was a grandfather who grew prize roses; for another, a neighbor who welcomed a little boy into her garden and gave him plants to take home; another was inspired by her uncle, an architect, "who should have been a garden designer," and another by a grandmother, who held spiderweb parties for her grandchildren. "A present would be hidden in the garden. It was tied to a string, and you had to untangle all the strings to find it, but you were not to walk in the flower beds."

I was an adult and had been gardening for several years before I found my mentor. Five feet tall and in her seventies at the time we met, Helen Gill was a shy, often abrupt New Englander with a sharp mind and a passion for plants. Her architect husband, Johnny, exuded southern charm and was as gregarious as Helen was reserved. Domestically and horticulturally, they were a superb team, and for many years their garden was a mecca for younger gardeners. They had transformed a few acres of abandoned farmland into a country garden that was both formal and informal.

It was surrounded on three sides by fieldstone walls. Openings in the walls were flanked by columnar yews and by matching borders thickly planted with a ravishing collection of trees, shrubs, bulbs, and perennials. The proportions were perfect; the layout, harmonious; and the beds filled with more plants than were dreamed of in my philosophy. Today, many of the Gills' plants still thrive in my garden.

I wrote about Helen and Johnny in my first book and, shortly after it was published, received a letter from Pennsylvania landscape architect Alice C. H. Farley. Her letter read: "Quite at random, I opened your book at a chapter entitled The Gills. At first, I thought, 'Oh, she knows some people named Gill, too. But not *my* Gills.' Reading about your friendship with them was like reliving *my* friendship with the two wonderful people who planted the seeds of my love of gardening twenty years ago."

Threadleaf coreopsis
(<u>Coreopsis</u>
<u>verticillata</u>)

Delicate foliage on
bushy plant covered
with long-blooming
yellow flowers.

When Alice Farley met her husband-to-be, she wanted to introduce him to her gardening mentors and arranged a visit with the Gills. "They were gracious and . . . adorable. We called them the 'cookie people.' Not because the food they served was homey—it was actually rather sophisticated—but because they were little and round, twinkly and crinkly—like homemade cookies. As I look at my garden, I am reminded of them over and over again. I've got lamb's ears, geraniums, Siberian iris, amsonia, campanula, and more—all from them."

Not all mentors are dear little old couples. But many are almost as lavish in their generosity as the Gills. I have recently met a group of young gardeners in their thirties who have plied me with plants and jolted me out of my comfortable rut. They have introduced me to unfamiliar annuals and whetted my appetite for tender perennials. They have traveled extensively, visiting gardens and botanizing in faraway places like Chile, New Zealand, and South Africa. They are extremely knowledgeable, and they share the richness of their experience with the same eagerness as their older counterparts.

Being a self-taught gardener does not mean gardening in a vacuum. There is a vast support system of gardeners out there waiting for you. But you may need a little help in finding these kindred spirits. If you are lucky enough to live near a botanical garden, arboretum, or nature center, start there. You will discover that their education departments offer a smorgasbord of classes, lectures, and seminars, and that gardeners of all levels of experience flock to them.

Community colleges and your state university also have educational programs of interest to gardeners. So-called land-grant colleges and universities have a Cooperative Extension System. Originally the federal government gave land to these institutions on the condition that they provide courses in agriculture and the mechanical arts. In addition, many offer courses in horticulture. Even if the university is miles away from you, the Extension System maintains a number of branches around the state. And many of them conduct master gardener classes.

The master gardener program is an example of the total immersion approach to horticulture. The classes are taught by professors from the sponsoring college or university and meet one day a week for twelve weeks. To become a certified master gardener, you have to volunteer a further sixty hours to answer gardening questions by phone at the Extension office. If you embark on the program, you will

Helen's flower
(*Helenium autumnale*)

Tall, leafy stalks topped
with small flowers,
distinct for their toothed
petals and round
central knob.

5

learn a great deal. You will also meet other gardeners, which, for my money, is the purpose of the exercise.

Joining a garden club is another way to meet gardeners. Some clubs have an active membership of outdoor gardeners. Others are long on flower arranging and short on horticulture. Try to attend a meeting before committing yourself. The majority of women's garden clubs meet in the daytime, and their ranks have been sorely depleted because so many younger members have full-time jobs. In my town, one club meets in the evening for the convenience of the working women.

Though fewer in number, there are also men's garden clubs. All garden clubs engage in civic projects, like planting sidewalk containers, beautifying traffic islands, and cleaning up parks. Some of the larger clubs undertake ambitious projects, like raising money for scholarships in the fields of horticulture and environmental studies.

Horticultural societies and plant societies are more information-oriented and are always coed. These groups hold plant shows and arrange trips, garden visits, and symposiums. I had never been much of a joiner until a friend sold me on membership in the North American Rock Garden Society. "Come to a meeting," she insisted. When I balked, she pointed out that I would meet wonderful gardeners. "Look," she said. "If you were interested in science, wouldn't you want to rub shoulders with people like Einstein?"

Her powers of persuasion won me over. I went, and on the strength of that experience, I now belong to no fewer than six plant societies and two botanical gardens. This is where the gardeners are. At meetings, you will find amateurs and professionals, people who have been gardening for years and people who are just starting out. Every organization I belong to welcomes new members with open arms.

For a rundown on horticultural groups and plant societies, invest in an invaluable paperback book called *Gardening by Mail: A Source Book* by Barbara J. Barton. Ms. Barton is a librarian who got mixed up with plants when a catalog from Wayside Gardens found its way into her mailbox. That was ten years ago. In the introduction to the fourth edition of her sourcebook, she explains what happened:

"As this insatiable habit was developing, one of my greatest frustrations was that there seemed to be no easy way to find out everything I wanted to know. If I saw a lovely plant, where could I get one to try to grow myself? Surely there must be wonderful gardening magazines, but there were very few on news-

Black-eyed Susan
(*Rudbeckia fulgida*
'Goldsturm')

Flowers are bigger and
handsomer than the
native species.

stands—what did *real* gardeners do? Were there plant
and horticultural societies?
Would they allow *me* to join?
Where might I find a horticultural library to browse in?
Even though I'm a longtime refer-
ence librarian myself, it all seemed so difficult! Only *old* gardeners knew—and it
took them years to find out."

Ms. Barton is a woman after my own heart. Having become hooked herself,
she wants to involve others in the engaging pastime of gardening. And because
she has been on the outside looking in, she appreciates the beginner's dilemma of
where to start. In *Gardening by Mail,* she methodically and meticulously shares
the resources she turned up in the course of her research. She provides listings for
dozens of horticultural societies and plant societies and their regional chapters.
There are clubs for everyone, from African violet fanciers to "the tomato crowd."
Dip into these entries. They include brief statements of purpose for each society
and the services they provide. Besides membership in one or more of these
groups, she urges you to ask at your favorite nursery, city recreation department,
or chamber of commerce to find out about local garden groups.

Lastly, Ms. Barton provides a very useful list of books. There is, of course, no
substitute for a gardening mentor, but some books are a real help, and Ms.
Barton separates the grain from the chaff. To be sure, her list is personal, but she
makes sound choices and arranges them in a sensible way: reference books; illustrated books that help in identifying plants; gardening encyclopedias; books on
plants for specific conditions, such as shade or woodland, city balcony or backyard, and plants for specific uses, such as hedges or ground covers. The book list
is relatively short but complete in terms of the areas it covers.

While books can provide information and even inspiration, you still need the encouragement of someone who has been down this road before. The best mentors are uncritical, enthusiastic types who like to see their protégés succeed. They don't lay down the law; they provide moral support and bolster your self-confidence. Ask them questions. If you are curious about something and are interested in the answer, there is no such thing as a stupid question. Mentors are flattered and happy to respond. There is no better way to learn than to stand in the middle of a beautiful garden with its creator and to listen to him or her speak with loving authority about the pleasures and problems of making that garden.

To initiate such a meeting requires chutzpah, but do try it. Walk around your neighborhood; look at foundation plantings, flower beds, trees and shrubs, front and back yards. If you see something you like, lurk around until the gardener appears. Then, express your admiration. You will almost certainly be invited in, because gardeners love to show off their gardens. And if you go home empty-handed, I'd be surprised. Most gardeners are quick with a trowel.

Even if you are loath to tackle neighbors, have not yet found a mentor, and have never taken a class, don't worry. You know more than you think. Everybody brings something unique to garden making—an eye for color, a talent for organizing space, the patience for nurturing plants, the hand-eye coordination needed for constructing cold frames, stone walls, paths, and decks—all these skills and more can be employed in the garden.

If you had asked me thirty-five years ago what I knew about gardening, I would have said, "Next to nothing." I had pulled weeds in my father's vegetable garden and mowed the lawn without enthusiasm. But I had lived in the country all my life, adored wildflowers as a child, and loved playing out-of-doors. Later, I visited my grandmother and aunts in England and fell under the spell of English gardens. These influences eventually found expression in my garden.

It was many years between my first visit to England and having a garden of my own, but the model of English gardens lodged in my subconscious. I had absorbed the idea of a garden as a unit that included the house and its immediate surroundings. Even before I lifted a spade to the rocky Connecticut soil, I felt that our garden must somehow tie together the house, barn, stone walls, rock outcrops, and incidental trees. Having no notion of how to go about making such a garden, I began by raking up sticks and leaves, cutting down brush, and digging flower beds. It wasn't a bad way to start.

Square One

For the sake of discussion, let's say you are in the same boat I was in thirty-five years ago. You are the proud possessors of a house and a piece of ground. Now what? The first step involves taking a good look at what you have. After that, you need to figure out what you want to do with it and how to go about it.

Three different approaches to sorting out the home landscape are available to you: plan making, substitution, and note taking. The first involves measuring and laying out your property on paper. However, many people have difficulty imagining the three-dimensional effect. If you are among them, try substitution. Use props and actual objects to replicate plants and garden structures. For instance, if you are contemplating the installation of a picket fence, put up a temporary fence made of garden stakes—anything to help you visualize the real thing.

Note taking is the easiest way to get a handle on your property. Write down everything that occurs to you. Make a note of ugly spots, things you don't like and want to change, and, conversely, things you want to feature. Get a good illustrated book of shrubs and trees (see Selected Further Reading), and identify those you have and those that you want to add. Jot down observations about your climate and site. If you notice that a howling wind comes in off the sea, you might consider a windbreak of some sort. Keep a notebook and write everything down in it.

I tried a combination of all three methods. First, I drew a ground plan. When

I found it less helpful than expected, I moved on to visual aids like stakes and string. Throughout, I took notes and highly recommend it. But there are other ways of tackling the landscape.

Our young friends the McKeons are dyed-in-the-wool do-it-yourself types. Bill simply fired up his chain saw and, without further ado, began clearing the land. Maureen and Dick McLachlan, who live a couple of miles away, took an entirely different approach. They collaborated with a contractor and a landscaper in the development of their home landscape. Every house on their street boasts well-kept foundation plantings. Narrow beds full of evergreens in the immediate vicinity of a house are always referred to as "foundation plantings." While the neighbors put in a few annuals for summer color, the McLachlans doubled the width of their foundation beds and planted perennials. Whenever I pass by, I notice new additions to the garden, and Maureen is always outside tending her plants.

The Eddison, McLachlan, and McKeon gardens are very different from one another, but each is appropriate in its own way. Your garden will be different from ours because you are who you are and because every piece of property has unique qualities and quirks. However, in New England, most fall into one of the following categories: an older home in a settled neighborhood; a newer home in a subdivision carved out of the woods; a modern Cape, colonial, or ranch in an open field; or a spanking new contemporary perched on a precipitous slope. The last is the most daunting, and seeking professional help may be your best bet (see Appendix A).

Our situation approximated the older-home scenario: a nineteenth-century house with a yard full of overgrown shrubs and mature maple trees. What made our place special was the 800-acre state forest surrounding it. The terrain is sloping, but there are no extreme changes in grade. So ours was not a problem site.

The term "older home" can equally well describe any house built before World War II. If yours belongs to the prewar era, it will almost certainly have full-grown shade trees. This being the case, you have to develop a philosophy about trees. It takes years for them to achieve their maximum beauty, but they are not sacred. If they block out needed sunlight or menace the septic system, it is not a sin to cut them down.

My husband and I have lived long enough to see a piece of land that we cleared thirty years ago turn into a woodland again. In parts of the country where trees are the climax vegetation, every backyard is a potential forest. If you need light or feel hemmed in by trees, go ahead and cut.

Assuming that you have an older home, there is a good chance that the site is relatively level. Level terrain is one of the advantages of a vintage property. Prior to World War II, good building land was abundant. Instead of clinging to cliffs and rock outcrops, houses sat firmly wedded to the ground. In those days, very little foundation showed aboveground. What did show was often constructed of brick or stone and quite handsome to look at.

Foundation planting came about largely in order to hide ugly new building materials, like cement block, and soon became a habit. Minnesota landscape architect C. Colston Burrell has another theory. He attributes the rise of foundation planting to the influence of British landscape designer "Capability" Brown. In the eighteenth century, Brown re-created nature as parkland with grand sweeps of turf and clusters of trees and shrubs. Transplanted to suburban America, this style resulted in the lawn-with-specimen-tree-and-house-hugging-shrubs syndrome.

If you have a perfectly presentable foundation and not too much of it shows, you don't need foundation planting. You certainly shouldn't feel obliged to preserve a stiff row of evergreens that do nothing for your house. Cut them down, and start again. On the other hand, an attractive mixture of evergreen and deciduous shrubs can enhance a house and provide a transition between the man-made structure and the natural landscape. Decide on an individual basis whether or not a foundation planting is in your future.

Outbuildings, such as barns, sheds, or detached garages, are common features of nineteenth- and early-twentieth-century properties. Most older homes have been tinkered with and added to by a succession of owners, so a variety of architectural features and building styles may be present on the same property. If you are wondering how to make these separate elements more cohesive, the easiest way is to tie them together with a system of paths and/or with a uniform ground cover. A ground cover can be a vigorous perennial, like pachysandra or a group of low-growing shrubs. Any desirable plant or group of plants that covers the bare soil with weed-defying vegetation can be described as a ground cover.

Another given with an older property is a collection of large, untidy shrubs. In the Northeast, huge mops of bridal wreath and forsythia are familiar sights, along with thickets of privet, lilac, and flowering quince. In the winter or early spring, cut these shrubs down to the ground, and they will resprout from the base. By the following year, they will look like new, small shrubs, and in three or four seasons they will resume flowering.

Evergreens fall into two categories, those with needles and those with true leaves. The latter are called broadleaf evergreens. Representative broadleaf evergreens include azaleas, rhododendrons, mountain laurels, and look-alike Japanese andromedas. These, along with juniper and gloomy, deer-ravaged yews, are almost mandatory in old-fashioned plantings.

The azaleas, rhododendrons, mountain laurels, and andromedas can be pruned as drastically as the deciduous shrubs previously mentioned. Cut them down to stubs. Again, it will take several years for them to recover, but it is worth the wait. You will have much better-looking shrubs in the end.

Yew is one of the few needled evergreens that respond to the same kind of cruelty. You can cut it right down, and it will put forth new growth from the base. In a few years, you'll be back in business. Juniper, spruce, and pine do not recover from harsh pruning. If these have been badly neglected, scrap them.

Our property had its share of tired, messy shrubs. In addition, there was a jungle of wild vegetation and a smattering of trees—here, there, and everywhere. House, barn, an outhouse, and a chicken coop completed our landscape. I had no idea what to do with any of it, but I knew that I wanted more order. At this point, I went out and bought a book about landscape design. It recommended making a ground plan of the property, which I did (see "How to Make a Base Plan" in Appendix A).

I spent a laborious spring vacation with tape measures and graph paper and finally completed a bird's-eye view of the 2 acres surrounding our house. Getting it all on paper was a magnum opus, and having done so, I was disappointed to find that the plan bore little resemblance to the actual landscape. The pronounced downward tilt of the land did not show on the plan.

Ground plans are like maps. They cannot help you visualize the lay of the land, but they can help you understand space and distance. From making the plan, I learned something about the scale of the out-of-doors. Dividing large garden areas with walls, hedges, and fences into "outdoor rooms" is a time-honored device for organizing space. But even a small backyard "room" is considerably larger than the average indoor room. So when you are dealing with the out-of-doors, *think big*. A bed that looks small on paper will look *tiny* on the ground.

Making a ground plan also shows you whether there are any logical connections among the elements in your landscape. Are the shrubs and trees arranged in groups or scattered around the lawn? Are there paths, and do they have destinations? Is there a convenient way to get from the garage to the kitchen? How do you know which is the front door, and is the route to the entrance well defined?

If you are dealing with level ground and a modest area, drawing a ground plan can be a worthwhile exercise. It is not difficult to figure out dimensions, and by taking measurements you become intimate with your land. You may not know what to do with the plan, but tuck it away for future reference. It contains useful information, and you may want to refer to it when you are considering the bigger picture.

Not everyone wants to tackle a ground plan. I agree with interior designer Jeffrey Bilhuber, who feels that unless you have a certain amount of experience, drawing a plan on graph paper isn't that much help. For homeowners in the throes of planning rooms, he recommends substituting real objects of about the right size for pieces of furniture and moving them around until a satisfactory arrangement results.

You can do the same thing in the backyard. Outline a flower bed or garden path with a flexible garden hose. If you want to see flowers from the terrace, and the outline of the bed doesn't show, move the hose until it is clearly visible. Likewise, if you catch yourself cutting corners and not walking within the outlines of your proposed path, put the path somewhere else.

To visualize the placement of trees, use posts or poles. Cut brush and stick it in the ground, or turn a garbage can upside down to replicate a shrub. Employ any movable object that suggests outline, form, and height. Live with your makeshift garden for a while. If you don't like it after a few days, rearrange your props.

If you get fed up with your garden looking like a junkyard, get out your notebook. It should be cheap and sturdy enough to hold up if it gets damp. Note taking will clear your head and help you establish garden priorities. Make your notes copious, detailed, and as specific as possible. Sometimes, the solution presents itself when you identify the problem.

For instance, if you don't like the terrace, analyze what you don't like about it. Ours was too narrow and got too much sun for midday comfort in the summer. In the end, we made a new seating area under one of the apple trees and used the terrace to display sun-loving container plants.

On your lists of things to do, there will be projects that you can do yourself and others that will require help. There will be things that you change your mind about and things that you shouldn't do at all. Anything that requires a permit is a job for professionals who are familiar with local building codes.

My husband and I had "his" and "hers" lists. His considerations were practical; mine were primarily aesthetic. Between us, we came up with a great many projects. But we soon discovered that our time, energy, knowledge, and financial resources were limited. Obviously, we couldn't do everything at once. For us, projects like clearing the brush and poison ivy took years.

We had high-priority projects that seemed to demand immediate attention. At the top of my husband's list was finding a better way to approach the house by car and on foot; mine was tearing out the old, ugly foundation planting around the house. Undertaking the first involved help. We got a truckload of gravel from the local sand and gravel company and had it distributed along the route we indicated between the house and the barn. At that time, we were still using the barn as a garage. When we added an attached garage and relocated the driveway, we grassed over the gravel. This involved importing a few yards of topsoil, raking it over the gravel, and sowing grass seed—all jobs within our limited expertise.

My foundation-planting project was easy, too. I cut down the barberry bushes around the house with loppers and grubbed out the roots with a mattock—the gardening implement of choice for many of the jobs confronting us. It was early in my gardening career, and the first replacements for the barberry bushes were not ideal, but they were an improvement. There have been many changes since. Be prepared to make changes and to accept change.

We tackled several of the projects on our lists prematurely. At the time, a walk to the front door seemed important, but we hadn't been in the house long enough for the pattern of our lives to emerge. As things turned out, the front door is only opened once in a blue moon. The first Christmas, a United Parcel Service driver made use of the new walk to deliver a side of smoked salmon. He stuffed the package between the storm door and the front door, where it languished for three months.

Our ill-considered swimming pool was a doomed project that we never should have attempted without expert advice. The upshot was a badly engineered blot on the landscape that we were stuck with for fifteen years. At the end of that time, the pool's fiberglass sides cracked and caved in. It was a great

relief, but the moral of this tale is: If a project on your list has lasting consequences, restrain yourself until you have more experience, more money, and
good professional counsel.

Maureen and Dick McLachlan's property was completely different from ours.
The beautiful open meadow within a stone's throw of town had been in Dick's
family for years, and when the tract was sold, he and Maureen kept the corner
lot of about an acre for themselves. Nine years ago, they built a modified Cape-
style house partway down a gentle slope.

Immediately, they realized that their number-one priority was privacy for the
deck on the east side of the house. They enclosed two sides with walls of airy lattice and planted honeysuckle at the foot of each section. "It was very pretty and
very fragrant," says Maureen, "but it didn't give us the privacy we wanted, so we
replaced it with wisteria instead." She is rueful about her second choice. "Privacy absolutely took over! I had no idea what we were getting into with the wisteria. There is a lot of work to keeping it chopped back, and in the fall, it's a
nuisance because it sheds its leaves constantly. I do like it, but I'm not sure that I
would do it again."

Maureen describes herself as "a very beginner" when it comes to gardening,
but certain things were important to her from the start. She didn't want to see
any house foundation, and she did want a planting that included evergreens to
welcome visitors and lead them to the front door. The contractor's careful siting
and grading accomplished the first goal. A knowledgeable landscaper provided
needled and broadleaf evergreens and a selection of deciduous shrubs—all in
good scale with the house.

While he was at it, Maureen asked the young man who did the planting to
make the beds extra deep. She wanted to put in flowers. "But," she says, "it
wasn't until quite recently that the shrubs were mature enough to give me a
background. Now, we have filled in among them with annuals and perennials."
The effect is a delightful dooryard garden that looks attractive all year.

Martha and Bill McKeon's property included a single-story house built in the
1930s and 4 acres of swampy woodland. The site is level but very wet. A small
stream runs down the north side of what is now their front lawn, curves abruptly
south, and fills the pond that lies a hundred feet or so from the front door.
When the young couple took possession, swamp maples came right up to the
house. "You couldn't even see the pond," says Martha. "We used to throw stones
into the water so that people would know it was there."

Making the beds of a foundation planting deeper and adding perennials, as the McLachlans have done here, is a good way to start a garden.

They wanted to see the pond; they also wanted a lawn; and Martha wanted a vegetable garden. At the time, Bill was working with his brother-in-law, who was a professional landscaper. Fortunately, both men were experienced with chain saws. To Martha's satisfaction, they mounted an attack on the encroaching forest. With every tree they cut, she could see more potential in the land.

"The first year we were here—we moved in July—it was too late to do anything except chip away at it. We had no kind of plan at all. We just knew we had to get rid of the trees. It wasn't a case of removing a tree because I realized we'd have more sky or more light. I had no idea what it would look like beforehand, but it always looked better and opened up a dozen possibilities I hadn't dreamed of."

This brings me to one of the most important things I have learned about garden making: One action inevitably leads to another. I call it the Scrabble Theory of Design. In the word-building game of Scrabble, you put down a few letters. Suddenly, you think, "I know a word." And you add to it. It works in the garden, too.

The minute you *do* something to the landscape, another project presents itself. You set to work on that, and another occurs to you. Gardens and gardeners are created by increments. Eventually, the cumulative increments reveal a pattern, and the pattern changes and grows with the gardener. There's no end to it.

For the moment, take the Scrabble Theory on faith. Go out in your garden and *do* something—move a shrub; cut down some brush; rake up bits of debris. If you have foundation plantings, make the beds wider and add some flowers. Start a planting area around a rock or tree that sticks out of the lawn. If you have a rock *and* a tree, link them together with ground cover, and see what happens next.

Tools of the Trade

✿

Naturally, gardening projects require tools, but most beginning gardeners buy too many. You don't need a lot of paraphernalia. Invest in a few good tools and don't pay for cachet. Save the money for plants. Although I enjoy poring over catalogs full of gorgeous English gardening implements, sturdy American-made tools fill the bill. A few years ago in a weak moment, I splurged on a beautiful imported spade from one of the mail-order catalogs. Today, the original green paint still adorns its blade, while the blade of a thirty-year-old shovel I got from the Newtown hardware store gleams with frequent use.

What you need in the way of tools depends to some extent on the kind of gardening you are going to do and on the type of soil you find on your property. If you are lucky enough to have eighteen inches of rock-free topsoil, you probably won't need a crowbar. But if you garden in rocky areas, this heavy steel rod with a wedge-shaped end is a godsend for prying out boulders.

Under normal gardening conditions, a dozen basic tools are all you need. For breaking ground in rocky, heavy, root-ridden soil, a pick or a mattock is required. A pick is familiar to anyone who has seen Walt Disney's *Snow White and the Seven Dwarfs*. It is a heavy tool with a long, narrow, slightly curved head, pointed at both ends. A stout wooden handle fits into a hole in the center. The pick is ideal for penetrating

A pick has a curved head pointed at both ends.
A mattock is similar, but with a cutting end instead of a point.

18

hardpan and getting out rocks. The mattock is similar. A 36-inch handle fits snugly into the center of a head that resembles a medieval weapon. One end has a blunt horizontal blade; the other is axlike. Use the horizontal blade to break through the compacted soil and the sharp end to chop off roots.

To prepare a flower bed or vegetable garden, you need a shovel with a pointed blade to cut through the sod and loosen the soil. As form follows function and a shovel is meant for lifting earth, the blade is rounded like a scoop. The shank between the handle and the blade is arched for easy handling. Handles can be either full length (48 inches) or short (from 27 inches upward to 32 or more inches). If you are tall, you will probably prefer the long handle.

The primary function of a spade is not earth lifting. It is used for working soil that has already been prepared and for tasks like planting, transplanting, and dividing mat-forming perennials. Both blade and shank are flat. Spades have handles from 27 to 32 or more inches in length with a "D" or "DY" grip at the top. The blades come in different configurations: straight edged; slightly curved; pointed; and with a rounded edge. I have two spades and never use either of them. Instead, I use my trusty shovel for everything, including the jobs usually assigned to a spade. It is a matter of habit and personal preference.

In addition to a shovel and/or a spade, you need a spading fork with four flat or square tines designed for lifting sod. It is also useful for moving perennials whose roots might be damaged by a shovel or spade, and it is by far the most efficient tool for digging manure into the soil. (Optional: a fork with many long, slightly curved oval tines. Twice the width of a spading fork, this type is intended for lifting large, relatively light loads, like hay and mulch.)

At the business end of digging and earth-moving tools, like shovels, spades, and forks, the head, shank, and socket

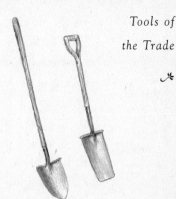

Shovels have curved, scoop-like blades intended for digging and lifting loose soil. Spades have flat blades for digging straight-sided holes.

The shank and head of any digging tool should be made of a single piece of metal that fits snugly around the handle with only a narrow seam at the back.

19

for the handle should be made of a single piece of metal. Where the shank meets the handle, look for a snug fit, and check the back of the socket. It should wrap completely around the handle for strength and have a narrow seam.

Good gardening tools should have sturdy handles made of hardwoods like ash or hickory. Fiberglass is another, more recent option. Lighter than steel, stronger than wood and somewhat heavier, fiberglass is often used for commercial-grade tools. I have a new shovel with a fiberglass handle that is a great success. The additional weight is manageable, and it is wonderful for tough jobs.

Moving on to the next step in preparing the garden bed, you need a steel grading rake to smooth and level the soil surface. (You will also need a hoe if you plan to have a vegetable garden.) Although it isn't strictly necessary, a cultivator is very useful in the final preparation for planting. It has a full-length handle and clawlike head with four 6-inch oval tines. The long tines are perfect for mixing compost and other soil amendments into the bed.

To put on the finishing touches, you need a turf edger with a long handle and a sharp, crescent-shaped blade to cut a clean outline of the new bed. The sharper the blade, the more precise the outline will be. I often cut out a narrow band of sod to define a proposed bed *before* beginning the soil preparation.

Turning to the lawn, you will need a light rake with thin, springy steel tines for sweeping up leaves, weeds, grass clippings, and other garden debris. Invest in two lawn rakes. Holding one in each hand, use them like a pair of salad servers to pick up large amounts of litter.

To transport the litter to the compost pile, you also need a tarpaulin at least 6 feet square. My "tarp" is a 7-foot square of woven polyethylene with corner loops for handles. The material is featherweight but durable. Garden totes called "BosBags" made of the same material are excellent for collecting smaller quantities of weeds and pruning detritus. Empty 5-gallon spackle buckets make the best totes for heavy garden rubbish, and they are free—if you have a friend in the construction business. You need lots of them, so never say no to more, even if you think you have enough.

Cutting down brush and pruning overgrown shrubs are often high on a new homeowner's agenda, so equip yourself right away with three tools for pruning—a pair of loppers, a pair of hand pruners (clippers), and a small pruning saw. If you get the best you can afford, you will be on the right track. In this particular case, the more expensive the equipment, the better it is apt to be. You are paying for superior-quality steel that keeps its edge. There are no costly "frills," just better material and craftsmanship.

Loppers are designed to cut branches up to an inch and a half thick and have handles between 20 and 30 inches long. Ratchet-action loppers have greater cutting power than single-action loppers, but they have more parts, and there is more to go wrong with them. Ratchet loppers will cut through a 2-inch branch without difficulty. For thicker branches, employ your pruning saw.

Clippers or hand pruners should be used only on material less than half an inch in diameter. *Make* yourself stick to the half-inch rule, or you will ruin your expensive pruners. I speak from sad experience. The pruners I favor have replaceable bypass blades that work like scissors. Only the broad blade requires sharpening, and *never, never* try to sharpen its flat side. You will interfere with the fit of the two blades. Sharpen the slightly rounded side with a fine stone. You will be doing yourself a service if you learn to perform this chore yourself. It means taking apart the pruners, but someone at your local hardware store will probably show you how.

Finally, a good wheelbarrow rounds out your collection of essential gardening tools. You will need it for moving loads of compost, manure, and wood chips. Some gardeners prefer a garden cart with two wheels, but I find a wheelbarrow easier to manage. If you get a wheelbarrow, choose one with a polyethylene tray and a large pneumatic tire. The plastic tray won't rust or chip, and a good-sized tire makes easy work of uneven ground and heavy loads. The tray should have a 6-cubic-foot capacity, the right size for most gardening projects.

I have not yet mentioned hand tools. Gardeners are funny about trowels, hand cultivators, forks, and weeders. All these small tools have 5-inch handles and, depending on their function, measure between 12 and 20 inches in overall length. Preferences among gardeners are strong and irrational.

Basic trowels have heads like elongated miniature shovels, measuring 6 inches in length and 3 inches in width. Specialized trowels for potting and for working in tight spaces in a rock garden have narrower heads. Cultivators come in different designs, but all have claws for scratching up the soil. Hand forks are just small versions of your basic digging fork, and weeders come in all designs. Most have blades, like a knife for gouging out deep-rooted garden invaders.

My most indispensable hand tool is a little wire rake with a plastic handle. It looks so flimsy and useless that I can't imagine why I bought it in the first place,

The

Self-

Taught

Gardener

✿

but I'm glad I did. It's a wonderful tool for scuffling up weeds, light cultivating, and cleaning out dead leaves among the perennials. I like it so much that I went back to our local garden center and bought several to give away. Everybody loves them. We were all desolated when the company that imported them from Japan went out of business. But I have recently found a replacement. Called a "whisk rake," it looks like a miniature lawn rake. Seventeen inches in length and 6 inches wide, it has long, supple, spring-steel tines.

Gardeners often wind up with a collection of gadgets that don't work. But there is no such thing as an excess of trowels. Trowels are easy to lose, even with red tape on the handles. I wrap stretchy, red plastic tape around the handles of all my small tools so that I can spot them if they get left in the garden.

In order to find the perfect trowel, you have to try different sizes and styles. Like other lifting and earth-moving tools, trowels should have tightly fitting handles and solid shank construction. Most of us also like to have a matching hand fork for weeding. One last word about tools: Don't be in too much of a hurry to fill up your garage with equipment. Start with the basics, and take it from there.

Part Two

*

How, When, Where, and What

Border Basics

꽃

Most gardening books approach the subject as if it were arithmetic—theory and technique first; plants and pleasure last. My idea is that you should go outside and play as soon as possible. Abandoning theory for practice gets you into the garden, where you belong, and satisfies the neophyte's craving for action.

Sooner or later, every gardener wants flowers. Usually sooner. Therefore, the next few chapters will be devoted to making flower beds. A flower bed serves as a self-teaching device. It is a lively, colorful, engaging textbook that provides experience and fosters confidence.

To avoid endless repetition of the same word, this typical plot of flowers will be referred to interchangeably as a bed or border. I looked up the word "border" in Hugh Johnson's admirable book *The Principles of Gardening* (Simon and Schuster, 1979). Johnson recalls the border's humble origin as a token strip of flowers in the vegetable garden.

"In the more extravagant Victorian gardens the flower beds were filled from the hothouses with spectacular displays of tender 'bedding.' Hardy perennial plants were forgotten, or relegated to borders round the kitchen garden and used simply for cutting." Then, at the turn of the century, Gertrude Jekyll, British painter–turned–garden designer, rescued perennials from the obscurity of the kitchen garden. In her gifted hands, the herbaceous border became the glory of English gardens.

The word "herbaceous" refers to nonwoody growth that dies back to the ground in the winter, and perennials are plants whose underground parts survive the cold season by remaining in a state of suspended activity. Growth resumes in the spring. Perennials can live for many years, while annuals germinate, flower, set seed, and die—all in one growing season. Biennials require two seasons to complete their life cycle. They make leafy growth the first year, flower and succumb after producing seed the second.

In this century, the great gardens of England boast impressive herbaceous borders of massed perennials, biennials, and annuals combined with shrubs to lend structure. Traditionally, these vast, flower-filled bands of color are backed by tall, exquisitely groomed hedges or mellow brick walls festooned with roses. As the name suggests, borders function as decorative floral edgings and are always much longer than they are wide.

So-called island beds also seem to have been a British invention. Free-form beds intended to be viewed from all sides were popularized by master gardener and nurseryman Alan Bloom. Bloom started his own business in 1930 and has been producing and selling delectable perennials for the garden ever since. The name Bressingham, which precedes many wonderful cultivars, is the village where the nursery is located. Bloom described his open-plan beds as islands to distinguish them from conventional one-sided borders, the distinction being in the absence of a solid background.

For the purpose of this book, the terms "bed," "border," and "flower garden" can be taken to mean exactly the same thing—a piece of ground of any shape, stripped of sod, prepared for planting, and filled with hardy perennials, a few annuals, and a handful of shrubs of the right scale.

From the moment we set foot on our land, I knew I wanted a garden that combined all kinds of plants. After one false start involving our septic tank (of which more later), I marked out a long, narrow rectangle about 6 feet wide and 30 feet long on the flattest spot I could find; removed the turf in pieces; industriously dug the underlying soil to a depth of 18 inches; worked in some manure and peat moss; and started planting. I found peonies and bearded irises on the property and transplanted them to the new bed. Generous neighbors contributed divisions of their perennials. The first year, I bought flats of annuals—marigolds, snapdragons, and sweet alyssum—to fill in the empty spaces.

The following year, I ordered phlox, Siberian irises, asters, and Shasta daisies by mail from Wayside Gardens and enlarged the bed. The result was pleasing enough to inspire a rash of photo taking. But the expanded garden was still too small for its setting. It just didn't look right, out in the middle of the lawn.

The third year, I moved it to the foot of an east-facing slope, where the ribbon of flowers looked more at home. Although the hillside was still covered with a tangle of brush, the bed looked far better against the shrubby green background than it had floating in a sea of lawn. Little by little, I extended the bed, skirting the base of the slope and following the natural contours of the land. The longer and wider this border became, the more sense it made in relation to its surroundings. Because it was wedded to the terrain and in scale with the rest of the garden, it made a more coherent contribution to the landscape.

In the process of digging and planting, tending and transplanting, moving and dividing, I learned something about growing hardy plants and acquired a repertoire of reliable perennials. Further down the road, I began to grapple with design and the larger landscape. But a border that incorporates perennials with annuals and shrubs teaches you a great deal of what you need to know in order to garden happily and successfully.

However, before you can start digging and buying plants, you have to decide what you want the flower garden to do for your landscape. Does this flower bed serve any special purpose? I started with the intention of cheering up the east side of the house and drawing attention to the entrance we used at that time. You might want to disguise a long blank garage wall or surround a patio with color. Obviously, having a specific purpose in mind dictates the placement of the bed. On the other hand, if its primary purpose is just to grow flowers and give you a chance to let off steam, the location is not so critical.

Whatever the location, you should find out if there are any limiting factors in terms of underground wires or water lines. Also, try to avoid your septic tank. I hit the steel cover of ours, assumed it was a rock, and set about prying it up. My husband intervened in the nick of time. Every state provides a service that can prevent calamity. In Connecticut, Call-Before-You-Dig will send a representative to your house and furnish you with a drawing that will show the location of wires and water lines.

In addition to physical obstacles, there are environmental conditions which impinge on your placement of a flower bed. Every piece of property has limitations. These are created by the amount of sun or shade, the position of the proposed garden in relation to the sun (exposure), and the type of soil. Don't be put off if you run into problems. There is usually a solution. Soil can be altered or plants found that can tolerate the light conditions you have to offer. You just have to do your homework and match the right plants to the site.

The most important thing you can do to ensure success is to study the patterns of sun and shade on your property. The more accurately you observe, the better your choice of plants will be and the better your garden will grow. If you buy plants at a garden center, the labels will describe their light requirements— "full sun," "shade," or "half shade." Mail-order catalogs include the same information, along with other tips about culture.

A sunny, open spot is the perfect place for a flower bed because most annuals and the majority of familiar garden perennials are sun-lovers. It is easy to recognize such a site. If it basks in the sun all day long, you have it made. Six hours of sun a day, preferably from mid-morning to mid-afternoon, is nearly ideal. And most perennials will cheerfully make do with either six hours of morning sun or six hours of afternoon sun. Even four or five hours of sun during the hot part of the day would be enough for some sun-lovers.

Shade is more difficult to evaluate. Despite years of experience, I still make mistakes. For example, I recently planted a young redbud tree in my woodland garden. My plan was to grow shade-loving primroses at its feet. But for one critical hour at midday, the sun reaches the ground. It is, therefore, too hot and too exposed for primroses, and they had to be moved. Remember that afternoon sun generates much more heat than morning sun. So look around at different times of day and see exactly when, where, and for how long the ground is shaded. Don't count on your memory, either. Make notes.

By definition, shade is a reduction in light. Most gardening books describe different degrees of shade as full shade, part shade, half shade, light shade, and dappled shade. I'm adding a category of my own: patchy shade. *Full shade* means a substantial reduction in light for the entire day. A southern New England hardwood forest creates full shade in summer; only the stray beam of sunlight manages to penetrate the thick canopy of overlapping leaves. A forest of spruce and fir produces *full shade* all year.

For my money, *part shade* is a cop-out. It doesn't tell you anything useful. Plants growing against the eastern wall of a house enjoy part shade—afternoon shade. Plants growing against a western wall also receive part shade—morning shade. The difference is that the western exposure, featuring shade all morning and sun all afternoon, constitutes almost *full sun* from a plant's point of view. Never choose shade-lovers for a western exposure. The heat is too great. *Half*

Cinnamon fern

The sterile fronds are tall, upright and lacy in texture; the fertile spore-bearing fronds turn cinnamon—brown after the spores are dispersed and remain attractive all year.

Christmas fern

Arching, leathery fronds are evergreen and provide color in winter; tolerates both sun and shade.

Maidenhair fern

Dainty fronds are made up of compound leaflets radiating outward from a wiry, semi-circular stem; the fans of foliage are held flat rather than upright.

shade at least tells you what it is: equal amounts of sunlight and shadow. Again, keep in mind exposure and time of day in selecting plants.

Light shade describes a delightful situation in which most plants would thrive—two or three hours of shade during the heat of the day. Even some ardent sun-lovers, like daylilies, benefit from a bit of protection at high noon, especially in the southern states. In cool parts of the country, a few hours of shade at this critical period would be enough for most true shade-lovers. *Dappled shade* is an often mentioned but rarely encountered phenomenon. A manicured, parklike woodland with well-spaced mature trees would result in dappled shade. Another example might be a grove of trees, such as birches, which have small, dainty leaves that move in the slightest breeze and admit light.

Patchy shade is commonplace. A large lawn tree casts a patch of shade to the west in the morning, to the north during the middle of the day, and to the east in the afternoon. A building does the same thing. In effect, patchy shade consists of alternating periods of full sun and full shade. What will grow in patchy shade depends as much on exposure as on light.

As gardeners are more interested in plants than in definitions, the bottom line is what will grow in different degrees of shade (see Some Easy Perennials for Shade). The Catch-22 is that all plants require light. Even ferns grow best in open woodland, although they tolerate full shade. And *all* flowering plants, including shade-lovers, demand adequate light in order to bloom well.

How much light is adequate light? Think of the problem this way: rhododendrons, mountain laurels, azaleas, and witch hazels are woodland plants, but they flower more profusely in clearings than deep in the forest. Let the bulldozer open up a road, and these denizens of the forest flower magnificently along the edge of the new road. Their backs are against the trees, and they are shaded by overhanging boughs, but they also receive a considerable amount of sunlight.

If you want a flower bed and your property is densely shaded, consider selectively removing some of the trees or limbing them up. Limbing up is a more conservative treatment in which the lower limbs are cut off to admit more light. Or if you can't bear to cut trees, you might look to nature for another solution.

Many of our loveliest native wildflowers are programmed to flower early, when abundant sunlight reaches the ground before the woodland trees leaf out. Later, as shade reclaims the forest floor, these spring bloomers either go dormant or cease to make active growth. You could follow a similar schedule with masses of spring-flowering bulbs paired with highly shade-tolerant hostas and ferns.

The bulbs bloom while there is ample sunlight. Then, as the leaves expand overhead, the hostas and ferns take over, concealing the remains of the bulb foliage with their lush summer greenery.

While we are on the subject of trees, take heart from another example in nature. Many plants grow well in the company of trees. In the woods, shrubs furnish the understory and herbaceous plants carpet the forest floor. The health and vigor of these plants depend on the amount of moisture and food available in the soil. As food is only useful to plants in solution, water is the key to gardening in the shade of trees.

It is worth noting that in southern New England, the forest floor is very dry. Our summers are relatively long and hot, and vegetation is sparse compared to the lush understory of northern deciduous forests. So it behooves the shade gardener to provide soil that holds moisture in order to grow plants successfully. Irrigation during hot, dry spells also helps.

Wherever you live, if you garden under trees, be sure that your herbaceous plants are receiving their fair share of moisture and nutrients. Because of their greater size, the extent of their root systems, and the abundance of their leaves, trees put heavy demands on these vital resources.

Nature provides another tip for shade gardeners. She abhors bare ground. Every year, the forest floor is mulched with fallen leaves. A mulch is a layer of any loose material spread over the open soil. Under trees, a layer of mulch goes a long way toward keeping the soil cool and damp in hot weather. Its benefits include retarding evaporation, preventing abrupt changes in soil temperature, and keeping down weeds. An organic mulch, such as chopped leaves, pine bark, shredded cedar bark, or aged wood chips, also adds nutrients to the soil as it decays.

Once you are familiar with the physical attributes of your land, you can begin to think about the size and shape of your border. The size should be determined by an honest answer to the question, "Do you actively *enjoy* getting hot, tired, and dirty?" Even if the answer is yes, it pays to start with something manageable.

On a city lot, a bed 5 or 6 feet wide and 20 feet long would probably do for a start. A larger suburban yard could accommodate a bed twice that long and up to 8 feet deep. In our country garden, the main border grew to 100 feet long and 12 to 15 feet wide, which is right for its setting in a former cow pasture surrounded by stone walls and acres of woodland.

Shape depends on site, surroundings, and personal preference. On a level piece of property, a geometric shape might be the best choice. In that case, try to tie it to some existing structural feature—a wall, a fence, or the edge of a patio. If the terrain is sloping and irregular, a bed that goes with the flow—echoing the contours of the land—might be more appropriate. If you don't like the shape, you can always change it. Cutting a new outline is easy. Relocating the bed if you are unhappy with the site is more trouble, but you can do that, too. I did it more than once.

Last, but far from least, ask yourself where a flower bed will give you the most pleasure. Siting a border for maximum enjoyment depends to some extent on your lifestyle. I never for a moment considered putting the garden in front of the house, because I wanted the color and excitement to be a secret and a surprise. The idea was to keep the front simple and save the fireworks for the back. Besides, the rooms we use most are at the back of the house.

At the time my perennial border finally found a permanent home, I was teaching and thought of the garden as a summer delight. For that reason, I wanted it to be visible from the terrace. I also wanted to look out on it from the kitchen windows. Siting the border at the foot of the slope in full view of both proved most satisfactory.

Once I stopped teaching, there were other considerations. The desire to have something to look at in the fall and winter inspired a new flurry of garden making. At about that time, we also replaced two meager little windows above the breakfast table with sliding glass doors. This wonderful change gave me the incentive to make two four-season borders at the far end of the lawn, where we could enjoy them during meals.

There is a lot to keep in mind when you are contemplating the site of a perennial border, but don't take it all too seriously. Remember that your first bed or border is your textbook. You may easily discard it as you become more proficient.

What to Grow

❧

In 1983, the New York Botanical Garden launched a series of symposiums dedicated to the use and culture of perennials. I went to one of the first programs. Prophetically entitled "Perennials: Plants for the '80's," it was well attended but by no means sold out. A few years later, a similar event drew a crowd that filled every seat in the auditorium. American gardeners had discovered perennials in a big way.

The immediate appeal of these plants is that they do not have to be replaced every season. But the notion that they are carefree subjects that last forever is seriously flawed. There are perennials and perennials. Frederick McGourty, noted horticulturist and author, and a lecturer with a wry sense of humor, provided the following definition of a perennial: "A plant that returns year after year—if it lives."

Some perennials are tough and durable. Orange daylilies worked their way from the gardens of early settlers all across the United States. Today, descendants of the original plants can be found thriving in ditches and fields in almost every state. Peonies are also survivors. Along with daylilies, they are often the only plants left in neglected, century-old New England gardens. Modern hybrids of these plants have retained much of their forebears' stamina.

By comparison, many other perennials are wimps. Beautiful sky-blue flax is as fragile as it looks. Blooming prolifically the first year, it dwindles after that and disappears about the third year. Unless you keep after Shasta daisies and divide them regularly, they peter out in two or three years. And delphiniums are so temperamental that many nurseries recommend treating them as annuals. Of course, the majority of perennials are neither as weak-willed as those above nor as persistent as daylilies and peonies.

Perennials have attracted a large following, thanks to their relative permanence and because most are easy to grow. They have straightforward cultural requirements and are not fussy about soils. But all demand a modicum of care. You can't just stick them in the ground and expect to have a lovely garden.

Sometimes, beginning gardeners are disappointed to learn that perennials do not bloom all summer. Each has a limited season—flowering for as short a period as a few days or for as long a spell as five or six weeks. Some flower intermittently all summer, but *no* perennial of my acquaintance remains in full bloom throughout the growing season.

Making the most of these great plants is like working out a fascinating puzzle. The trick is to combine them into a living collage that changes throughout the season and from year to year. There are different approaches to this vital art form. One is the big bang school of massed bloom. You get this effect by limiting yourself to large numbers of a single plant. Daylily gardens knock your socks off in the middle of the summer but leave much to be desired for the rest of the season. Another scheme is to practice restraint and go for something in bloom from the first breath of spring until the snow flies. Such a garden will never have the impact of the daylily garden, but it will provide something to look at throughout the growing season.

I stumbled on yet another way to use perennials—the four-season approach, featuring periods of peak bloom supplemented by restful periods when plants with superior foliage carry the day. This scheme depends on a spring bulb display; peonies and Siberian irises for early June; a mid-season blast of color from the daylilies and other summer-blooming perennials; grasses and sedum for fall. And a few evergreens, deciduous shrubs, and ornamental grasses for year-round appeal.

No matter how you use perennials, you have to take into account their everchanging, all-season presence in the garden. When you plant a perennial, you are planting for keeps—if the plant lives! It is there in the winter awaiting the return of warm weather. It is there in the spring, when the shoots push through the cold ground, and in summer when the leaves unfurl. At this stage, it takes up more room than it did in the spring. Next year, it will take up even more room.

Finally, in its appointed season, the perennial favors you with its flowers. After their moment of glory, the blossoms wither, and the foliage goes through a ratty stage. Tidy gardeners usually do something about this—either cut it down or reduce its height. Many perennials get a new lease on life a few weeks after being cut back and put forth fresh leaves. A few produce a second flush of bloom. But flowers or no flowers, these plants occupy their space until repeated frosts kill the aboveground portions.

Bulbs, of course, are the exception. By midsummer their foliage disappears, leaving room for the leafy perennials. As for longevity, daffodils can certainly be considered perennial. Our garden is now thirty-five years old, and the daffodils planted here by our predecessors still bloom every spring. Despite their reputation for impermanence, tulips last five or six years if they are planted about 10 inches deep.

Little bulbs, like glory-of-the-snow, grape hyacinths, and scillas, are not ideal subjects for a perennial border. It is too hard to keep track of them. They get moved around in the course of weeding, dividing, and transplanting the perennials. They also self-sow and turn up in unexpected places. I would describe them as permanent but elusive.

In order to have a perennial garden that looks respectable throughout the growing season, you have to make careful plant choices. Eschew those—however gorgeous—whose foliage makes a mess for weeks at a time. I have in mind Oriental poppies—so glorious in bloom; so miserable as they are going dormant. Nor can you afford to give too much room to large plants that only flower for a week or so. You pay dearly for that brief period.

In my own garden, I have finally given away many of the big double peonies. Each plant takes up a 4-by-4-foot area, flowers for only a few days, and requires staking. Even if the stems have been staked individually, they often snap just above the stake and plunge the huge, full flower heads to the ground. I have come to prefer the single peonies, which take up less room and stand on their own much better.

As flowers are the high point of a perennial border, the most intriguing aspect of this kind of gardening is orchestrating the sequence of bloom. You have to really know your plants to get it right. That means taking notes, learning as you go along, and finding out exactly when each blooms in order to contrive mutually enhancing associations. Add to this the fun of playing with color, texture, shape, and height and you have some idea of how all-consuming the perennial game can be.

But do not underrate annuals. Although they only last for a season, they have many virtues. Cheaper than perennials, they flower longer—most really do bloom all summer, and they come in more patterns and styles than you can imagine. There are the flat daisy shapes of zinnias and blanket flowers; the spires of larkspurs and snapdragons; the pincushions of scabiosa; the fuzzy heads of ageratum; the tubular flowers of nicotiana; and the frilly trumpets of petunias. There are pompoms, disks, bells, and balls. And colors that rival the rainbow.

True annuals flower from seed the first year and die with the arrival of heavy frost. The term is also used to describe a plant that blooms the first year from seed, whether or not it completes its life cycle in a single growing season. Snapdragons are actually perennials from the Mediterranean, but generally they are not cold-tolerant enough to survive in the Northeast. Here in Connecticut, they rarely make it through the winter. In other words, they behave like annuals and, therefore, are classed with them.

Unlike perennials, which are always changing, annuals are a stable, reliable presence in the garden. Once they reach maturity, they stay about the same until frost kills them. Their greatest charm, of course, is that they bloom, and bloom, and bloom. And the more you pick them, the more they bloom.

Annuals are invaluable fillers in a newly planted perennial garden that has plenty of room. In a mature perennial garden, it is hard to find enough open space. But it is worth making places for them. I purposely leave gaps at the back of the border for tall, airy cosmos and white Italian sunflowers, a branched variety with creamy, dark-centered blossoms. These annuals are at their best in August, when many of the perennials are going through their after-flowering angst.

For seed-sowing purposes, annuals are classified as hardy, half-hardy, and tender. Seed of those described as hardy can be planted before the last frost, while seed of tender annuals cannot go into the ground until the soil has warmed up and the danger of frost has passed. Seed designated as half-hardy is somewhere in between. It can withstand some cold but not prolonged cold.

Growing annuals from seed is fun and easy, but steer clear of those requiring special treatment to induce germination. Seed companies usually identify the easy ones, and the packages provide simple instructions for planting. Old favorites like sunflowers, cosmos, cleome, zinnias, marigolds, nasturtiums, and nicotianas (along with most vegetables) germinate quickly and can be sown right where you want them in the garden. Or you can take a shortcut and get six-packs of young plants from the garden center.

Annuals are particularly useful to new homeowners. A few six-packs can do wonders for a flowerless landscape. But just as there are perennials and perennials, all annuals are not created equal. Some have beautiful flowers on leggy, awkward plants. I love sunflowers but hide them at the back of the garden because of their ungainly growth habit.

Some annuals have poor foliage—zinnias are prone to fungal diseases that spot the leaves; nasturtiums get horrible aphids, and their leaves turn yellow. In short, you have to experiment to find annuals with appealing flowers and good-looking foliage that holds up well all season. I have found blue salvias, nicotianas, marigolds, and cosmos among the best all-round annuals.

Biennials have a timetable that makes them frustrating plants for a border. Seed sown in the spring or summer germinates, produces vegetative growth that season, and flowers the following year. After blooming and producing seed, the mature plant dies. This is tiresome behavior, because a biennial takes up space the first year without earning it. The third year, you have to start all over again.

However, in an informal setting where they can be allowed to self-sow, biennials can be an asset. I particularly love foxgloves. In my woodland garden, they eventually settle into a routine. Mature plants bloom in June and drop seed that germinates in the summer. By fall, the seedlings are substantial little plants that will bloom the following June. *Their* seedlings will bloom a year later, and so on.

Whether you choose annuals, biennials, or perennials, you must get to know your plants. You must also know yourself. How much time are you willing to devote to maintenance? Do you like to putter in the garden, or do you just like the end result? Are you a happy-go-lucky gardener who is easily pleased, or are you a control freak? Answers to these questions will steer you toward suitable plants. For instance, a control freak would object to annuals and biennials that self-sow everywhere.

Gardening is full of contradictions and conundrums. Here's one for you. You have to grow plants to know plants. So how do you get started? By asking questions. Find out if the plant you are interested in is an annual, perennial, or biennial. When does this plant bloom, and for how long? What does it look like in flower and out of flower? What is its foliage like? If the plant is a perennial, does the foliage get shabby after the plant blooms? If so, for how long, and what is the gardener supposed to do about it? How tall will this plant grow, and how big do the clumps get at maturity? How much maintenance does this plant require? Does it need to be dug up, separated into smaller sections, and replanted in order to maintain its vigor? Does it have to be staked? Do the dead flowers have to be removed daily, or not at all?

You will need to consult books for information about the character, growth habits, and blooming seasons of plants you like and want to grow (see Selected Further Reading). But in the end, you will find your own homemade notebook more valuable and truthful. Start gathering information by visiting other gardens. Roam the nearest public garden, botanical garden, or arboretum. Keep an eye open for garden tours. Visit nurseries, garden centers, and the gardens of friends. Study the plants and combinations of plants. Talk to other gardeners. Gardeners love to talk about their gardens and are unstinting with their time and advice.

At first, you may feel intimidated by beautiful gardens. You will be bowled over by the masses of bloom; the unfamiliar plants and their sheer numbers. Keep your head and look at specifics. Is there one plant that you admire? Ask its name or look for a label. Failing that, write a description of it in your garden notebook; make a crude sketch; or take a photograph. And look it up later. What are its approximate dimensions? A pocket tape measure is useful because size, spread, and height are vital bits of information. Does this plant take up a lot of room horizontally, or does it occupy a tall, narrow space? Is it growing in bright sunshine or under trees? Find out everything you can about your chosen plant, and *write it down.*

If you learn about one or two new plants in every garden or nursery you visit, you will soon have a collection of plants to play with. The next step is to actually grow some of them. Now, we're getting someplace. But first, a word about nomenclature.

Alas, Gertrude Stein did gardeners a disservice by proclaiming that "a rose is a rose is a rose." Quite often a rose is *not* a rose. A rose-of-Sharon is a shrub or small tree related to the hollyhock; a Christmas rose is a member of the butter-cup family; and a primrose is a spring flower so named because Chaucer angli-cized the French 'Primverole', which means "first flower of spring" to Primerole, thence to primrose. So who are you going to believe?

The only safe course is to take it from Linnaeus, the eighteenth-century

Swedish botanist who standardized the binomial system of nomenclature. As you struggle to master it, you may be comforted to know that Linnaeus came from a gardening family and adored plants. His intention was not to bewilder gardeners but to create order out of botanical chaos. His system replaced dozens of different names and descriptions rendered in different languages. To eliminate confusion, he substituted a two-part Latin or Latinized Greek descriptive name recognizable throughout the world. Many of the names he selected make so much sense that they are still in use today.

The plant kingdom has many divisions and subdivisions, but only two are of immediate concern to gardeners: genus (plural, genera) and species (singular and plural are the same: one species; ten species). Genus describes a group of plants linked together by botanical similarities. The genus is always capitalized and precedes the specific name. A genus may contain many species.

Species describes a close-knit group of individuals belonging to the same genus but distinguished from other members by one or more unique characteristics. Usually, the genders of genus and species agree; thus both end in the feminine "a," the masculine "us," or the neuter "um." In print, generic and specific names are both italicized.

Here's how it works. The scientific name of the Japanese candelabra primrose is *Primula japonica*. It belongs to the genus *Primula* and the species *japonica*, distinguished from other primroses by its tall stems with tiers of blossom in shades of pink and red. Its two-part name is recognized by gardeners around the world and applies only to this particular primrose.

If several species of the same genus are listed in print, only the first initial of the generic name is repeated. Having written out *Primula japonica*, other primula would be identified only by the initial and the specific name. For instance, *P. pulverulenta* is a primrose from China, similar to *P. japonica* but distinguished from it by a heavy dusting of silver powder on its stems and the back of its leaves.

Knowing and using Latin names does not make you a better gardener, but it does make you more accurate in identifying plants, and it opens up a new world. Generic and specific names introduce you to people, places, and habitats.

When I first joined the North American Rock Garden Society, I was completely floored by names like *Campanula portenschlagiana*. However, when I learned that the specific name honors the Austrian botanist Franz von Portenschlag-Ledermayer, my courage returned. Often, gardeners find the biggest

Botanical Latin

These 3 members of the genus <u>Primula</u> (primroses) have traits in common, but are different enough to belong to separate species.

Drumstick Primrose
<u>Primula</u> <u>denticulata</u>

Latin name means "toothed" and refers to the leaf edges.

Polyanthus Primrose-<u>Primula</u> x <u>polyantha</u>

Botanical name means "many-flowered"; the "x" indicates that other primrose species were crossed to produce this plant.

Candelabra Primrose
<u>Primula</u> <u>japonica</u>

The plants are native to Japan, hence the epithet <u>japonica</u>.

stumbling block to using scientific names is fear of mispronouncing them. But *any* pronunciation delivered with confidence serves the purpose. So give it a whirl.

Demystification is the first step to making botanical nomenclature manageable. Look for the obvious. What could be easier than the specific names *japonicus* and *nipponicus* for plants native to Japan? Or *chinensis* for those indigenous to China? The specific name often gives you useful tips about growing conditions. *Sylvestris* means "of the woods," from the same root as "sylvan." *Palustris* means "of the swamp." In addition, the names can be descriptive: *grandiflorus* means "large-flowered"; *globosus* "globe-shaped"; and *pulchellus* "pretty." The latter comes from the same root as pulchritude.

Having been a hopeless student of Latin myself, I have every sympathy with gardeners who balk at learning botanical nomenclature. But mastering frequently used generic and specific names is much easier than it appears. Moreover, it is part of knowing your plants. It is like knowing the city and street address of your friends. You need that information in order to reach them. Henceforth, you will find Latin names beginning to creep into the text. They appear in parenthesis following the common name.

In the next two chapters, you will meet the perennials that carry a garden through the growing season. In order to obtain the same plants for your own garden, you will need to know their correct botanical names. You will find them all in Appendix B.

Every gardening book provides plant lists, but with time and experience, you will accumulate your own. Shaped by trial and error, observation, note taking, and personal taste, it will be the most valuable and reliable. I hope some of my favorites will still be on it.

Some Easy Perennials for Sun

❧

The building blocks of a beautiful garden are happy, healthy plants. Depending on the plants you choose, maintaining their health and happiness can be relatively easy or it can be exacting and labor-intensive.

Take alpines, for example. Tiny plants from mountainous regions of the world demand low humidity and bone-dry foliage, but their roots must be kept constantly moist. These contradictory requirements make alpines hard to please. Rock gardeners devote their lives to replicating the native habitats of their finicky charges and catering to their whims. If you like the challenge of growing difficult plants, more power to you. But if your aim is to make an attractive garden without resorting to heroic measures, choose sturdy, adaptable plants instead.

Of course, all plants have basic requirements in terms of sun, shade, soil, and moisture, and even the most amenable do best within a prescribed temperature range. To guide gardeners in selecting plants for their particular climate, the United States Department of Agriculture devised a map establishing hardiness zones (see the Hardiness Zone Map, opposite).

In general, the farther north you live, the lower your winter temperatures and the lower your zone number on the hardiness map. The coldest part of the country lies in an irregular band along the Canadian border, from northern Wisconsin to northern Montana. This section, with an average annual minimum temperature of minus 50 degrees Fahrenheit, is designated Zone 1. At the oppo-

Hardiness Zone Map

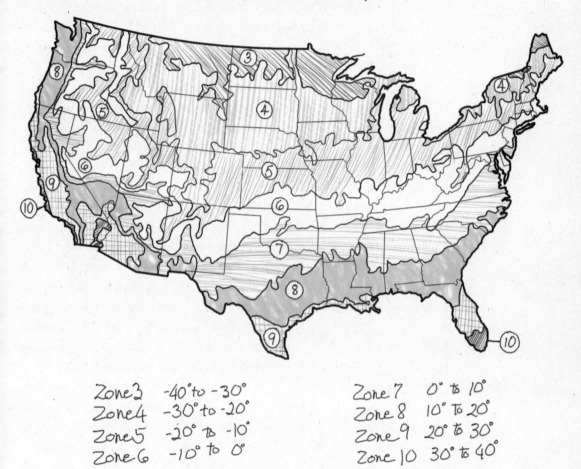

Zone 3	-40° to -30°		Zone 7	0° to 10°
Zone 4	-30° to -20°		Zone 8	10° to 20°
Zone 5	-20° to -10°		Zone 9	20° to 30°
Zone 6	-10° to 0°		Zone 10	30° to 40°

site extreme, in Zone 9, southern Florida enjoys average minimum temperatures of between 30 and 40 degrees Fahrenheit, while my Connecticut garden belongs in Zone 6, with minimum lows of 0 degrees Fahrenheit to minus 10 degrees Fahrenheit.

Tolerance of a wide range of temperatures indicates adaptability. Gardening books and catalogs usually assign zone ratings to the plants they list. Use only those that can be grown within your zone, and avoid plants with a rigidly narrow range, unless your climate is just right for them. The same applies to plants with uncompromising requirements in terms of soil and moisture. Unless you have wet, very acid soil, forget about bog plants.

43

The acid or alkaline content of soils is largely determined by the chemistry of the underlying rock: limestone rocks, like chalk and marble, make the soil alkaline; eroded granite makes the soil acid. Climate and vegetation also affect soil chemistry. In climates with relatively high rainfall, decomposing forest vegetation produces acid soil, while deserts are usually alkaline.

Degrees of soil acidity and alkalinity are indicated by numbers and the symbol "pH." A pH of 4 is very acid; 8 is highly alkaline. But don't worry too much about the pH of your soil—anywhere from 5 (moderately acid) to 7 (neutral) will suit the vast majority of perennials. Normal soils fall within this range. If you still want reassurance, you can have your soil tested by your Cooperative Extension Service (see "Moral Support").

Let's look at some dependable perennials whose basic needs are met by average soil and six hours of sun a day. (See Appendix B for other easy, sun-loving perennials and recommended cultivars of those mentioned in this chapter.)

As daylilies were among the first and most successful perennials I planted, we'll begin with them. Their botanical name, *Hemerocallis,* comes from the Greek *hemera,* meaning day, and *kallos,* beauty. Each flower lasts for only twenty-four glorious hours. But even a modest clump of daylilies can produce upwards of a hundred flowers that open over a period of from three to five weeks.

Hardy from Zone 3 to Zone 10, daylilies have masses of fleshy roots—some thonglike; others, plump and fingerlike. These provide ample reserves of food and water for the long haul. In the wild, they permit daylilies to

Daylily
(*Hemerocallis* hybrids)

A rainbow of flower colors; also many sizes and shapes; note modern form with wide petals and ruffles.

cling to cliffs and steep slopes and enable them to endure drought. While infinitely preferring sun, daylilies will survive even in deep shade, though they may not flower.

Leafless stems, called "scapes," arise from the foliage and carry up to thirty or more flowers. The colors include every known shade of yellow, from creamy-primrose to rich golden-yellow. You can have Day-Glo orange, tangerine, cantaloupe, and bronze. Reds range from scarlet to crimson to American Beauty. There are wonderful pinks: true summer-phlox-pink and blush-pink; rose and peach. Purple is a relatively new addition in shades from pansy to palest lavender; and, finally, there are the oh-so-nearly-whites.

In addition to countless colors, daylily flowers boast variations in patterns, shapes, and sizes. Some are edged with a darker color that complements the basic hue. And many have ruffles or tiny pleats. Heights run from dwarf plants only 12 inches high to soaring 6-footers; and flower sizes vary from "miniatures" under 3 inches across to large flowered cultivars fully 8 inches in diameter.

Daylily leaves are long and tapering. They emerge in pairs from the crown, where the roots and foliage meet. A division consisting of a sturdy pair of leaves, complete with roots, is aptly called a "fan." Several fans become an arching mound of foliage.

In daylily catalogs you will meet three foliage types: dormant, evergreen, and semi-evergreen. Dormant means that in the North, the leaves die back to the ground in winter. "Dormants" are the hardiest and the most suitable for northern gardens. Most dormants also do well in the South.

"Evergreen" applies to foliage that remains green and growing all winter, a southern phenomenon. As a rule of thumb, evergreens are the least hardy. While some are cold-tolerant enough to be grown successfully in the North, others are not. You have to know which are which. Semi-evergreens are alleged to do well in most parts of the country, though their hardiness also varies. To be on the safe side, visit a local daylily garden and see which types and cultivars do best in your area. A list of daylily display gardens is available from the American Hemerocallis Society (see Appendix B under *Hemerocallis*).

There are numerous daylily specialists, usually amateur breeders who must sell plants in order to support their habit. Their catalogs provide a wealth of useful data—foliage type, flower size, color, height, and blooming time. They also identify cultivars as either "diploid" or "tetraploid." Tetraploids have four sets of chromosomes in each cell, instead of the diploid's basic complement of two sets. For breeders, this information is vital because "tets" can only be crossed with tets and "dips" with dips. As a gardener, it doesn't matter whether you grow tets or dips. They are all beautiful. Your only problem is being faced with an embarrassment of riches. There are about 15,000 named cultivars available.

Peonies are almost as popular as daylilies and hardy from Zone 3 to Zone 8. They are not a good choice for the Deep South, because excessive heat wilts their flowers. Eager hybridizers have developed innumerable cultivars from which to choose. Although they bloom for a week or two only, by selecting early, mid-season, and late-flowering types you can eke out a month of spectacular beauty. In the Northeast, this four-week period begins in May and runs through late June.

As everyone knows, peony flowers are magnificent. But not everyone knows that the American Peony Society recognizes four different forms—singles, doubles, semi-doubles, and Japanese types.

'Krinkled White', with five or more pristine petals surrounding a tuft of golden pollen-bearing stamens, is one of my favorite singles. It blooms early.

Peony (<u>Paeonia</u>)

Very large, showy, red,
white and pink flowers;
shapes include single,
double, semi-double and
Japanese.

Doubles are as big as the head of a baby and a solid mass of petals. Pale pink 'Mrs. Franklin D. Roosevelt' is my pick of the early doubles.

Semi-doubles have an outer ring of guard petals around a cluster of smaller petals interlaced with yellow stamens. I love fluffy, white 'Minnie Shaylor'.

The guard petals of Japanese types surround a floppy boss of non-pollen-bearing stamens called "staminodes." Sometimes, the staminodes masquerade as

Siberian iris
(*Iris sibirica*)

Finely crafted flowers and
tall, narrow, upright foliage.

a wispy cluster of petals the same
color as the guard petals or a tint of
that color. Cream-centered white
'Cheddar Gold' is gorgeous.

I can attest to the longevity of peonies. Only 'Cheddar Gold' is a recent in-
dulgence. 'Krinkled White', 'Mrs. Franklin
D. Roosevelt', and 'Minnie Shaylor' have
been in my garden for at least twenty-five
years. And I still have old rose-red peonies that I
found on the property when we came here. That's
the good news. Peonies are durable.

Now, the bad news. Peonies are not trouble-
and maintenance-free. Staking is mandatory, and the trouble is a fungus disease
called botrytis blight. Botrytis rots the base of new stems, spots the leaves, and
affects the buds, which wither without opening. Treatment with a fungicide is
recommended.

Peonies bloom at the same time as irises and provide a brief but wonderful
period of peak bloom in my garden. The peony colors seem to have been made
for the Siberian irises, which have a range of wonderful blues and purples. The
sky-blues and ocean-blues have underlying tints of turquoise and peacock, while
the purples range from royal to pastel lavender, and there are reddish-purples,
like 'Eric the Red' and 'Cabernet'. A recent breakthrough has added butter-
yellow to this list.

Siberian irises are elegant, easy perennials with strong constitutions. They
are hardy from Zones 3 to 9. Their small, finely crafted flowers resemble the
fleur-de-lis, with three upright segments called "standards" and three drooping
"falls." The flowering stems are straight and tall, rising 2 to 4 feet, and the blos-

soms hover just above the foliage. One cultivar name says it all—'Flight of Butterflies'.

Although the period of bloom is not long—a week or two, at best—the foliage is an asset all season. The narrow leaf blades shoot up from a thick mat of fibrous roots and underground stems called rhizomes and form an attractive clump.

You will notice that bearded irises are absent from this list of good and easy perennials. I regret this omission, because the flowers are unbelievably lovely. They have more frills than a negligee, and the colors make your mouth water. But these beauties ask too much for too little. Each stem has to be staked in order to support the extravagant blossoms, and the bloom season is fleeting. Afterward, the relentless iris borers turn the leaves into slimy tatters. Despite all this, I still grow one bearded iris called 'Allegiance'. The purple velvet flowers are so stunning that I can't help myself, but I hide the plants behind clumps of daylilies.

Ornamental grasses are near the top of my list of perennials that give high value for low upkeep. Currently, these graceful plants are receiving the recognition they deserve. As a group, they are among the most accommodating of perennials. They come in all sizes, from small tufts of stiff foliage to great fountains of gracefully arching blades; and in all heights, from a few inches to 10 feet. For color, there are blue grasses, gold grasses, or variegated grasses. The variegations come in shades of yellow, ivory, and white and may be in the form of thin, vertical stripes or broad horizontal bands.

In the wild, grasses inhabit meadows, prairies, and steppes. They also grow in the mountains and along streams. They are part of the earth's natural ground cover and well equipped to deal with harsh climates. Often, their wiry roots descend to great depths—which is worth remembering when you plant grasses. They are easy to grow but not easy to move. Hardiness varies. (See Appendix B for recommended cultivars and hardiness ratings.)

Most sedums are easy-care perennials. There are low-growing types for the front of the border and tall mid-border candidates. All are hardy in Zones 4 to 10. They bear starry yellow, orange, red, or pink flowers in clusters. One of the best garden subjects of all time is *Sedum spectabile* 'Autumn Joy'. At 2 feet or more, it is a beautiful plant with succulent blue-green leaves and flat heads of pink flowers. Trouble-free and long-lived, it should be in every garden from Maine to Florida and westward. This sedum makes a contribution to the landscape from the moment its ice-blue rosettes emerge in the spring until the flower heads turn pink in August, russet-red in September, brown in October, and support cones of snow in the winter.

Some gardeners shun members of the mint family because common peppermint is an aggressive spreader. But catmints, which belong to the genus *Nepeta*, are hardy (Zones 3 to 10), reliable, well-behaved plants with a long season of usefulness. The most familiar kinds are bushy and low-growing. For weeks at a time, a haze of little lavender-blue flowers covers billowing mops of small, toothed gray-green leaves.

When the flowers shrivel, the whole flowering stem should be cut to the ground and the remaining foliage given a haircut with a pair of scissors. New leafy stems will come from the base of the plant, repairing the damage within a very short time. And you can expect at least two or three subsequent periods of bloom. A cultivar called 'Six Hills Giant' is particularly desirable because it blooms all summer without being cut back, though it looks better if occasionally trimmed. It is a big plant, rapidly spreading to 3 feet across in one season, so leave it enough room.

The genus *Calamintha* also provides gardeners with neat, bushy, nonspreading mints for the front of the border. My favorite is *Calamintha nepetoides* (it is also sold as *C. nepeta nepeta*). Its naturally rounded growth habit is just about ideal, and the foliage is shiny, dark green, and intensely peppermint-scented. Until August, it looks like a low green bush. Then, sprays of flowers, so small and myriad that they might be baby's breath, cover it completely. At first their color is almost white, but it deepens to lavender as the cool weather arrives. In winter, I treasure calamint for its dainty skeleton against the snow.

I am a sucker for carefree daisies. If you ask a child to draw a flower, they inevitably surround a disc with rays. Daisylike plants have centers composed of minute, tightly packed tubular flowers—the part of a daisy that children color yellow. The white "love me, love me not" rays may look like petals, but in fact they are individual flowers.

This touchingly naive design goes with everything in the garden. And there are many different kinds of daisies to choose from—sneezeweed, coreopsis, coneflowers, sunflowers, and black-eyed Susans. As they have only recently left the fields and grasslands for the garden, daisies are undemanding. Accustomed to root competition from the grasses, they make do when moisture is scarce. Sneezeweed is the exception. It prefers moist soil but tolerates normal garden conditions. All those mentioned withstand extremes of heat and cold and are hardy from Zone 3 to Zone 10.

Sneezeweed is an unflattering misnomer for a beautiful native plant. Its botanical name, *Helenium autumnale*, means "Helen's flower," and a very pretty flower it is. Short yellow, bronze, or chestnut-red rays encircle the little round knob of disc florets. As the specific epithet suggests, Helen's flower blooms late—August into September in my garden. Tall, leafy stems from 2 to 5 feet high bear terminal clusters of 2-inch flowers. The flowers open over a period of weeks.

Several species of coreopsis have been civilized and introduced into the garden, but *Coreopsis verticillata* is by far the best. In 1993, a cultivar called 'Moonbeam' was named Perennial Plant of the Year by the Perennial Plant Association, a group of nursery professionals. And no wonder. Colonies of fine stems with threadlike leaves (it is called threadleaf coreopsis) form a patch of green lace covered with small, pale yellow flowers. This color seems to appeal to everybody, but a golden-yellow cultivar called 'Zagreb' and another called 'Golden Showers' have a better plant habit. Both are tighter as a clump, more upright, and more persistent. I sometimes lose patches of 'Moonbeam' for no known reason. All the cultivars are under 2 feet.

I love purple coneflowers. The plants are rangy, with rough stems clad in coarse, dark green leaves, but the large daisy flowers are wonderful. They have rays the color of crushed raspberries surrounding prickly, prominent, bright orange cones. The sheer audacity of such a color combination appeals to me, to say nothing of the length of the blooming season. The flowers just go on and on. For gardeners who don't like bizarre color schemes, there are a couple of lovely white cultivars with orange centers: 'White Luster' and 'White Swan'. Heights vary from plant to plant, but most of mine grow to around 3 feet.

I grow a lot of different sunflowers and am always ready to try a new one. *Helianthus* x *multiflorus* 'Flore Pleno' is an old-fashioned favorite. The first part of the botanical name is easy to understand: in Greek, "helios" means sun, and "anthos," flower. Linnaeus brought it into the classification system by combining the names and providing a Latin ending. That little "x" identifies the species *multiflorus* as a hybrid of two parents belonging to different varieties, species, or genera. The cultivar name 'Flore Pleno' means "with double flowers."

The flowers are very double, like pom-poms, bright yellow and numerous, and the stems are tall—4 to 6 feet. The only problem with this sunflower is that it spreads. Just below the soil surface, it sends out stolons—horizontal stems, each ending in a new upright shoot. I just chop them off with a shovel.

Heliopsis helianthoides is the botanical name of the false sunflower. The ending "oides" in any botanical name means "like," and the flowers are sunflowerlike. I have grown this plant for years and would be lost without its single, double, or semi-double yellow flowers. It begins blooming in mid-June and, if the faded blossoms are removed, goes on for fully two months. There are several fine cultivars, including double 'Golden Greenheart' and semi-double 'Light of Lodden'. Neither is stoloniferous.

So many people love black-eyed Susans that they have made *Rudbeckia fulgida* 'Goldsturm' a garden cliché. Don't be put off. In the garden, a cliché is just a popular success. 'Goldsturm' ('Goldstorm') has all the cheerful appeal of the wildflower, but the dark-eyed, golden-yellow flowers are larger, handsomer, and more numerous, and at 2 feet, the overall plant is more compact.

Please note that all the daisies above are American native plants. It may surprise you to know that many other popular garden perennials are American wildflowers—achillea, boltonia, blazing star, bee balm, evening primrose, mallow, gallardia, aster, and false indigo, to mention a few. The more difficult your site and climate, the more you should think in terms of tough, indigenous plants.

Some Easy Perennials
for Shade

❧

Shade-tolerant perennials are just as appealing as sun-lovers. But you have to adjust your expectations. Plants that naturally prefer shade to sun tend to bloom in the spring, when temperatures are cool. Many are woodland plants that produce flowers when the trees are leafless, allowing sunlight to pour down through the bare branches. Once the leaves expand overhead, the herbaceous plants settle into their green phase.

Sun-lovers have more colorful summer flowers and thrive in warm temperatures. But if you can bring yourself to accept spring as the brilliant season in your shady garden, you can have a border as bright as a bed of nasturtiums. For color, primroses are the answer to a shade gardener's prayer.

Hardy at least to Zone 5 (many are hardy to Zone 4), primroses bloom at the same time as tulips, when other perennials are mere tufts and sprouts of green. I grow primroses under trees and around a little pond in a moist, wooded hollow behind our barn. But they would be just as happy in shade on the north or east side of a house or at the foot of shrubs.

The genus *Primula,* to which hardy primroses belong, contains over 500 species. They come in all sizes, shapes, and colors and are found in cool, damp places from the Rocky Mountains to the British Isles, from the Swiss Alps to the Himalayas and throughout China and Japan. Many have compound flower heads with the typical five-petaled blossoms arranged in different configurations: tight round balls, horizontal tiers, vertical spires, and flattened or loose clusters.

Most primroses grow from rosettes of leaves, which may be as small as a silver dollar or as large as a robust clump of hosta. Like all flowering plants, they need light to bloom profusely and bask in the gentle spring sunshine. But they also need summer shade and moisture-retentive soil (see "The Good Earth"). Water them well in hot, dry weather.

The most readily available primroses are colorful polyanthus hybrids with sturdy 10-inch stalks bearing large, rounded flower clusters. In Greek compound words, *poly* signifies many; *anthus* means flowered. Hybridizers have had a field day with this primrose, and many colors have resulted from their ministrations: pink, mauve, purple, blue, yellow, gold, orange, and red.

Hybrids of the common English primrose have a similar color range, but the flowers are borne singly on stems about 6 inches high. You will find these primroses under two different botanical names. Most often they are sold as *Primula acaulis*, but sometimes the same plant is called *Primula vulgaris* (preferable according to about 80 percent of the members of the American Primrose Society). By either name, they smell as sweet and have as many lovely colors.

Drumstick primroses (*P. denticulata*) are some of the easiest to grow and are readily available. They bloom very early—mid-April in my garden—and their tight round balls of flowers last for three weeks. The shape of the flower head atop stems that reach 18 inches gives this primrose its common name. The colors are shades of mauve, lavender, magenta, deep red-violet, and white. The leaves form a rosette as large as a flattened head of romaine lettuce.

Japanese candelabra primroses (*P. japonica*) are among the easiest to grow and most ravishing. But they *must* have constantly moist soil. They are perfect plants for the edge of a pond or stream. These water-lovers grow well around my pond. Although the water disappears in the summer, the soil remains damp all season and provides them with adequate moisture.

It's hard not to go overboard in describing the flowers of *P. japonica*. Their blossoms are arranged in circular tiers around a stout stalk that rises to a height of 2 feet. This elegant form combines with luscious colors—every permutation of red and pink, from the deepest wine-red and magenta to the palest pink. There is also a white form. If content with their site, Japanese candelabra primroses self-sow liberally.

You could have a beautiful shady garden and something to look at for eight months of the year if you grew only hostas and ferns. By interspersing these foolproof shade-lovers with spring-flowering bulbs—hosta and ferns are the perfect

Hosta (<u>Hosta</u>)

Tremendous variety
of handsome leaves
in numerous shades
of green, blue, and gold.

disguise for withering bulb foliage—you can have your cake and eat it, too. Brilliantly colored tulips, sky-blue scillas, and sunny yellow daffodils bloom early and eventually make way for the cool, green leaves of these superb foliage plants.

Although they have conspicuous spikes of drooping white or lavender bell-shaped flowers, hostas are chiefly grown for their splendid leaves. The flowers are marred by their habit of bloom. Opening from bottom to top, the faded flowers detract from the fresh ones above them. Passionate hosta enthusiasts—and they are many—will probably take exception to this criticism. But I could do without the flowers. Who needs them when the foliage is so magnificent?

All by themselves, hostas can make a garden. They come in a range of size, shape, texture, and color variation—bold and subtle—that would stun Victorian gardeners. "Funkias," as they were called in those days, lined front walks to many late-nineteenth-century houses. The mounds of plain green leaves, used without imagination, gave hostas a bad name, and for years they were out of fashion. Today, they are "in" and then some.

Thanks to American hybridizers, you can now have a choice of tiny hostas or giant hostas and every size in between. The leaves can be narrow and lance-shaped, elongated and heart-shaped, or as broad and round as a Ping-Pong paddle. Some are wavy-edged, others are plain. The surface texture is often an outstanding feature. Some cultivars have deeply incised parallel veining; others are as dimpled and shirred as seersucker; still others have an almost satin sheen.

Solid colors run the gamut from powdery-blue in the case of 'Blue Cadet' to the gray-blue of 'Krossa Regal' to all shades of green. Most cultivars with the word "gold" in their name are, in fact, shades of yellow, cream, or chartreuse. However, one of the most golden is the cultivar 'Midas Touch', with huge, rounded, puckered golden-green leaves. 'Wogon Gold' has small, smooth, immaculately tailored golden-green leaves. 'Gold Standard', one of my favorites, has large, pointed, oval leaves of chartreuse edged in dark green. In the spring, the narrow, wavy leaves of 'Kabitan' are bright yellow with a dark green edge. Later in the season, the color turns more chartreuse and the dark edging becomes less pronounced.

The variegations in 'Kabitan' and 'Gold Standard' are confined to neat, narrow edgings. But in the gorgeous, much-sought-after 'Frances Williams', the bright chartreuse edge is broad, bold, and irregular and surrounds a blue-green center; 'Fascination' is green splashed with cream and yellow; and 'Aureomarginata' has wide brushstrokes of yellow along the edges of the elongated heart-shaped green leaves.

Like peonies, hostas are long-lived. There is a price to pay for this boon. Unless you buy large plants—and large plants are expensive—you have to wait about three years for a young hosta to come into its own. I bought a small plant of 'Frances Williams' and was disappointed the first year. I even thought I had been sold the wrong cultivar. Instead of being broad and rounded, the leaves were pointed ovals, longer than wide. However, within two or three years, the immature foliage had been replaced by the characteristic paddles with their flashy chartreuse edges.

Ferns are perfect companions for hostas because their cultural requirements are the same—shade and moisture-retentive soil (see "The Good Earth")—and their forms are entirely different. While the leaves of hostas are solid and substantial, ferns have intricately cut, featherlike fronds. Instead of spreading into low mounds, tall ferns spout upward in cool green jets of foliage. Dainty maidenhair ferns hold their fronds flat, like green doilies, and leather-textured Christmas ferns are upright to arching.

The ferns I grow are all native northeastern woodland plants with no problems or pests and a wide natural range from Canada to the Deep South and across the Midwest. They are tough, cold-hardy, and easy to grow. Although they prefer shade, they can take a certain amount of sun if the soil is moist.

Ostrich ferns grow best in soil with a high moisture content, but they survive in the drier parts of my woodland garden. They send up a ring of 4- to 6-foot fronds of great beauty and symmetry from a knob of wiry roots and underground runners.

The regal fern is also a moisture-lover, often found in swamps. It tolerates drier soil grudgingly and appreciates supplementary watering during the summer. It is one of the most elegant ferns because the leaflets are spaced well apart, and the broad fronds are light and airy. Unlike the ostrich fern, which can travel considerable distances via its underground runners, the regal fern stays in a clump and increases slowly.

Cinnamon ferns have pretty fronds, tapering at both ends, with finely toothed leaflets. The outstanding feature of this fern is the separate spore-bearing stalk. Instead of seeds, ferns produce dustlike spores encapsulated in small sacks called sporangia. In this fern, clusters of sporangia are grouped together at the top of the fertile stem. After the spores have been disbursed, the whole stem turns brown, giving the cinnamon fern its nickname.

The sterile fronds of the interrupted fern are very similar to those of the cinnamon fern, but the fertile fronds are so distinctive you can't confuse the two. In the middle of the frond, a few pairs of leaflets (pinnae) develop sporangia. These eventually release their spores and turn brown, creating an interruption between the green top of the frond and the green pinnae at the bottom. Both interrupted ferns and cinnamon ferns are tall, handsome subjects for the shady garden.

Christmas ferns are virtually indestructible. They will grow almost anywhere, sun or shade, though they prefer shade, and they put up with dry shade. An excellent choice for under trees, they have arching fronds up to 36 inches long that remain green all winter.

The genus *Helleborus* provides shade gardeners in Zones 3 to 8 with the Lenten rose, an almost perfect perennial, and the Christmas rose, just slightly less than perfect. Both bloom in March in my garden. The Lenten rose has shiny, palm-shaped leaves borne on 15- to 18-inch stalks. They are very handsome and, during a mild winter, retain their looks. If they become battered or burned by winter sun, cut them to the ground in March. Within a month, a new crop will emerge, following the appearance of leafless, branched flower stalks.

The flowers are nothing short of exquisite. A shallow cup of five broad, pointed petals embraces a cluster of purple stamens. Because so little is in bloom

at the time hellebores flower, you can take time to study and appreciate the fascinating, complex blossoms.

The only colors generally available are creamy-green to white, and a curious,
crushed raspberry-purple. The Christmas rose is not quite as sturdy a plant, in
my experience, but the waxy white flowers are matchless, and the foliage is a
marvelous dark green. Being poisonous, the hellebores are not bothered by any
pests.

Certainly no shade garden should be without
epimediums. These spring-blooming plants from
Japan and Korea are adaptable and hardy from Zones
4 to 8. They are about a foot tall and have dark, wiry
stems clothed in thin-textured leaflets shaped like
narrow, lopsided hearts. In some species,
these are tinged with red in
the spring and turn
bronze in the fall.

Hellebore
(*Helleborus orientalis*)

Very early flowers; superb,
almost evergreen foliage.

The plants belie the
somewhat fragile ap-
pearance of the fo-
liage. Though they
prefer a moist, wood-
sy type of soil, epi-
mediums can tolerate
even the dry shade of
maple trees. The flowers,
which precede the leaves in the spring, are small, spidery, and carried in airy
clusters on thin stems. There are several different species that offer charming
flowers in shades of red, pink, lavender, white, and yellow. 'Rose Queen' and
'White Queen' are desirable cultivars.

To give height and summer color to the shade garden, there is nothing like
astilbe. But the soil must be moisture-retentive. A dry astilbe is a dead astilbe. I
speak from bitter experience. No astilbe is going to prosper under a maple tree.
However, given the right soil and a bit of shade, this fine plant produces wonderful pink, red, and white spires that rise out of handsome, compound foliage
divided into toothed leaflets.

Some cultivars have tight heads of minute flowers; others, like 'Bridal Veil',

57

boast loose, airy heads. The majority of astilbes are 2 to 3 feet tall and bloom in June. Astilbe foliage is an asset to the shade garden all season.

Astilbelike in both flower and foliage, but much taller—4 to 6 feet—and more robust, goat's beard is an invaluable addition to the shade garden. It blooms in June—attractively but briefly, with large, lacy, cream-colored plumes. The individual flowers are insignificant, but taken as a whole the flower head is striking for about a week. After that, the tall, good-looking foliage provides an interesting background for large-leaved hostas.

Snakeroot, with not dissimilar compound foliage, divided and subdivided into toothed leaflets, sends up tall, narrow white flower spikes in July. I love this plant. The flower spike is no thicker than a stalk of asparagus and tapers to a point. It is at its loveliest when the tiny white flowers are still tight buds and look exactly like seed pearls.

A sentimental favorite for shade is old-fashioned bleeding heart, a large plant 30 inches tall by about the same across. It blooms in late May and contin-

Astilbe
(Astilbe x *arendsii*)

Tall, colorful flower plumes and attractive divided leaves.

ues into June but usually goes dormant in the summer. Compensate for this habit by planting it behind hostas and ferns. The foliage of bleeding heart is blue-green, and everybody loves the heart-shaped flowers that dangle in a single row from drooping stems. There is a pure white cultivar called 'Pantaloons', but the classic flower is pink tipped with white.

A smaller relation, fringed bleeding heart does not go dormant and blooms for a much longer season. Instead of single hearts, little clusters of somewhat heart-shaped flowers nod from the tips of the stems. The stems arise from mounds of ferny leaves. The whole clump reaches about a foot in height and the same or more across. 'Luxuriant' and 'Bountiful' have bluish-green foliage and deep reddish-pink flowers. Both the fringed and the old-fashioned bleeding heart are very hardy—Zones 3–9.

Corydalis has a common name that is no more familiar than its botanical name. At least, I had never heard of fumitory or fumewort. Anyway, the yellow species called *lutea* is a plant so charming and adaptable that I'm including it in the hope that it will become more familiar and more popular.

The foliage is a dead ringer for the fringed bleeding heart, only more delicate and a bluer-green; the flowers are small, tubular, and gathered in little clusters at the tip of the stems. What is so grand about this plant is that it flowers nonstop from April to November, and the foliage looks lovely all season.

Corydalis lutea was given to me twenty years ago by the Fosters. H. Lincoln Foster and his wife, Timmy, were the team that collaborated on *Rock Gardening: A Guide to Growing Alpines and Other Wildflowers in the American Garden*. Their literary and horticultural skills were matched only by their legendary kindness to beginning gardeners. The retaining walls around the Fosters' driveway billowed with *Corydalis lutea*—"Linc's weed," everyone called it. And he gave away seedlings by the shovelful. It has to be moved when tiny because the water-filled stems and roots are fragile. Mature plants self-sow, and seedlings turn up in every shady nook and cranny. Use it as a lacy edging for hostas. I wish I could give every beginning gardener a few little plants of Linc's weed.

Part Three

✤

The Art and Craft
of Gardening

✤ ✤

Design: Setting the Jewels in the Crown

*

Design is a word that strikes fear into the hearts of many. It shouldn't. To design means to contrive a plan. In deciding on the location of your flower bed, you have already completed part of the plan. By this time, you also know whether you need sun worshipers or plants that prefer shade. Ahead of you lies the happy task of assembling plants that you think will work well together. This is the frosting on the cake.

There is one more hurdle. As you have not yet grown the perennials you are about to plant, how are you to know when they will bloom in your area? It is all very well for me to give blooming dates for my Zone 6 garden in southwestern Connecticut, but elsewhere the same plants will have a different schedule. When will they bloom farther north in Maine? Or farther south in North Carolina? The ruler of Siam in the 1950s musical *The King and I* described this sort of problem as "a puzzlement."

Fortunately, landscape architect Joseph Hudak solves the puzzle for gardeners. In his invaluable book *Gardening with Perennials Month by Month* (see Selected Further Reading), he explains that for every degree of latitude, there can be three or four days' difference in flowering time. Thus when plants bloom in his Zone 6 garden in Boston, Massachusetts—at approximately 41 degrees latitude—they bloom two to three weeks later in Montreal at 46 degrees latitude. In Dallas, Texas, at 33 degrees latitude, the same plants flower as much as four weeks earlier than in Boston. With time, experience, and faithful note taking, you will be able to pinpoint blooming times for your own garden.

As you think about flowers and blooming times, don't forget foliage. It's easy to get swept away by a pretty face. But leaves are just as important as flowers. Because no perennial blooms all the time, you have to seek out those with foliage that retains its carriage and color throughout the season. This is especially important in edging plants. Any plant used at the front of the border can be considered an edging plant. And edgers have a heavy responsibility. They *must always* look respectable. Healthy, attractive edging plants can mask the flaws of the plants behind them and cover up a multitude of sins. Few casual viewers look beyond a clean, tidy edge.

As a perennial bed is a year-round proposition, it behooves gardeners to add a few year-round plants. For winter, there are ornamental grasses. Their tall, graceful sheaves of foliage dry and turn lovely shades of wheat, parchment, and tan. A few small deciduous shrubs change the flat winter bed to a three-dimensional addition to the landscape. They furnish the bed with intricate, twiggy skeletons and provide elevation when the herbaceous plants have died to the ground. Evergreens give the winter border geometry and lasting color—not just green, either. There are suitable evergreens in shades of gold, blue, and bronze.

Because making a flower garden is similar to making a painting, artists and gardeners work with many of the same elements: color, line, form, and texture. But for the gardener, there is an additional ingredient—plant habit. The phrase describes a combination of shape, outline, and texture that results in an overall impression.

Of course, the unique challenge for gardeners is using living materials that change with the season, during the season, and from year to year. Painters would throw up their hands if the canvas went from chartreuse to green to scarlet to brown to white. In many sections of the country, that's what happens from spring to fall in the garden. And that's the fun of it.

As color is one of the gardener's most beguiling playthings, a nodding acquaintance with rudimentary color theory is useful. In the seventeenth century, British physicist Sir Isaac Newton established that sunlight contains all the colors of the rainbow. His experiments involved intercepting beams of sunlight with a glass prism, which split the white light into bands of its respective colors: red, orange, yellow, green, blue, and violet. He described the colors collectively as the "solar spectrum."

It wasn't a big step from the arc of the rainbow to the color wheel, the chart he devised to demonstrate color relationships. The colors appear in the same order, but they are laid out in a circle and divided into wedges, each showing the various intensities of that color.

There are three primary colors—so-called because all other colors can be made from them: red, yellow, and blue. The secondary colors are orange, a combination of red and yellow; green, a combination of blue and yellow; and violet, made by mixing red and blue.

Colors that appear opposite each other on the color wheel are called complementary colors. And paired complementary colors intensify each other. This is of interest to gardeners, because putting complementary colors together creates contrast, drama, and excitement. Green is the complement of red; orange, the complement of blue; and violet, the complement of yellow.

While complementary colors are unrelated by pigment, harmonies are based on a sequence of colors that may (or may not) share a common pigment and are adjacent to each other on the color wheel. For instance, blue, blue-violet, violet, red-violet, and red is a color harmony. Blue and red are unrelated to each other, but violet in all its ramifications is related by pigment to both.

Colors can be either warm or cool. The warm colors seem to advance toward you, while the cool colors appear to recede into the distance. If you want your garden to look bigger, use cool colors. Red and orange are the hot spots; blue and green their cool counterparts. Yellow and violet can be either warm or cool. Greenish-yellow leans toward its cool neighbor, green; brassy yellow leans toward its warm neighbor, orange. Red-violet is warm and blue-violet cool.

The component of line in a garden can be found in the two-dimensional pattern of any man-made structure, like a trellis, wall, or fence. Also think of line as a pattern on the ground: the edge of a path or the outline of a garden bed. In winter, we suddenly become more aware of this element. We delight in the two-dimensional design of bare tree branches against the sky. Leafless trees and shrubs also trace designs on the ground against the snow or throw interesting shadows.

By form, I mean the solid contours of a plant. Ornamental evergreens make solid, flat silhouettes, but they also furnish the landscape with three-dimensional geometric shapes—cones, cylinders, pyramids, and globes. These forms abound in the natural world: Tree trunks are cylindrical; fir trees, conical, and many shrubs have a naturally rounded habit. Low mound shapes, fountain

Edging Plants

A good edger is any plant that retains its looks and habit all season.

Lady's-mantle (Alchemilla mollis)

Lovely, pleated, gray-green leaves and frothy yellow-green flowers.

Lilyturf (Liriope muscari)

Neat clumps of narrow green or green-and-yellow variegated leaves; wonderful all year.

Lamb's ears (Stachys byzantina)

Downy, silver-gray leaves; needs good drainage.

shapes, tall spear shapes and spreading fan shapes also appear frequently in the natural landscape and in garden plants.

Texture is a subtle aspect of gardening. It takes years to be aware enough and skilled enough to explore the nuances of texture, but start thinking about the different surface qualities of leaves and petals. The word "texture" comes from the Latin verb *texere*, meaning to weave. Originally, it had to do with the finish of woven fabric, but it has come to mean a variety of surface qualities. As you weave your garden, be on the alert for textural differences. Lamb's ears (*Stachys byzantina*) have velvet-textured leaves; holly, leaves that gleam like polished furniture. Daylily blossoms are surfaced with a glittering layer of diamond dust that sparkles in the sunlight, while prickly globe thistle flowers absorb rather than reflect the sunlight.

Of all the design components used by the gardener, none is more important than plant habit. There are soft filler plants that form airy masses of delicate foliage and flowers—just right to close an irregular gap in the border. Blocky plants with large leaves and uncomplicated flower shapes offer another look and screen out unwanted sights, like withering bulb foliage. There are sprawling, mound-forming plants, and spiky, upright ones; plants with a graceful arching habit, and plants whose natural shape is dense and formal.

Putting together the elements of line and form, color, texture, and plant habit is what garden making is all about. And there are as many ways of doing it as there are gardeners. But the following tips and techniques may help you get started.

It is natural for gardeners to think in terms of variety. The plant world is rich in wonderful shapes—those cones, fans, globes, and cylinders. Use them all. Employ all the fanciful flower shapes: the chic fleur-de-lis of the iris, the lily's trumpets, and the flat flower heads of sedum and yarrow. Variety gives life and energy to a flower bed, but too much can result in chaos. And the one-of-each-kind approach is interesting but not satisfying.

Because nature has made lavish provision for variety, it is important to establish a focus in your bed. Otherwise, the confused eye wanders aimlessly over a rich array of plants without differentiating among them. To anchor the viewer's roving gaze, you need either a big, eye-catching plant or a group of smaller plants of the same kind. Strategically placed, this focal point will give the eye something to rest on. Slowing down the viewer's visual sweep of the garden encourages appreciation of the plants surrounding the focal point or points.

Repetition is another way to still the overactive eye and lead it gently and enjoyably along the length of a perennial border. To establish rhythm in a long mixed border, repeat blocks of color; groups of similar structural forms; clumps of the same kind of plant; or a series of well-spaced evergreens. Even an intentionally exuberant, unruly bed in the cottage garden style benefits from repetition, to keep the eye content.

Unity is another device that can be used to contain chaos. By planting a single plant as an edging, the wildness within is kept under control. If that seems too boring, try different plants all of the same color. A single color theme can successfully hold together a multicolored border. Or try different colors but in plants all of the same size and texture. Another ploy is to establish a strong, clean edge. A tiny boxwood hedge, a stone strip, or just crisply cut turf serves exactly the same purpose. It reassures the viewer that this mélange of plants is actually loved and cared for, not just a colorful wilderness.

At first glance, Peter Wooster's northwestern Connecticut garden looks like a colorful wilderness enclosed by a picket fence. But controlled wilderness is the key. Inside strict boundaries—the fence on three sides and a stone wall on the fourth—there are eight free-standing rectangular beds: six large, two smaller, and a long bed next to the wall. All are stuffed with outrageous, wonderful plant combinations.

One year, the long bed boasted soaring clumps of purple-stemmed joe-pye weed, tobacco plants 12 feet high, and amaranths taller than I am. The leaves of the amaranths were green and the stalks red. From the tip of each terminal shoot, long clusters of red chenille cords dangled down and mingled with the red and purple leaves of coleus planted at its feet.

To contain the outlandish vigor of the plants and the daring of the color schemes, Peter edges the beds to within an inch of their lives. The lines are as straight as a ruler and painstakingly trimmed with long-handled grass shears every few days. In addition, each bed has structure provided by plants with solid, weighty forms or strong linear patterns.

An interior designer by profession, and an inspired amateur gardener by choice, Peter has this to say about deploying plants in a flower bed: "If they are all about the same size, you need something big to hold it all down. You need height in the middle from evergreens or shrubs. Then, each bed has corners that should be addressed."

Lynden B. Miller, a professional garden designer specializing in public spaces, says the same thing in a slightly different way: "If you made a brand-new garden and put in a couple of vertical dwarf evergreens and a couple of rounded ones, you'd be halfway there because you'd have given it geometry."

My own contribution is this: Good edging plants and superior foliage are the secrets of an effective perennial border. Look to the leaves and the edges, and the rest of the garden will fall into place.

I should be embarrassed to admit that what I have learned about designing a perennial garden can be summed up in six sentences, but here goes:

1. Include evergreen shrubs for geometry.
2. Use deciduous shrubs for linear structure and bulk.
3. Include variegated foliage as a substitute for flowers.
4. Address the centers, corners, and ends of beds.
5. Choose the best possible edgers. And use only those perennials whose foliage is acceptable all season.
6. Repeat plants, groupings, or colors to give purpose and unity to the border.

As you can see, some of these ideas are begged, borrowed, and stolen from gardening friends. Others I have picked up in the course of tinkering endlessly with my own perennial border. But I've tried them all, and they work.

Mull over the tips and techniques offered in this chapter. Then, pick and choose. As a gardener, you have to be an adventurer and an opportunist. Take what you need from other gardens and gardeners, from books, or from classes. But discover your own principles. Whatever works for you goes. Finally, as you feel your way, you will undoubtedly change the garden to fit your emerging personal style. At its best, a flower bed is a small private world in which you alone are the arbiter of beauty.

Putting It Together

❧

The last three chapters were intended to give you the wherewithal to carry out the next step—putting a flower bed together. You can choose to do this first on paper or you can do what Peter Wooster does. When the ground has been prepared and the bed is ready for planting, he and an accomplice assemble all the plants they have grown, bought, or acquired. "Then, we drag around a million pots and argue about where everything should go. It's not on paper, it's all in the garden with the plants in front of you. You come up with ideas and combinations in the heat of planting."

The reality is that most gardens are planted piecemeal with specimens found on the property, divisions from friends and neighbors, purchases from mail-order nurseries, and impulse buys from local garden centers. But starting with a plan on paper does help, no matter how far you stray from it. Drawing up a whole landscape design is daunting, but sketching a freehand map of a 6-foot-by-30-foot flower bed is not difficult.

I recommend drawing a bird's-eye view of the proposed bed on graph paper, using a half inch to equal a foot. The squares will keep you mindful of one of the few ironclad rules in gardening: You can't have it all. A perennial bed is like a checkerboard. If a square is occupied, it is occupied for the whole season. So you can't have hundreds of daylilies in the squares where you want phlox, delphiniums, and roses. You have to decide what you want most from your garden—a daylily display or a mixed border—and apportion the squares accordingly.

The squared paper also acts as a guide to spacing and plant numbers. If your plants are on the small side, three of a kind make a more satisfying picture than a single specimen. And odd numbers are easier to place in an informal arrangement than even numbers. Spacing is a very inexact science, but if you are using groups of three or more plants of one kind, leave more space around each group than between each plant in the group. The average planting space between plants is from a foot to 18 inches. Between groups, try 20 inches to 2 feet.

If somebody brings you a big clump of daylilies or a huge hunk of ornamental grass, treat it as a group, and give it additional room. But don't fuss too much about spacing. If you find you have planted too closely—an almost mandatory mistake—you can always change things around. Most perennials are easy to move. (Moving trees and shrubs is another story.) Finally, plot out approximate positions on your squared paper and draw the outline of the plants and plant groupings.

At this point, rather than present you with an arbitrary garden plan, I am going to analyze three gardens that illustrate some of the principles discussed in the previous chapters. There are dozens of wonderful perennial gardens I could have selected for this exercise, but I chose my own because I know it so well; Lynden B. Miller's because if there is such a thing as the perfect perennial garden, this is it; and Martha McKeon's because it is a promising, five-year-old work-in-progress.

We are different sorts of people at different stages in our gardening careers. Martha and I are amateurs; Lynden is a professional. Martha and I made our gardens in the same way that many of you will make yours—by trial and error and doing the work ourselves.

Lynden started out that way. She began her Connecticut country garden in 1980 but soon combined her training as a painter with her skills as a gardener. Her career as a designer of public gardens was launched in 1982 by an invitation to restore the Conservatory Garden in New York City's Central Park, at 105th Street and Fifth Avenue. Today, she is at the top of her field.

As Lynden is a New Yorker, much of her work graces that city. There is a great deal to learn from her magnificent perennial borders in Bryant Park behind the New York Public Library and in the lovely Conservatory Garden. But her own private garden is the perfect teaching garden because the scale is not too intimidating.

Like me, Martha is a part-time gardener and passionate do-it-yourselfer. She has a husband, two young daughters, a pair of Jack Russell terriers, a seasonal job at a nursery, and limited leisure. She began planting her 100-foot-long perennial border in 1990. Her struggles and triumphs, observations and insights, are particularly relevant because she has recently been through the early stages of making a new bed.

If your garden is not in Zone 6, like Martha's and mine, or Zone 5, like Lynden's, use Joseph Hudak's method of figuring out when the same plants will bloom in your garden. Look up their heights and other information in the back of the book or in one of the books suggested in Selected Further Reading.

I hope that you will take ideas from our gardens. Jot down plant names and plant groupings that appeal to you. Try some of the edging plants. Plant a few of the shrubs. Experiment with the color schemes. Don't worry about copying us. Any fleeting resemblance to the originals will disappear as your garden becomes increasingly personal.

My garden mentor, Helen Gill, was too diffident to foist her ideas on anyone, but she was notoriously generous with her plants. Years ago, she gave two other local gardeners and myself more plants than you can shake a stick at. We hauled off acres of lamb's ears and hosta; bags, boxes, and flats of hardy geraniums, irises, veronica, blue star, goldenstar, Memorial daisies, and catmint. In terms of plant material, our gardens were extensions of Helen's garden. But not one of the three remotely resembled hers. Nor were they like each other. In fact, our respective gardens were so different that it's hard to believe they were furnished with so many of the same plants.

With respect to my present garden, Peter Wooster's advice about addressing the corners of a rectangular flower bed can be applied even to my long border. While there are no corners, there are the two ends, which are very important in establishing the beginning and end of the garden.

A purple smoke bush holds down the end nearest the house, and a threadleaf Japanese maple with garnet-red foliage finishes off the other end. The maple is 25 years old and 9 feet across. Because of its commanding size and rich, deep color, it makes a good stopping place. You know that you have come to the end of the border. The maple is just over 3 feet in height, and its low, mounding habit links it to the gently sloping lawn and to the surrounding garden landscape.

Focus in my garden is largely a matter of color during the growing season. You look at what's in bloom, and what's in bloom depends on the time of year; but the eye is guided in its tour by the undulating bands of color, which run from one end of the border to the other. Peonies are repeated along the front, and their flowers take center stage in May and early June. They are large plants for the front of a bed, but their foliage is not as tall as the daylily scapes that rise behind them in July and August. Also the large, lobed peony leaves are valuable for hiding the foliage of spring-flowering bulbs and concealing the after-bloom flaws of the daylilies.

I am proud of my edging plants. They do yeoman service. Loose mounds of catmint alternate with neat clumps of calamint and low-growing sedums. 'Ruby Glow' and 'Vera Jameson' are favorite sedums for their succulent, smoky-green foliage tinged with purple. Also at the front of the bed, there are a couple of stands of threadleaf coreopsis; a few ornamental onion plants with flat swirls of blue-green leaves; and one clump of blue oat grass, which grows in a dense, spiky hummock. The catmints and coreopsis have naturally rounded forms and can be trimmed without violating their habit.

Catmints need shearing about three times a summer, but they are back in business within a couple of weeks. The fine, dense foliage of the coreopsis stays neat and green but is improved by being cut by about half when the main flush of bloom dwindles to a few flowers. The sedums benefit from having their stems shortened early in the season so that they sprawl less; after that, their fleshy leaves look attractive all summer. Except for chivelike flower heads late in the summer, the ornamental onions hardly change at all. The interesting vortex-pattern of their leaves needs no help in staying presentable. That's one of the traits you want in edgers—consistency.

Because my husband and I live in our house year-round, we want a year-round garden, and a good many squares in our checkerboard are now devoted to four-season plants, like ornamental grasses and shrubs. For years, though, I didn't bother too much about the fall and winter seasons because I was teaching full-time. I concentrated on summer. And because I have always been obsessed with daylilies, midsummer became the high point of my garden year. Many, many squares are still filled with daylilies. The two other periods of peak bloom when color is abundant are in early spring and from the end of May to the middle of June.

During April and the first part of May, white, cream, and yellow narcissus and tulips glow in the pale spring sunlight. Because their foliage dies down in the summer, there is room for them among the daylilies, and the daylily leaves hide the ripening bulb foliage.

Beginning in mid-May, the rhododendrons behind the border flaunt trusses of pink and red flowers. Soon, these are echoed in miniature by peonies at the front of the bed. All the reds and pinks tend toward the cool side of the spectrum. They bloom at the same time and harmonize with catmints and irises in shades of lavender-blue, violet, and purple.

From mid-June until the beginning of July, there is a pause in the flowering sequence. For at least two weeks, colorful foliage, contrasting leaf shapes, and different textures are responsible for keeping the garden attractive. The foliage of the smoke bush and the Japanese maple is dense, dark, and weighty. Elsewhere in the bed, self-sown seedlings of purple-leafed perilla turn up, adding flecks of the same purple as the smoke bush.

At intervals in the back of the border, variegated dogwood and three tall clumps of variegated ornamental grass provide so much light and life, they almost seem to be in bloom. The repetition of cream and green maintains interest throughout the length of the bed.

Repeated along the front of the border, *Sedum* 'Autumn Joy' has achieved its full stature by mid-June. Its blue-green leaves and immature flower heads look like giant bunches of broccoli. In contrast to the blocky forms of the sedum plants, the Siberian iris foliage rises up tall, slim, and grasslike. The dark green peony leaves are large, shiny, and cut into lobes, while the medium-green leaves of the daylilies are arched and ground-sweeping. The catmints have masses of small gray-green leaves; the calamints, small, shiny, deep green leaves.

The making of the whole bed is a 2-foot-wide band of silver-gray lamb's ears that runs the length of the border at the foot of a little retaining wall. From late spring through summer and fall into the early part of winter, this bright ribbon of foliage plays a dominant role in the perennial bed and in the larger garden landscape.

The presence of the lamb's ears at the foot of the wall illustrates the Scrabble Theory of design in action. Years ago, a huge shovelful of lamb's ears was one of Helen Gill's many gifts. The perennial border was much shorter then and already jammed with plants. It was too crowded for the lamb's ears. Like many gray- and silver-leaved plants, lamb's ears need good air circulation or they rot.

In desperation, I dug up a bit of lawn at the foot of the wall and stuck in the lamb's ears. At first, they looked out of place, but as the perennial border grew in length, following the contours of the slope, so did the band of lamb's ears. Today, they are the most photographed plants in my garden. They draw the eye purposefully along, providing unity and setting the border off from the surrounding green lawn.

Blue Oat Grass
(Helictotrichon sempervirens)

Spiky, low-growing clump, holds its steel-blue color in winter.

Fountain Grass (Pennisetum alopecuroides)

Cascading mound with stiff stalks and fuzzy flower heads.

Variegated Eulalia Grass
(Miscanthus sinensis 'Variegatus')

Tall, elegant sheaf of green-and-cream blades.

Midsummer is daylily time. Large clumps weave through the center of the garden, from one end to the other. Their blossoms, in closely related hot colors—red, orange, gold, bronze, and yellow—ignite the whole bed. Backup plants for the season include sunflowers in coordinating shades of gold and yellow; contrasting lavender-blue globe thistles; and spikes of shocking-pink gayfeather and loosestrife.

After this explosion of color, the month of August is something of an anticlimax. But yellow daisy-shaped flowers, like sneezeweed, rudbeckia, and sunflowers, combined with blue mist shrub and clumps of *Sedum* 'Autumn Joy', provide a modest display. This trio of plants with yellow, blue, and pink flowers is repeated three times in the border—at each end and near the middle. The blue mist shrub blooms from mid-August to mid-September and overlaps with the pink-to-rose stage of the sedum flowers.

Ornamental grasses, mostly members of the genus *Miscanthus*, are beautiful all year, but their graceful forms begin to be noticed more as the color from the daylilies subsides. In late August and September, the plumed flower heads rise above the foliage, unfurl, and, finally, produce silver seeds enveloped in fine silk floss.

In winter, these seed heads and the shocks of beige foliage persist and stand out against the rhododendrons. At the front of the border, low-growing blue oat grass pierces the snow with steel-blue blades that hold their color until spring.

Without its leaves, the red twig dogwood adds color to the winter landscape. And I enjoy the pattern of the blue mist shrub's bare, twiggy branches. After a snowstorm, the calyces, which once held flowers, rebloom with white cotton tufts of snow. Among the perennials, *Sedum* 'Autumn Joy' is handsome in winter, and I love the calamint's spidery network of fine, bare stems.

If you live where there are four distinct seasons, a garden like mine may appeal to you. If so, it is not a bad idea to start backward, choosing plants that will enhance the winter landscape first. All the winter winners make a substantial contribution to the summer garden as well.

In thinking about periods of peak bloom, consult your own schedule. If you travel in the summer, you might want to concentrate on spring bulbs and a fall garden full of late-blooming perennials and ornamental grasses. If you're away all winter and don't return until May, forget about bulbs and devote the majority of your checkerboard to summer bloomers.

Lynden Miller's garden has it all: waves of bloom, superior foliage plants, good edgers, year-round substance, entrancing color harmonies, soothing repetition, variety, and focus. It owes much of its all-season beauty to a magnificent 175-foot yew hedge that holds the garden in its semicircular embrace. The hedge acts as a boundary and background. "I look at the outline of the plants against it," says Lynden. "I like the negative and positive spaces, and what I see in my mind is the green shape around the plants."

The hedge has three openings from which paths fan out, like the spokes of a wheel, into the field beyond. The main opening is furnished with an elegant white arbor and gate. The two lesser openings have gates only. Matched conical arborvitae—a dwarf form that remains in scale with the perennials—mark the gate openings, like pairs of bookends.

The herbaceous plants on either side of the openings have been chosen with as much care and purpose as the shrubs. Some of them should sound familiar by now. Edging the beds on either side of the main gate are mats of lamb's ears, and holding down the front corners of the bed are clumps of catmint.

Strong, linear Siberian iris foliage stands tall behind the catmint and lamb's ears, and next to the irises there are bold clumps of peonies. Front-of-the-border plants include some of my favorites: blue oat grass, and the sedums—'Autumn Joy', 'Vera Jameson', and 'Ruby Glow'. Several variegated *Miscanthus* grasses are used as exclamation points at the back of the border.

Also at the back, the vivid bark of the versatile red twig dogwood looks handsome in the winter and gorgeous in summer with its wonderful cream and green leaves. You will find specimens of purple smoke bush in prominent positions near the openings. As befits a painter, Lynden is masterful in her deployment of evergreens and shrubs with colored foliage. Her palette includes: red-leaved barberry (*Berberis thunbergii* 'Rose Glow'), purpleleaf sand cherry (*Prunus* x *cistena*), dwarf forms of blue spruce, and globes of dark green holly. In addition to color, the subtle geometry of these shrubs, repeated in various combinations, gives her perennial plantings authority and yearlong beauty.

If you are lucky enough to visit any of the New York City public gardens Lynden has designed, you will see some of the same shrubs in action. In Bryant Park, she uses red twig dogwoods, hollies, and vertical yews pruned into flame shapes for both winter and summer structure.

Spiraea thunbergii is another shrub she likes "because it is one of the best four-season plants known to man. It gets to be six feet tall with white spring flowers and feathery green foliage for summer. Such a wonderful plant! It has warm, reddish-brown stems for winter interest and a very dense growth habit." She used groups of three to disguise the park's smoke vents.

The dark red barberries in the Conservatory Garden are her pride and joy. "They are beautiful, tight globes, pruned by the people who work for me," she says, "and we repeat them in each bed. In the winter, they're just fantastic the way they maintain the design." Using globe shapes to provide contrast among all the upright perennials is one of Lynden's design secrets. "Most plants read as vertical stems," she observes. "I think you need to take some and make them into rounds."

Another trick she favors is the use of big leaves. She grows oakleaf hydrangea (*Hydrangea quercifolia*) in all her gardens. It is a medium-sized shrub, 4 to 6 feet tall, with large, shapely leaves that relieve the busyness of a perennial border. Another signature foliage plant in Lynden's gardens is biennial Scotch thistle, with huge, carved silver leaves. The size and definition of the leaves rivet the attention instead of letting it drift away.

If you were to make seasonal visits to Lynden's garden, you would find many of the same plants I use, but blooming a little later in her Zone 5 climate. But in midsummer, when my garden is on fire with the hot hues of daylilies, cool colors dominate Lynden's garden. In July and early August, her border is like an exquisite length of watered silk. Close harmonies in mauve, lavender-blue, plum-purple, smoky-pink, bright pink, gray, and silver ripple against the dark green background of the hedge.

Silver is a recurring theme here. Lynden's repertoire of cool silver leaves includes lamb's ears, artemisia, and Russian sage, which brings silver-gray to the middle of the border. Its 3-foot stems are light gray and clad in slightly darker leaves. Although it is prized chiefly for the long, loose clusters of dainty lavender-blue flowers, Lynden loves the ethereal frost-color of the stems in winter. They make a beautiful pattern against the dark yew hedge.

A word of warning about plants with silver foliage. Most demand good drainage. If your soil gets soggy at any time, they are not the plants for you. But do realize what lovely blenders they make.

For the pink shades, Lynden counts on garden phlox 'Bright Eyes' and a few clumps of deep pink loosestrife—a cultivar called 'Morden's Pink'. Favorite cool colors are provided by annuals: "lots of blue salvia—a tall one for the back called *Salvia guaranitica*, petunia 'Blue Skies', and violet heliotrope." There are touches of cream from the variegated grasses, but yellow plays no part in this

The spring bulb display in my garden features tulips and daffodils.

Peonies, Siberian irises, and daisies repeated throughout the border hold sway in early June. The diagram opposite identifies important plants already in bloom and others waiting in the wings.

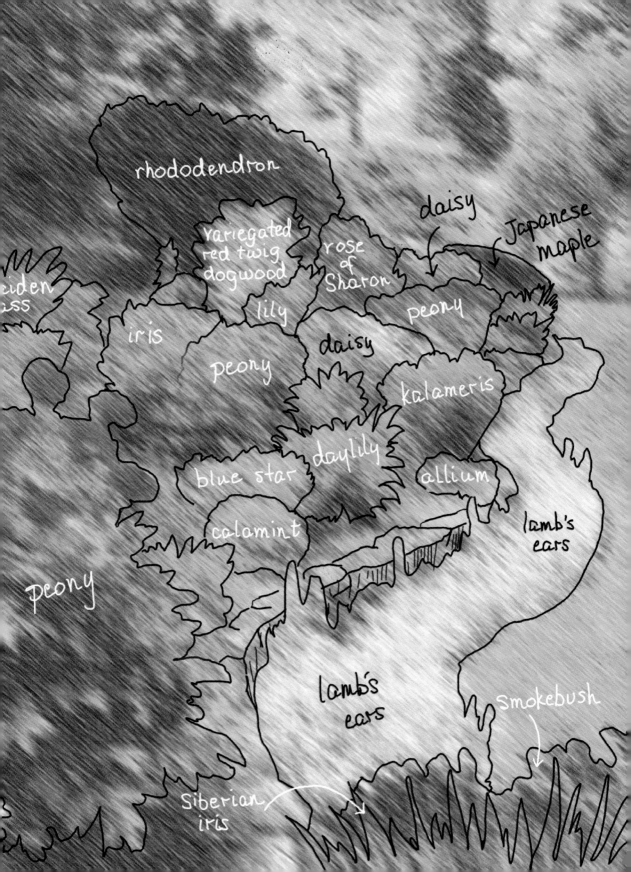

By mid-June, gray, red, and purple foliage and variegated leaves are the border's chief attraction.

Color returns with the beginning of the daylily season.

Sedum 'Autumn Joy' brightens the fall border, along with blue mist shrub, annual sunflowers, and tall joe-pye weed.

Grasses and snow-capped sedum give stellar performances in the winter.

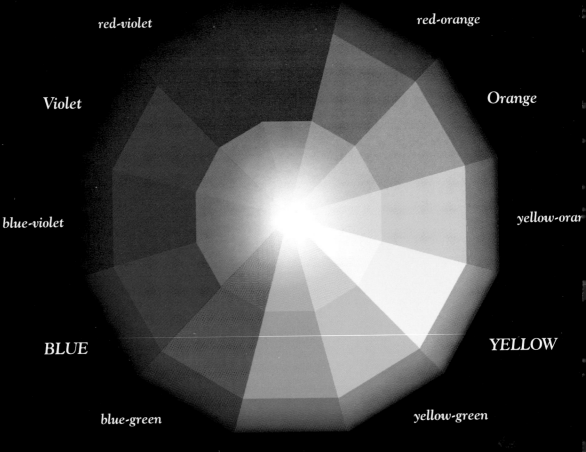

RED

red-violet   red-orange

Violet   Orange

blue-violet   yellow-orar

BLUE   YELLOW

blue-green   yellow-green

Green

In the eighteenth century, Sir Isaac Newton discovered that white sunlight contains every color in the rainbow: red, orange, yellow, green, blue, and violet. He also observed that the first and last colors share a common pigment—red. To illustrate this relationship and other color relationships, he rearranged the color spectrum into a wheel.

scheme, whereas yellow and the colors on the warm side of yellow are the central motif in my summer border.

In 1990, Martha McKeon wrote me a letter: "I would love to see your garden and also to have you come to our place. We moved here 14 years ago to a house my English grandmother still refers to as a 'sort of bungalow.' The woods come up to the doors and windows, but we are trying to make some sense of our Connecticut wilderness."

By the time I saw the property in June 1991, sense already prevailed. From the front of the house, a broad expanse of lawn sloped down to the little pond. At the edge of the lawn, facing due south, a long perennial bed stretched from the driveway to the pond. Behind it lay swampy woodland. In order to make the bed, Martha's husband, Bill, had cut down no fewer than sixteen red maples. Six years later, they are still pulling maple roots out of the bed.

Beautifully sited, with the woods as a background, the border is nearly a hundred feet long. Remembering my own timid beginnings, I was impressed by Martha's daring in making the bed so long. It is the rare beginner who can work in scale with nature. But from the start, she sensed that the garden had to divide the wilderness from the civilized area.

"I really didn't want it that long or that big," she admits with a laugh. "But there was no logical place to stop, except the pond. Actually, we stopped a few feet short of the water because the tiller broke down. God, what an awful job! The maple roots kept twining around the blades, and we had to cut them out with clippers. Running the tiller was like riding a bucking bronco. At one point, it almost took Bill into the pond."

From the very beginning, Martha intended to widen the bed. "It was about six feet deep the first year, and I knew right away that it was too narrow. Now, it's ten feet deep, and it varies because I use the stream as the back boundary. Where the stream curves away, the garden's wider, and where it curves inward, toward the lawn, the garden's narrower." Today, the proportions of the bed are just right—ample and satisfying.

The first plants went into the new bed in the fall of 1989. They were all from Bill's sister Karen, who was moving to Florida. The next spring, Bill's mother gave Martha more plants, old-fashioned blue lupines and ornamental grasses that had been in the family for years. Martha bought daylilies, phlox, delphiniums, and other perennials from the local garden center. "The daylilies and phlox are probably the only plants I bought that year that I still have," she says ruefully. "I tried lots of things . . . delphiniums, bee balm. The delphiniums rotted, and the bee balm got so tall it fell over and was a mess. So I gave up on them."

Excited as she was about the garden that first spring, she became discouraged by August. "When I began making the garden, I thought I only liked flowers. But after they grew, I realized that you can't just have little flowers against a background of tall, skinny trees. You need shrubs. But Bill said, 'I've just cut down all the trees and brush. I don't want any shrubs!' That's when we went to your house. I remember coming home and saying, 'Didn't you see all those rhododendrons? You *have* to have shrubs.' And finally, he said, 'All right.' "

The second year Martha made changes that reinforced her feelings about the shrub background. She put some of the tall ornamental grasses her mother-in-law had given her at the back of the bed. "I had them all lined up like soldiers, and they looked horrible," she says. "But even though they weren't in the right places, I could see how much their bulk and height improved the transition between the flower bed and the woods. The grasses helped me to understand why the shrubs were so important." She is still adding shrubs—butterfly bush, where it is not too wet; red twig dogwood, sweet pepperbush, and lacy, golden-leafed elderberry in the damp spots. And new grasses have joined her old favorites.

Having figured out what needed to be done to the rear of the border, Martha turned her attention to the front. The edge is as straight as a die, except at the far end, where it curves to meet the edge of the water, and at the near end, where a matching curve meets the driveway.

Within a couple of years, she had hit upon a very successful combination of plants. Among them, you will find lamb's ears and threadleaf coreopsis, but Martha worked out exceptionally attractive, varied groupings that include hostas next to lady's-mantle. This pairing is wonderful in June, when the lady's-mantle produces frothy heads of chartreuse flowers. The rest of the season, the scalloped, pleated, gray-green leaves of the lady's-mantle offer a pleasing contrast to the large solid green leaves of the hosta.

Variegated lilyturf is an outstanding companion for lady's-mantle and, in its own right, a world-class edger. About a foot tall, it looks like a compact ornamental grass with broad, slightly arching blades striped in green and primrose-yellow. The small spikes of tiny lavender flowers that appear in the fall won't take your breath away, but the foliage is striking all year long; and the combination of the lilyturf's striped leaves and the chartreuse flowers of lady's-mantle is perfectly lovely. I would steal this idea in a minute, if lady's-mantle didn't resent the dry soil in my border.

The foliage of coral bells makes an important contribution to the front of Martha's border. The leaves are generally round, scalloped, or toothed along the margins, and marbled with frosty patterns. They form a tidy mound from which the wiry flower stalks arise. The flowers are charming—tiny bells in loose spikes, and they come in pink, red, and white—but as edgers, their foliage is the main attraction.

Martha is triumphant about the front of the bed, and well she should be. The contrasting foliage shapes, varied textures, and limited color range—green, gray-green, silver, yellow, and chartreuse—result in a serene, orderly, interesting edge.

"Once I got down the edging plants," she says, "I didn't have to change that part of the garden much again. It's been about the same for four years. Repetition unifies it. I think you could take any bunch of plants and just plop them in, as long as you had a single theme or one type of ground cover uniting them all."

Discovering the charms of *Spiraea* x *bumalda* 'Anthony Waterer' and *Spiraea japonica* 'Little Princess' constituted another breakthrough for Martha. She had been complaining that the border looked "too fluffy" and needed more form. Enter the spiraeas and the clippers. Finely twigged, orderly in growth pattern, and densely covered with small, delicate leaves, both these spiraeas are invaluable shrubs for the perennial border. Their flowers are pretty—flat heads of tiny, fuzzy blossoms—but almost incidental to their superb plant habit.

Now, tightly clipped cushions of 'Little Princess' provide those valuable round forms at the front of the border, while 'Anthony Waterer' does the same for the middle of one of the island beds. Because these spiraeas bloom on new shoots, Martha prunes them heavily in the early spring, before growth begins, to give them a good shape. After flowering, she cuts them back by a couple of inches to remove the dead flowers and maintain their neat forms.

Don't be put off by the scale of the Eddison, Miller, and McKeon gardens. Mine was made in increments of about 10 feet a year. Take a section of one of our gardens to study. For a single segment, you need only half a dozen four-season plants; a handsome edger; one shrub for structure, and an evergreen for geometry. Mix and match from the plants mentioned in this chapter, and then branch out on your own.

Acquiring Plants

Y ou shouldn't be thinking about plants until the ground has been broken and the bed is ready for them. But you're only human. Besides, making long, expensive wish lists is harmless and educational. As I write, snow blankets the garden, and the landscape is a study in black and white. But indoors, the kitchen table is awash with color. The trickle of nursery catalogs that began before Christmas has reached flood stage. These tempting brochures find their way into my post office box because I am a garden writer. If they don't find you, you can find them by looking in Barbara Barton's *Gardening by Mail*.

Nearly a third of *Gardening by Mail* is devoted to plant and seed sources. Page after alluring page describes the offerings of mail-order nurseries. The entries include information about their catalogs—how much they cost (some are free, others cost a dollar or two) and whether or not they are illustrated in color. If they specialize in certain plants, these are listed, along with other useful information.

You will find sources of native plants and exotic plants; tender perennials and hardy perennials; prairie plants and aquatics; fruit trees and ornamentals. Because the choice is so overwhelming, I'm going to suggest three not-to-be-missed catalogs. The following have high-quality color photographs, extravagant but accurate plant descriptions, and good cultural information.

Always first in my mailbox and in my affections is the sumptuous Wayside Gardens catalog. It isn't just that I'm a sucker for gorgeous color pictures of plants—which, of course, I am. Wayside and I go back a long way together. Many of the ornamental trees and shrubs in our garden were ordered from them when the company was still in Mentor, Ohio. And that was many years ago. Since that time, I have never failed to receive a catalog—free of charge—whether or not I have placed an order within a couple of years.

Now located in Hodges, South Carolina, Wayside continues to produce a first-class publication handsomely illustrating their tremendous selection of herbaceous perennials, trees, shrubs, and vines. Often, Wayside is the only source of rare and hard-to-find plants. In addition to the general spring and fall catalogs, they send out a separate rose catalog. Graham Stuart Thomas, British rosarian and plantsman extraordinaire, acts as consulting editor for *The Complete Rose Catalog*. The text includes tidbits of rose lore and history, and practical advice about pruning.

Connecticut is home to White Flower Farm, which produces a lavish garden catalog twice a year and a once-a-year Christmas gift catalog. Customers who have made a purchase within the previous two years receive copies at no charge. Others wishing to obtain the catalogs pay $5 a year; the fee may be used as a credit toward any purchase.

Lately, White Flower Farm's choice of perennials has become increasingly adventurous, though there are plenty of solid classics for the beginner. Excellent plant descriptions and reliable tips on culture are a help to the novice. In addition to perennials, the spring catalog offers a collection of unusual annuals. The fall catalog features all kinds of bulbs; peonies; lilies; and irises.

The Klehm family has been in the nursery business in Illinois for 150 years, and they know what they are about. In their catalog, you will find extensive listings of the plants for which they have long been famous—peonies, daylilies, and hostas—but they also offer a limited collection of other surefire garden perennials: the best of the best. There is a fine group of Siberian irises from which to choose, and a select list of ornamental grasses. They are also expanding their shrub section. The catalog has a new look, which I love. There are color photos—you have to see the incandescent red blooms of the single peony 'Burma Ruby' to believe them. Artwork by Marcella J. Spanogle gives the Klehm catalog its special charm.

Klehm Nursery, Wayside Gardens, and White Flower Farm are large, reliable, well-known firms. They have many years of experience in storing and shipping plants, and you should be satisfied with your orders. Their guarantees are similar—one-time refund or replacement of any plant that has been properly taken care of but fails to grow. I have ordered from all three over a period of years and have found their service and plants most satisfactory. Plants are shipped either bare-rooted or in containers.

Your first sight of a bare-rooted plant in its dormant state can be a shock. It's hard to believe that soaking the roots in a bucket of water for a few hours and settling the plant into a prepared hole is anything but a waste of time. Dormant plants, and especially shrubs, look dead on arrival. But many can take the rigors of travel much better in this inactive state. Roses are usually shipped without soil. They arrive with only a few shortened canes rising from the woody crown and bare roots dangling below it.

Always unpack your plants carefully and keep an eye open for instructions. The recommended procedure for roses and other bare-rooted shrubs is to keep their roots moist and wrapped in damp newspaper or whatever packing material came with them until you are ready to plant. Although they should be planted as soon as possible, they can be stored like this in a shady, sheltered place for up to a week. Then soak the roots for a few hours before putting them into the ground.

Many perennials are shipped in pots these days, but a few still arrive bare-rooted. Peonies, bearded irises, and daylilies are almost always shipped without soil. Peony roots are stout and ugly with red or white sprouts called "eyes" at the top end. These sprouts are next year's stems, leaves, and flowers packaged and ready to grow. The only proper time to plant bare-rooted peonies is in the fall, any time before the ground freezes. Depth of planting is critical. The eyes must be at the top end, and *no deeper than two inches beneath the soil surface*. In the south, one inch below the surface is recommended. Peonies that are planted too deeply fail to flower.

If you are starting a new garden in the spring and want to grow peonies, leave a spot for them and order plants for fall. In the meantime, fill their space with annuals. Or you may be able to find potted peony plants at your local garden center. Garden centers often carry a few container-grown peonies, but your choices of cultivars will be limited.

Like peonies, bearded irises are particular about planting time. Although plants growing in containers can be purchased from local garden centers in the spring, iris nurseries usually ship in mid- to late summer, after flowering. The plants should be put in the ground promptly. Bearded irises are shallow-rooted

Bare-rooted Plants

Bare-rooted plants arrive from the nursery with the roots cleaned of earth and the foliage cut back to about 8".

Mail-order daylily nurseries furnish single (illustrated) or double "fans".

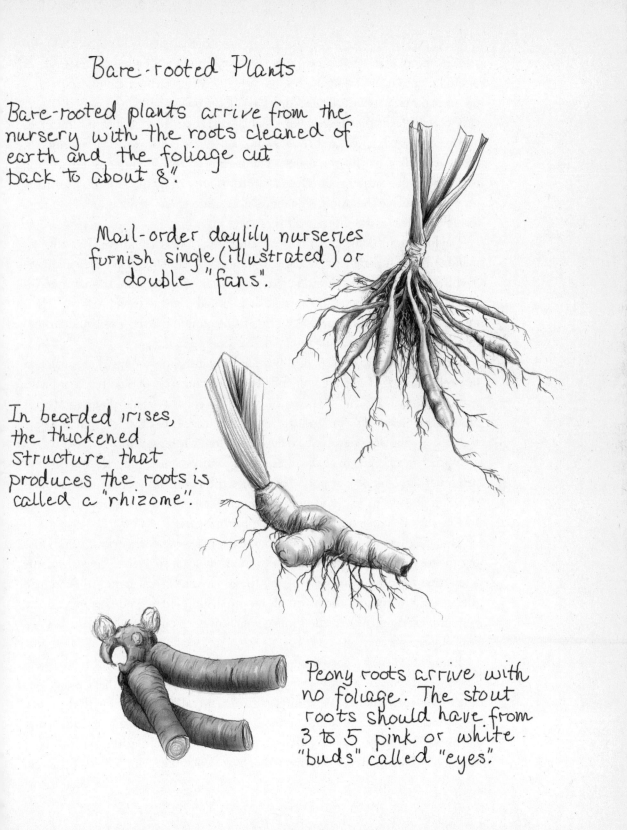

In bearded irises, the thickened structure that produces the roots is called a "rhizome".

Peony roots arrive with no foliage. The stout roots should have from 3 to 5 pink or white "buds" called "eyes."

and, in the North, need time to become established before the deadly cycle of alternate freezing and thawing begins. When loose cultivated soil freezes, it rises up, like the dome of an ice cube, dragging plant roots with it.

On arrival, iris plants are a sorry sight, with their thick, horizontal rhizomes and pale roots exposed and their swordlike leaves cut down to a few inches. However, this is par for the course. Plants shipped in leaf are constantly losing moisture through their foliage. As their roots are not in the ground, they have no way to replace the water. The more leaf surface there is, the more water they lose. So the leaves are shortened to conserve moisture.

Daylilies don't look much better than irises when they arrive. I vividly remember my first shipment. I made an irate entry in my garden notebook: "the daylilies look terrible." However, new foliage soon appeared, and they all bloomed the first summer. Like irises, bare-rooted daylilies travel best with their foliage cut down to 8 inches and with nothing around the roots except dry shavings. Moist packing material around fleshy roots encourages rot.

Unlike peonies and irises, daylilies can be planted almost any time, although late fall planting is not recommended in cold climates. I've gotten away with planting in early November by putting 4 or 5 inches of shredded autumn leaves around the plants. The ground will eventually freeze, but the leaf mulch delays the process, allowing new roots to develop before winter sets in.

With the exception of daylilies, irises, and peonies, the vast majority of perennials are shipped in pots. Sometimes the plants are dormant; sometimes they are already in leaf and growing. Even container-grown plants that have traveled any distance need a little tender, loving care.

Unpack them and set their pots in a shady place out of the wind. Wind dries out the foliage. Keep the soil in the pots moist but not soggy, and give the plants a few days to recover before bringing them out into bright light. You can ease the shock by exposing them first to morning sun. Then, gradually extend the period of exposure. When their foliage remains crisp and turgid all day, they are ready for the garden.

Being able to buy potted perennials at the garden center and plant them whenever the mood moves is very appealing to gardeners, but there is a downside to this convenience. Beginning gardeners literally lose touch with the roots. No wonder people are confused about the difference between true lilies and daylilies. The most obvious difference is underground. True lilies, members of the genus *Lilium*, develop from bulbs that look like giant cloves of garlic.

Daylilies, which belong to the genus *Hemerocallis*, grow from fleshy thongs and fingerlike storage roots.

In time you will get to know your roots, because you will meet them when you are moving and dividing your perennials. There are many desirable perennials that increase rapidly, and gardeners are relieved to find good homes for extra daylilies, irises, ornamental grasses, lamb's ears, and other vigorous perennials. When I'm dividing plants, I put extra divisions into plastic bags, add a bit of soil, write the cultivar name on the bag with a Magic Marker, and stash them away out of sight under a tree. Then they are ready when someone wants them.

Although my giveaway divisions are not absolutely bare-rooted, the soil will probably fall off when the recipient takes them out of the bag. Divisions received in this state should be potted up and given the same treatment afforded mail-order plants that arrive bare-rooted: moisture, shade, and shelter from drying winds.

On the whole, you can safely and gratefully accept divisions of your neighbors' perennials. Most experienced gardeners are truly generous and well meaning. They won't give you a "dog." But there are a few plants that multiply so fast they will take your breath, and most of your garden, away. These can be useful in the right place, but if you receive divisions of the following, be aware that given good, friable garden soil, they will take over.

Gooseneck loosestrife is such a plant. It is extremely pretty, a wonderful cut flower and a perfect menace if it has its way. The underground stems weave an impenetrable network from which close ranks of leafy stems arise. The long, white flower heads all face the same direction. They curve forward and downward, then up again at the tip, hence the common name of gooseneck. In very dry soil, this plant is controllable, but it tends to wilt. In damp soil, it will overrun a large area quickly. Mint and bee balm have a similar tendency, though they are easier to discourage than gooseneck.

I love but fear the magnificent plume poppy. Peter Wooster dares to include this huge, assertive plant in his bold border, but he keeps attacking its wandering roots with a sharp spade. Plume poppy has wonderful lobed blue-green foliage and elongated, pinkish-tan heads of tiny flowers. It grows to 8 feet and will colonize your entire garden if you don't keep after it.

If you find plantings already on your property, you can have a bit of instant garden by moving entire clumps of perennials to your new bed. Plants with masses of relatively shallow, fibrous or fleshy roots, like daylilies, Siberian irises, lady's-mantle, veronica, sunflowers, sedums, ferns, and hostas, are easy to move. (Plants like balloon flower and gas plant have deep roots and resent relocation, except when small.)

Late summer is the best time to divide plants. That subject will be covered later, but early spring is the best time to move whole clumps. At that time, the leaves are just emerging; every moisture-filled root is bursting with vitality; the weather is cool; and the surrounding earth is damp. Damp soil clings to the roots better than dry soil does. Your aim is to remove the clump intact, retaining as much soil as possible. If the ground is dry, water the plant beforehand.

Drive the blade of a sharp shovel or spade straight down all around the perimeter of the clump, but not too close to the stems. Then, thrust the blade forward under the roots to loosen the clump. Because the ball of damp earth will be heavy, use a tarpaulin to haul away your prize. I learned the value of a tarpaulin from a young gardener who used to help me once a week. Ann's motto was, Never carry what you can drag.

If, despite your best efforts, the clump falls apart, treat the pieces like new arrivals: pot them, water them, shade them, and in a few days introduce them into the garden.

The Good Earth

Soil is to plants what hearth and home, air, food, and water are to us. Some orchids and bromeliads manufacture their own food and find physical support where they can. But most plants depend on the soil for everything. The particles of rock that make up the mineral content provide anchorage for their roots. The spaces between these mineral particles hold life-sustaining air and water.

Plants are about 70 percent water. Water fills their cells and holds them upright; it dissolves the nutrients in soil and transports them to the plant's stems, leaves, and flowers. Air is just as important. In order to function, roots must have oxygen. But vital as oxygen, water, and rock are, they are of no use to plants without a fourth component—organic matter.

Organic matter is derived from plant and animal waste. In the presence of moisture and air, bacteria go to work on dead animal and vegetable tissue—a mouse that has died, weeds that have been killed by frost—eventually transforming them into a soft, brown material called humus.

Gardeners say the word "humus" with reverence. It is the magical substance that renders hard soil friable and stabilizes sand. It provides food for plant roots and holds water for their future use. It looks good, feels good, smells good, and does good. Best of all, you can make your own by salvaging vegetable scraps, grass clippings, autumn leaves, and garden debris and putting them somewhere out of sight until they rot (see "Compost: Let It Rot").

The end product of complete decomposition is a sticky liquid called humic acid. Humic acid coats the mineral particles in soil and binds them together in units of different sizes. You know that humic acid has done its work when the soil is soft and crumbly. If you squeeze together a handful of good garden soil, it should hold its shape for a few seconds, then fall apart. This means there is enough moisture but not too much and that the soil particles are different sizes instead of uniform.

A handful of clay will hold its shape indefinitely, indicating the presence of moisture but no air. And a handful of sand just falls apart. In the best of all possible soils, water travels through the interstices between clusters of mineral particles and adheres to the sides of these units, permitting air to fill the remaining spaces.

There is a formula for good garden soil: 45 percent sand, silt, and clay (mineral particles); 5 percent organic matter; 30 percent air; and 20 percent water. But a lot about soil quality can be determined by exercising the senses. Really look at your soil. Humus gives good soil its rich color and chocolate-cake texture. If the soil is gray, yellow, or tan, it is probably lacking in humus.

Earthworms are a promising sight. Their presence indicates an abundance of organic matter, and their network of tunnels conducts water and air to plant roots. Moreover, as worms stitch their way up and down through the soil layers, they distribute decomposed animal and vegetable wastes to the barren subsoil.

Touching the soil tells you something about its mineral content. Take a pinch between your fingers. If it feels grainy, it probably contains a high proportion of sand; if silky, the chances are that silt or clay predominates. Sand particles are relatively large; silt particles are almost invisible to the naked eye. Clay particles are so fine they can only be seen with a high-powered microscope.

Sandy soils have their virtues. Being loose and porous, they are easily penetrated by the frailest of roots. Water passes quickly through the pores between grains, and air is abundant. But as gravity conducts the water speedily downward, pulling it from the sides of each grain of sand, all the nutrients go with it. This flushing of the soil is called leaching. And leaching robs the roots of sustenance. Worse, it can cause death. As the water drains away, the empty spaces fill with air, and most plants cannot live on air alone. They wilt and die.

Clayey soils are just the opposite—dense, heavy, and hard for roots to penetrate. The microscopic clay particles cover the soil surface with a water-repellent dust, delaying water absorption. Puddles sit for a long time before percolating down through the minute pores. Even as moisture begins to move downward, it is in no hurry. Once wet, clay stays wet. Slowly draining clay soils are rich in nutrients, but if every tiny pore is filled with water, plants literally drown, and their roots rot.

Every gardening book I have ever consulted extols the virtues of "a well-drained, moisture-retentive soil." But only one has explained this riddle to my satisfaction. In *Wildflowers in Your Garden* (Random House, 1993), Viki Ferreniea discusses soil in a way that anyone can understand. She explains that a plant requires a balance between moisture retention and good drainage. "At first, this sounds like a contradiction: what it is saying, however, is that the plant needs a soil that has enough organic matter (humus, compost, manure, and the like) mixed into it to absorb and retain water, and at the same time has enough drainage material (sand, small stones, or gravel) in it to allow excess moisture to drain off after the organic matter has soaked up all the water it can." There now.

The organic matter acts as a sponge; the sponge serves as a reservoir for the plants; and the drainage material allows the remaining water to escape, instead of filling every pore. Some soils are well-drained and moisture-retentive because nature made them that way. Others are dense and dreadful for the same reason. But all soils can be improved.

At the New York Botanical Garden, the natural soil is heavy clay. Michael Ruggiero knows this soil as well as he knows the soil in his own backyard. He has worked at the Garden since he was sixteen. The secret of his success with plants is passion, knowledge, and good soil.

Recently, he showed me how he and his crew amend the soil at the Garden. Out behind the propagation range there are three huge bins with wooden sides. Mike buried his big hands in a heap of crumbly black stuff that filled one bin. "This is leaf mold," he said, "from our own leaves. We make our own compost, too."

Moving on to the next bin, he seized a handful of soil and let it run through his fingers. "We buy a lot of soil from Long Island because of its sandy quality. Sandy soil doesn't hold together at all." He squeezed a handful to no avail. "It drains too well and won't hold any moisture, while our clay soil holds all the moisture and doesn't have any air. We mix the two with compost and leaf mold and end up with a hybrid. The combination with the organic matter is what makes it good."

The senior curator of the Peggy Rockefeller Rose Garden dusted his hands on his work pants and grinned. "It's a Catch-22. To straighten out this sandy soil, you add organic matter. What do you think you add to clayey soil?" Fearing an ignorant reply, he answered his own question. "Organic matter. If you add sand without compost or leaf mold, you have two-thirds of the recipe for concrete."

The natural texture of my garden soil is clayey rather than sandy. In the spring, it looks dark and promising because it stays damp for a long time. But moisture rather than adequate organic matter gives it its healthy color. In a hot, dry summer, the surface sheds water like a duck's back. Or it used to, until I discovered the benefits of an organic mulch.

A mulch is any material employed to cover the bare ground. A layer of loose, airy material spread over the soil prevents erosion, protects plant roots from abrupt changes in temperature, retains moisture by retarding evaporation, and discourages the germination of weed seeds.

Nature mulches with leaves and vegetation—living and dead. Man has devised a variety of synthetic mulches that do the same job but add nothing to the soil. Organic mulches gradually decompose and contribute precious humus to the garden.

It is almost impossible to overstate the case for an organic mulch. I say almost because mulch can provide a haven for small rodents. However, the benefits outweigh the risks, and despite vole damage, I continue to mulch the perennial border.

You can use almost anything from leaves shredded with the lawn mower to compost to pine needles, buckwheat hulls, or ground corncobs. Ruth Stout, whose book *How to Have a Green Thumb without an Aching Back* put mulch on the map and on the gardens of her readers, used anything and everything.

It was my good fortune that, in spite of all warnings against it, I had formed the habit of leaving all the vegetable waste, such as corn stalks, right there in the garden and had spread leaves all over it in the fall and vegetable garbage all winter long. Now, when I raked this mass of stuff aside to make a row for the spinach I found the ground so soft and moist that I made a tiny drill with my finger.

Louise Marston, an early disciple of Ruth Stout's mulching technique, came into my life in the early eighties. I had already been gardening for twenty years, but without benefit of mulch. Within weeks, she had convinced me to cover every inch of exposed soil in my perennial border with a 3-inch layer of partially decayed leaves. The returns were immeasurable and immediate.

Beneath the leaves, the soil surface remained loose and open, instead of turning to dust. Rain easily found its way through the mulch and into the soil. Moist soil takes up water; dry soil doesn't. In addition, the mulch delayed evaporation and kept the soil cool, damp, and almost weed-free. Weed seeds need light to germinate. By eliminating the light, we reduced the population to a few weak, straggling things that could easily be tweaked out. I haven't really weeded in years.

Since I began using a mulch, there has been a gradual improvement in the top inch or two of soil in my perennial beds. It would take eons to make a deep layer of humus-filled soil, but every year, the decaying leaves deposit at least a thin residue of organic matter, which is incorporated into the soil. The job is never done. Soil is created by constant renewal.

In the natural course of things, plants die, and their remains are recycled by living bacteria. Seeds germinate in the humus created by these microscopic organisms, and a new generation of plants uses up the supply. When they die, the stock of organic matter is replenished by their remains. This is not what happens in the garden.

Tidy gardeners interrupt the cycle of birth and death by cleaning up the garden in the fall. Applying an organic mulch in the spring simply returns to the soil what nature would have provided. Good soil is made year by year. While farmers don't mulch their cornfields, they do renew the organic matter in their soil every spring by spreading manure. No aspect of gardening is as important as the care of your soil.

Louise Marston actually makes soil from scratch. Her garden perches precariously on a bulge of bedrock high above the street. Initially, the rock was swept clean of soil by wind and weather, but this patient, painstaking gardener built low retaining walls and backfilled them with layers of hay and manure. Year after year, layer after layer—first the hay, then the manure, along with any soil she could scrape off the rock.

Using bales of hay by the hundred and truckloads of manure, she is usually able to plant within a year or two. The work has been grueling, but the payoff is the most glorious, rich, soft, dark soil and the biggest, healthiest, most beautiful plants I have ever seen. A telephone pole would sprout leaves in Lou's soil.

How I wish I had understood the importance of organic matter when I began my main perennial garden! The digging was tough, and I was impatient. I charged along the hillside, stripping off the sod, prying out rocks, and, where I could, loosening the soil to the depth of the shovel. But I never prepared the whole bed (see "Breaking Ground").

I prepared the planting holes with a bit more care, adding compost and peat moss. I feel obliged here to say a word about peat moss. In my day, virtually all gardening books recommended peat moss as a soil amendment. Although it has no nutritional value, it adds organic matter to the soil and improves moisture retention. Being readily available, clean, and odor-free, it is still popular.

Today, it is politically incorrect to use peat moss. While there is justifiable concern about depleting the supply, *peat moss is a slowly renewable resource*. Be that as it may, there are better, less controversial sources of organic matter. Try composted cow manure or bagged humus from the local garden center instead. There are also private companies that sell bulk compost. Check the classified pages of your newspaper.

Back to my garden. My selection of plants was better than my soil preparation. I chose strong, adaptable plants that have, on the whole, prospered. However, periods of drought are far more damaging in my garden than they are in Lou's. Her plants come through with flying colors, thanks to the high moisture content of her rich, humus-filled soil. If you want to grow perennials, nothing, but nothing, is as important as good soil.

Having said that, I must add that many alpine plants subsist on a meager diet of broken stone and mineral crumbs, while sun-loving native wildflowers, like coreopsis, black-eyed Susans, and coneflowers, and some silver-leaved plants, can make do with quite poor, dry soil. However, most common garden subjects crave the stuff that Lou makes—soil that is both moisture-retentive and well-drained.

In a long gardening life, I have enjoyed myself, learned from my mistakes, and have few regrets. But I devoutly wish I had understood from the start the importance of good soil. While I continue to believe in the dig-a-hole-and-plant-something approach to gardening, be forewarned: At some point, you will have to give serious consideration to your soil. The more you do now, the less you will have to do later, and the better your first plants will grow.

Breaking Ground

※

Preparing a new bed is hard work. There is no getting around it. Most beds are carved out of existing lawn. More often than not, the soil underneath has been packed down by foot traffic or, worse, heavy equipment. Soil that has suffered this treatment is dense and airless. It may also be full of rocks, roots, and building debris. Human intervention is necessary in order to make this hostile environment suitable for plants.

Usually, this means stripping off sod. I have always done it manually, but there are other methods, and in the right hands, power equipment can be a boon. Rental sources of power equipment can be found in the Yellow Pages of the phone book.

If the area is large, level, and open and the proposed bed is bounded by straight lines, you might consider renting a sod cutter. Be advised, however, that transporting the 300-pound machine to the site is usually the renter's problem. Unless you are fit, strong, and mechanically inclined, you would do well to rent an operator, too.

This machine is gasoline-powered and self-propelled, with a blade that shaves off the sod in neat strips a foot wide and a couple of inches deep. Each strip can be rolled up as easily as rolling up a rug, leaving behind a bed with beautiful, sharp, straight edges. But the corners still have to be dug by hand, because the sod cutter is too cumbersome to make tight turns.

For an inexperienced operator, the sod cutter's drawbacks outnumber its virtues. Chris Curless, a young, able-bodied friend of mine, rented one in order to review its performance for an article in *Fine Gardening*. He told readers that it was a real struggle to maneuver the thing because it has no reverse gear. He also found that it mangled the turf on a curve and was hopeless on a slope. "Keeping it upright on even a slight grade would require prodigious strength," he wrote. These reservations would—and should—discourage many gardeners.

However, in half an hour, working on level terrain, Chris stripped the sod from an area that would have taken him an entire afternoon by hand. Make no mistake, stripping sod by hand is time-consuming. But if the area is relatively small or among trees or near the house, where there may be hidden utility lines, it is the best method. It is safe, cheap, and thorough.

First, mark out your bed with string stretched taut between short stakes driven into the ground. You want the string close to the ground in order to use it as a guide. If the bed has curved lines, use a hose to outline the shape. Then, take an edger with a crescent-shaped blade or a sharp spade with a straight edge and make vertical cuts into the sod, following the course of the string or hose. Drive the edger or spade 3 inches into the ground. Make a grid pattern of verti-cal cuts so that you can lift out pieces of sod about a foot square. Loosen them by thrusting the spade underneath them as nearly parallel to the ground as possible. You don't want to rob the bed of any more soil than you can help.

Now, pry up the pieces by hand, and shake off the earth. Collect the sod in a wheelbarrow, and find an out-of-the-way place where you can start a compost pile. Stack the pieces of sod grass side to grass side, to encourage decomposition. Compost piles are discussed in another chapter (see "Compost: Let It Rot").

Removing sod is only the first step in preparing a bed for planting. The soil still has to be loosened, fertilized, and amended with organic matter. Once it has been laid bare, dig the whole area to the depth of a shovel blade. Most books recommend deeper digging, but realistically, most common perennials will do well in 8 to 10 inches of loose, humus-rich soil.

Turn the soil over, shovelful by shovelful. Break up each clod of earth with the back of the shovel, and remove roots, rocks, and any remaining sod. Rake the surface level and sprinkle it with granules of a complete fertilizer at the rec-ommended rate, usually 2 pounds per 100 square feet.

A quick word about "complete" fertilizers. There are fifteen elements neces-sary for healthy plant growth. Three are obtained from water or from the air: carbon, hydrogen, and oxygen. The rest have to come from the soil. The three most important are: nitrogen to stimulate luxuriant green leaves and stems; phosphorus, which is required for strong root development; and potassium, which promotes general good health and disease resistance.

The hyphenated numbers on fertilizer bags refer to these three elements, always in that order: nitrogen, phosphorus, and potassium. As perennials need less nitrogen and potassium than phosphorus, general-purpose fertilizers are tailored to these needs. The most often recommended is 5-10-5.

Next, add 2 inches of organic matter: compost, composted manure, mushroom compost, or whatever is available locally. Now, dig the organic matter into the bed, along with the fertilizer. I prefer a long-handled shovel to a spade for this operation. Digging in the soil amendments puts nutrients where the plants need them—near the roots. Moisture in the soil dissolves the mineral nutrients in the fertilizer and makes them available to the plants.

All my flower beds have been prepared by hand—not, alas, as thoroughly as the method I have just described, but you live and learn. The more recent the bed, the better the soil preparation. The vegetable garden was the only departure from hand preparation. In the early days, we succumbed to the notion that because we lived in the country and had enough room, we needed a large vegetable patch.

I marked out a 30-by-60-foot area of the former cow pasture with stakes and string. My engineer husband, who is skilled with power equipment, churned it up with a rotary plow mounted on our Gravely tractor. Driven by the tractor's powerful 7.5-horsepower engine, the plow tore through the rough field turf like a giant brace and bit, flinging around small stones and striking noisy blows on the remaining boulders.

We were young then, but even so, we found that initial foray into the vegetable garden strenuous. So was the handwork that followed. The soil was full of stones and hunks of undigested sod. I picked out the stones, carted them off in the wheelbarrow, and dumped them in the woods.

The sod had to be raked up and taken to the compost pile, but I missed pieces. Perennial barnyard grass is tough, and any that I overlooked soon took root and thrived in the newly cultivated soil. Pulling it out took a lot of time the first couple of years. An organic mulch would have solved the problem by smothering it, but I had not yet made that discovery. Admittedly, the task of preparing the vegetable garden was less work every year, even without the mulch.

No one is better equipped to tell you about preparing a new bed than Rita Buchanan. Since I have known her, she has started two different gardens from scratch. Rita has made vegetable and flower gardens wherever she has lived and figures that she must have broken at least an acre of new ground in the last ten years. She has always done it with a tiller. I value her view on tillers because when she was the editor of *Fine Gardening*, she ran field tests on a range of small tillers. Her 60-pound Honda is the joy of her life.

"Overwhelmingly, I think the Hondas are best. Compared to other tillers that I've used, Hondas are far the easiest to start. I found that all those mini-tillers were cranky to start and noisy, noisy, noisy. I've had my Honda for nine years now. It has always started on the first or second pull, and it has a little muffler so it isn't noisy."

Rita's enthusiasm for tillers goes back a long way, almost as far back as her gardening roots on a farm in upstate New York. Growing food came with the territory. "My love of tillers surely comes from having spent many years doing lots of vegetable gardening. In that context, a tiller is just indispensable," she says. She is the first to admit that making a new bed takes a considerable amount of work, even with a good tiller. But she emphasizes that the machine provides the muscle; the operator only has to exercise patience.

"You have to realize from the start that it takes time. You have to make many, many passes with the tiller. But remember that tilling does not require brute force. The machine does the work. That is what people find hard to accept. Everybody panics and tries to grip it or force it. But the secret to using a tiller is letting it bite down gradually and of its own accord. On every pass, it bites deeper.

"After you've gone back and forth four times—sometimes it's only twice, sometimes it's six times—the tines start going deeper and deeper into the soil, and eventually, as deep as they will go. By this time, the machine is moving forward very slowly. You could twiddle your thumbs as you are walking behind it. Now, it is doing a deep, thorough job."

The ease or difficulty of breaking ground depends to some extent on soil moisture. Obviously, you don't want to work wet soil. It will clog the tines of the tiller and make the job slower and harder. Nor is dry soil easy to work. Rita says the ideal time to break ground is after a rain but when the soil has had a chance to dry out again.

Her tiller takes a beating in the rocky soil of her Connecticut garden. She regularly meets rocks the size of grapefruit. "The tiller is a great tool for removing rocks that size," she says gleefully. "It bumps them loose. The only thing that can go wrong is that smaller rocks can get stuck between the tines. And the machine stalls. You have to stop the motor and jiggle the rock loose. If you grit your teeth and convince yourself that it is not going to hurt the tiller, you can deal with a rock the size of a watermelon. Let the tiller bump it a few times, and the rock will come loose. Then, put the tiller on idle, while you pry it out with a digging fork."

Coping with rocks is a fact of life in New England. Rita always equips herself with a fork and a wheelbarrow when she is making a new bed. As she follows behind the tiller, she tosses loosened rocks into the wheelbarrow. If she hits a big rock, and it comes loose, she gouges it out with the fork. "Whenever you see a rock, get it out so that you won't hit it again and again," she advises.

I was interested in how she dealt with sod. She had to admit that the tiller won't slice up chunks of coarse perennial barnyard grass. These have to be collected and put on the compost pile. But it reduces lawn grasses, like fescues and bluegrass, to clumps the size of your fist. Left on the surface, the clumps usually dry out and disintegrate, while those left in the soil decompose, adding more organic matter. If the bed is planted and mulched immediately, any remaining grass is smothered by the mulch.

As Rita likes to dig for the sake of digging, she sometimes employs a combination of tilling and hand preparation. "There are times when I'll do an initial digging by hand, either because I feel like it or because I expect there are a lot of rocks. But when it comes to serious soil preparation and incorporating organic materials into the garden, I think that my little Honda tiller is the best tool I've ever bought."

For the gardener with foresight, there is yet another way of breaking ground. I discovered this alternate route by accident. Despite the excitement and haste with which I first threw myself into gardening, taming our whole property all at one time was obviously impossible. So to keep the weeds down along a stretch of stone wall where I planned one day to have a bed, I got a few bales of mulch hay. Unfit for consumption by livestock, mulch hay is available by the bale wherever there still are farms. I broke open the bales and laid down 6-inch-thick mats of hay at the foot of the wall.

For a year, the mats just sat there. Then, a few weeds began to sprout in the decomposing hay. I still couldn't get to that part of the garden, so I got some more hay and piled on another 6 inches. The next year, I did the same thing. It was about four years before I could turn my attention to that area. By that time, something wonderful had happened. Without my lifting a finger, the hay had broken down into beautiful compost, at the same time killing the grass beneath it and turning it into humus.

At this point, a tiller would have breezed through its work and done a better job of loosening the soil and mixing in fertilizer and organic matter than I could by hand. But even digging was easy. The small rocks were loose and the soil was rich and fluffy.

I wish I could relate that ever thereafter I used this method of preparing beds. But impulse still gets the best of me. I offer this alternative to wiser gardeners than myself. Another tip for the wise is to let the newly prepared soil settle for a few weeks before planting. The best thing you can possibly do is to prepare the new bed in the fall, add the soil amendments, till or dig them in, and leave the bed until spring. Then, when the weather warms up and the soil has dried out, add another 2-inch layer of soil amendments; dig or till it in; wait a few days; and plant.

Planting

&

Before turning to the happy task of planting, I want to relate a bit of history from my first garden notebook. The year was 1962. It was our second spring in Newtown. After tangling with the lid of our septic tank, I seeded over the spot and on May 8 dug a new bed "12 to 18 inches deep with rotted manure and peat moss on top." I forked in the soil amendments and transplanted the peonies that came with the house to the new bed. It could hardly have been a worse time to move them, but, miraculously, they survived.

On May 22, I made an excursion to White Flower Farm and recklessly bought: 2 yellow hybrid lilies called 'Prosperity'; 3 pots of pink phlox 'Dodo Hansbury Forbes'; 2 red phlox 'Floreat' and a white phlox called 'Everest'; 3 Siberian irises—2 purple 'Caesar's Brother' and 1 white 'Snow Queen'; and three pots of Shasta daisies (the cultivar was 'Alaska').

Arriving home with this collection, I planted them all at once. That was the first, last, and only time I have ever planted an entire bed in one operation.

I started out with a rough plan on paper and an idea of when things bloomed. The irises and Shasta daisies were supposed to bloom with the peonies, which they did not. By the time the peonies opened, the irises were long gone. The phlox and the lilies were for summer, but the lilies were over before the phlox came into its full glory.

Later that spring, a toolmaker at the factory where my husband worked gave me half a dozen dwarf dahlias, some canna roots, and a flat of pansies. I stuck his offerings in among the perennials, then bought annuals—yellow marigolds and dark red snapdragons—and a lot of gladiolus corms. I edged the bed with yellow marigolds. The "snaps" and "glads" went in at the back. In July, a neighbor was dividing bearded irises, and she gave me some. That was my garden in 1962.

The point is that even if you have a plan, you will almost certainly end up improvising. You may succumb to some impulse buy or be given plants you are too embarrassed to turn down. That's all right. Plant everything, and sort it all out later. My perennial border didn't find a permanent home until 1965. At that time, I finally gathered up the plants that had done well from different parts of the property and put them all together.

Try not to let the detours get you down. You are learning all the time. To minimize frustration with your first flower bed, I offer the following tips. These fall into two categories: a few last words on design—there are no hard-and-fast rules; and nitty-gritty instructions for dealing with the transition from pot to plot. First things first.

Before you do anything else, you have to decide how many plants you are going to use. Most authorities recommend three, five, or seven of one kind of plant. This is negotiable. It is true that gardeners err on the side of too many kinds of plants and too few of one kind. It is an endearing trait. It means you love plants and want one of everything. Try it. But I don't think you will like it.

My early notebooks are full of complaints: "The trouble with the garden is that this whole place is so big that it needs large splashes of color. The solid daylily bed is the right idea, I think, but maybe I should stick to one color." Well, naturally, I couldn't stick to one color or just a few kinds of plants, but I was on the right track.

In an informal border, the three-five-seven rule has something to recommend it. Try starting with three to five of a kind. Seven is too much of a good thing unless the bed is very large. Besides, strong growers, like daylilies, can soon be divided to increase your stock. The numbers should depend on how big the garden is, how rapidly specific plants grow, and how long the gardener is willing to wait for them to fill in. Big plants, like the *Miscanthus* grasses and other back-of-the-border subjects, can be planted as individual specimens.

"Drifts" are dear to the hearts of gardeners. A drift is an irregular arrangement of plants—usually all of one kind—planted on the diagonal. This creates a layered effect. Looking at the border head-on, you don't notice gaps between plants because instead of being side by side in parallel rows, the groupings are angled back into the bed behind other plants. The same effect is achieved by siting the border so that it is viewed at a diagonal. Looking at an angle down the long dimension of a border, plants that are actually side by side appear to be one behind the other. It is easier to make drifts with uneven rather than even numbers of plants.

However, the odd-number rule immediately breaks down when you consider the requirements of a formal bed. The language spoken here is even numbers and symmetry instead; matched pairs of identical plants or quartets for the corners of a rectilinear bed.

Having decided on plant numbers, you are ready to consider spacing. There are many variables—the expectations of the gardener, the size and vigor of the particular plant, its suitability for the site, the nutrient and moisture content of the soil, and other factors.

If the plants are small enough to be planted at the front of a bed, I plant them 1 foot apart. Three 1-quart containers of coreopsis 'Moonbeam' planted a foot apart will become a solid mass in a year or two, but that's fine. I would also plant clump-forming plants like garden pinks, scabiosa 'Butterfly Blue', lamb's ears, lilyturf, and lady's-mantle a foot apart.

Bigger plants, like daylilies, purple coneflowers, sedum 'Autumn Joy', false sunflower, sneezeweed, and gayfeather, would get 2 feet between plants. Big babies, like globe thistles, peonies, and Siberian irises, the *Miscanthus* grasses, joe-pye weed, and tall coneflowers, would get 3 feet. Some of the grasses really take off and need 4 feet.

In a nutshell: Small, medium, and large plants = 1 foot, 2 feet, 3 feet between them. This spacing scheme leans toward the instant garden. The plants fill in quickly and need dividing sooner than they would if you planted them farther apart. The 1-2-3 system is not very precise, but it gives you somewhere to start.

Plant height is another consideration. Before you pop those perennials out of their containers and into the ground, think about relative heights. In formal gardens made up of complex geometric patterns, the plants have to be uniform in height. This is quite a different approach from the informal perennial border. In the border, I like to see ups and downs, rather than graduated steps, like bleachers.

Martha McKeon found placing plants according to height a knotty design problem, and her experience is a common one. "When a book tells you that something is four feet tall, it means nothing if you have to cut the stems down after the plant has bloomed. As soon as you cut the stems, there is a gap. You might just as well have that plant in the front of the bed. There's no point in putting it behind something that's two and a half feet tall, because when the flower stalks are gone, it won't show anyway."

Quite a few plants that bloom early in the summer get cut back after blooming. Yarrow, evening primroses, perennial bachelor's buttons, and Shasta daisies are among them. Despite their flowering heights of from 18 inches to 3 feet, they belong near the front of the border, because after being cut down, their new growth remains low.

Actually, it is an advantage to have a few tall subjects in the foreground of a border. To relieve the monotony of graduated tiers, British horticulturist and writer Christopher Lloyd recommends planting a few "see-through" plants at the front of the bed. Russian sage is a good candidate. Its graceful stems, sparsely clad in small, ferny, gray-green leaves, end in loose, open-flower clusters. The veil of tiny lavender-blue flowers enhances the plants behind it without hiding them. As an alternative, try a few spikes of mullein. The rosette of foliage is low to the ground, but the flowering stalk shoots up tall and narrow.

Now, for the nitty-gritty. Both spring and fall are good planting times, because the weather is comparatively settled. In cold climates like ours, I prefer spring planting for most perennials; they have a whole season to acclimate themselves before facing the rigors of winter. In the South, where summers are beastly hot, the long, gentle fall season is the best time to plant a new perennial bed. Cool but not cold temperatures and a moist atmosphere are ideal for establishing a new bed. So choose the time when your climate approximates those conditions.

Even if you have labored long and hard to make humus-rich, moisture-retentive, well-drained soil for your perennials, moving them into the new bed is hard on their systems. No matter how carefully you plant them, you are disturbing the fine, hairlike feeder roots. Feeder roots do most of the work of taking up water and nutrients, and until the plant puts new ones into the surrounding soil, its water and nutrient supply is at risk.

Moisture is critical to plants at planting time. Water the bed a couple of days before you are going to plant. Ideally, the soil should be slightly damp. If your plants are bare-rooted, soak the roots overnight in a bucket of water; if you purchased plants in containers, water them several hours ahead of time.

If possible, choose a cool, overcast day or wait until late afternoon on a

A Shade Frame

¼" dowels for hinges

1"×2" furring strips for legs

nail lath to furring strips with wire nails

Plaster lath for slats

dimensions of both frames are the same

Leave 3" at the top for a hole for the hinge dowels.

Lath comes by the bundle in 4' lengths; pre-cut furring strips 8' long are also available by the bundle. Frames 2 feet square are the most economical size.

1"

3"

105

sunny day. Even container-grown plants suffer shock at the time they are removed from their pots and set in the ground. They lose water through their foliage but are unable to replace it because their roots are not yet established. Sun and wind rob them of moisture and cause them to wilt. Therefore, shading newly planted perennials is a good practice.

However, your shading device should admit light and air. Plants feed themselves by converting the sun's rays into oxygen and sugar, and they need fresh air to ward off fungus diseases. To meet these requirements, my husband designed simple A-frame shades made of cheap lumber and lath, which I assemble in the winter. These A-frames are the most often borrowed and least often returned items in my garden shed. They replace tents made from bedsheets, upturned flats and bushel baskets, and even old garden furniture. The shades are a great improvement, and everybody admires them.

When you have all your plants collected and your tools handy—shovel or spade, trowel, watering can, tarp, and wheelbarrow—you are ready to begin. Probably the majority of the plants are in plastic pots, so you don't have to worry too much about them drying while you are planting, but if they are bare-rooted, keep them moist, shaded, and out of the wind until you are ready to put them in the ground.

Now, let the fun begin. With your plants still in their pots, arrange and rearrange them in the bed until you are satisfied or else tired of trying to find the perfect spot. To remove a perennial from its container, cover the top with your hand, fingers spread apart, allowing the stem of the plant to emerge from between your fingers. Turn the pot upside down and tap the bottom with the other hand. The root ball will fall into your open hand. If the roots have started to grow around in a circle, tease them loose so that they will reach out into the soil when you put the plant in the ground.

In the prepared bed, make a generous hole to give the roots room to expand outward and slightly downward. But don't make the hole so deep that the plant sinks way below ground level. You want the top of the soil in the container to be level with the surface of the garden soil. If you plant too deeply, the crown (the place where the roots and stems meet) may rot. If you don't plant deeply enough, the plant could dry out. Level with the soil in the bed is just right.

Fill in the hole, firming the earth around the roots with your hands to eliminate air pockets. Roots need air but not air pockets; in order to get air and water from the soil, the roots have to be in close contact with it.

If you are planting bare-rooted daylilies, make the hole large enough to spread the roots out in every direction. Scrape up enough soil from the bottom of the hole to make a mound in the center, and perch the plant on the mound. Spread the roots outward and downward. Backfill the hole and firm the soil around the roots.

You can water as soon as you have completed the planting operation or after spreading a 2-inch layer of organic mulch. Water each plant either by hand with a watering can or with a water wand attached to the hose. A water wand is a long pipe. The far end is angled to reach under plants or into pots, and it is fitted with a head that delivers a gentle but soaking shower of water.

Planting shrubs and small trees is a very similar operation. However, the stakes are higher—shrubs and trees live longer than perennials, grow bigger, and represent a larger financial investment. In terms of practical differences, the holes have to be bigger—a container shrub needs a hole at least a third wider and deeper than the container itself. And the safest way to release the plant is to cut the container off the root ball with a pair of old scissors or utility shears.

When the ball of earth has been exposed, you will usually find that the roots fill it entirely. It is vital that they be encouraged to grow outward rather than in on themselves. Scratch the sides of the root ball vigorously with your fingers. If that doesn't free the roots, attack the ball with a hand cultivator.

Before setting the plant in the prepared hole, tamp—do not stomp—down the soil in the bottom of the hole so that the plant won't settle too much. Then, position the plant and lay a yardstick or garden stake across the top of the hole. The soil on the surface of the root ball must be at ground level. Backfill around the root ball, firming the soil as you go. With a shrub or small tree, you can do this with your feet. You want the earth snug against the roots but not trodden down so firmly that the structure of the soil is compromised. Tramping around on soft, friable soil eliminates the spaces between mineral particles and ruins its loose, open texture. Try to think like a plant. What would make your roots happy?

Bare-rooted shrubs require slightly different handling. Make a cone of earth in the bottom of the hole, perch the plant on top with its roots dangling down, and start backfilling with the loose soil. Shake the plant so that the soil fills in around the roots. Push it down among the roots with your fingers, tamping it down as you go along. The bare roots *must* be in firm contact with the soil.

Plants that come from the nursery "balled-and-burlapped" (abbreviated in catalogs to "B & B") have to be well watered before planting, and you have to remove their wrappings. Some are encased in heavy wire corsets designed to hold the burlap in place. To remove this cage of steel, you will need wire cutters. Other B & B specimens are bound with string held in place by common nails. Cut the string and remove the nails.

Natural burlap made of jute or hemp will eventually rot in the planting hole, but if the ball is wrapped in *plastic burlap*, remove it before planting. I heard one horror story of a landscaper who planted a 300-foot hemlock hedge without taking the plastic burlap off the root balls, and his client wondered why every tree died.

Plant balled-and-burlapped shrubs and trees the same way you plant container-grown material. Settle the plant in the hole. Use a stake or yardstick to determine the proper level. The top of the earth ball *must* be level with the ground. Spread open the natural burlap and backfill so that the soil, not the burlap, is in direct contact with the root ball. Fill the hole and firm the loose soil with your feet.

Mike Ruggiero of the New York Botanical Garden has a tip about watering and mulching newly planted shrubs, especially those with low branches. "Mulch *before* you water," he says. "That way, you don't spray mud all over the place. If the foliage is covered with dirt, it doesn't photosynthesize properly." Photosynthesis is the process by which the leaves use the sun's energy to manufacture food.

Mike also belongs to the school of thought that favors making an earth collar called a "well" around shrubs and trees to guide water to their roots. Make the collar at some distance from the trunk or crown. After mulching, flood the depression with a gentle stream from the hose or water wand. For trees and shrubs, the layer of mulch can be as deep as 3 or 6 inches, but keep it away from trunks and crowns. On a flower bed, 2 inches is enough.

One last word about planting. If you know in your heart that you have not put as much effort into preparing the bed as you should have, you have another chance to improve the shining hour. Excavate each planting hole to twice the size of the pot or twice the spread of the bare roots; ladle bagged or homemade compost into the holes, and stir it all around with the existing soil. Now, dig some of this lovely stuff out, put the plant in, and backfill.

$\mathcal{TLC}$:
Spring and Summer

✿

Finally, your garden is planted. You are filled with anticipation and apprehension. "I've spent a fortune," you grumble to yourself. "I wonder if any of this stuff is going to grow?" Another sobering thought crosses your mind: "I hope this isn't going to be a lot more work than I bargained for." I hope not, too.

To put your fears in perspective, I'm going to tell you how Lynden Miller, Martha McKeon, and I manage our gardens. In each case, the perennial borders are part of larger garden landscapes. These are country gardens with many different cultivated areas. Lynden has an allée of crabapple trees with solid swaths of daylilies planted under them and, among the daylilies, daffodils for spring. She also has gardens around a swimming pool; a tiny formal herb garden; and a garden where she tries out new shrubs and perennials.

I have extensive shade plantings; Martha has her pond, a vegetable garden, and what she describes as "a bullet-proof rose garden." We both have little woodland gardens. All three of us have other commitments and limited help. Lynden's work takes her away from her own garden during the week, and she employs a part-time gardener. For the last few years, I have had help once a week, and my husband does the mowing. Diane Campbell and I do everything else from pruning to fall cleanup. Martha's spouse cuts their grass; otherwise she is a one-man band.

In short, our perennial borders do not take up every waking moment of our time, and they are big borders. Lynden's is 175 feet by 12 feet; my old border is

100 feet long and 15 feet wide and the new one about 50 by 10; Martha's is 100 feet by 10 to 12 feet. The reason these gardens can be maintained with relative ease is that they are full of low-maintenance plants. We all want and need plants that thrive without heroic measures. But there are no such things as maintenance-free perennials, and if there were, we wouldn't want them. We grow plants because we love them and enjoy looking after them.

Ongoing care of a perennial garden involves the following: deadheading (removing spent blossoms), pinching back, staking, watering—if you can afford the water—and a little weeding. Weeding is a task that beginning gardeners dread unnecessarily. I weed twice a year: in the spring, when the mulch of shredded leaves has broken down or been raked away during fall cleanup, and again in August, when Diane and I have been dividing perennials, and the mulch gets lost in the shuffle.

If given a chance, weeds pop up in the bald spots. But they can be scraped off the soil with the edge of a trowel. Without their tiny green leaves, they soon die. A new application of mulch will smother any that escape the trowel. In general, when you apply an organic mulch in the spring or immediately after planting, you can almost forget about weeding.

A few dandelions find their way from the lawn into the lamb's ears in front of the perennial bed. These aren't easy to get out. If you break the root, leaving even the tiniest piece, a new plant appears. However, you can often remove them whole if you do it early enough in the spring. Frost heaves work in the gardener's favor, loosening the dandelion's stubborn roots. Drive an old kitchen knife or a very narrow trowel straight into the ground next to the dandelion and loosen the soil. Grasp the rosette of leaves and wiggle the offending weed back and forth until it comes out. Keeping lawn grass out of the lamb's ears is a routine exercise that has to be performed several times during the season. The best way is to cut a new edge with a sharp spade or the edging tool and pull the grass out by hand.

One of my keenest pleasures on a summer evening is breaking off the flowers of my daylilies. I fill the wheelbarrow with heaps of red, yellow, orange, gold, cream, peach, pink, and purple blossoms. Some are too exquisite to put on the compost pile, and I bring them indoors to savor their last few hours. The next morning, they will be dead anyway.

The other way to look at what I do for pleasure is to regard it as a gardening chore. Deadheading is performed in order to prevent seed formation. Producing

Deadheading and Shearing

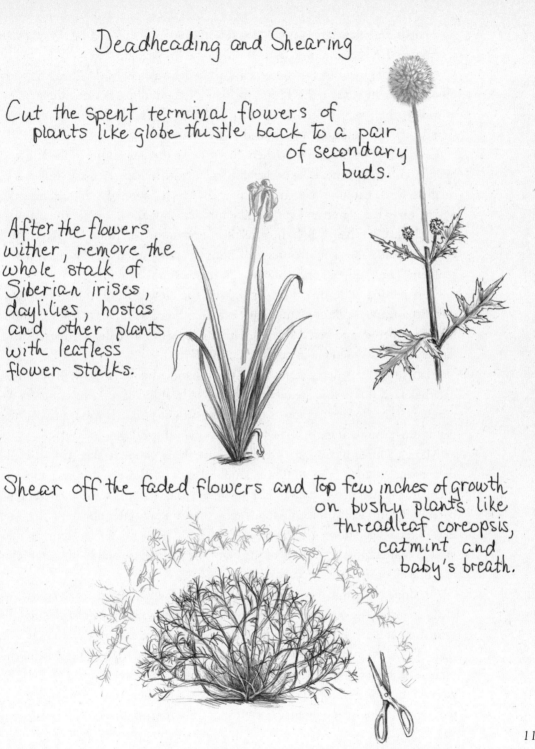

Cut the spent terminal flowers of plants like globe thistle back to a pair of secondary buds.

After the flowers wither, remove the whole stalk of Siberian irises, daylilies, hostas and other plants with leafless flower stalks.

Shear off the faded flowers and top few inches of growth on bushy plants like threadleaf coreopsis, catmint and baby's breath.

111

seed puts a drain on the plant's food and water supply. Deadheading allows these raw materials to be employed in revitalizing the whole plant.

One of your first tasks as the season gets under way will be deadheading early bloomers. In my garden, this means the daffodils and tulips. Because their stems, as well as their leaves, are involved in food making for the future, it is best to simply pick off the wilted flower heads, leaving the rest.

Catmints start flowering at the same time as the late spring bulbs and will need attention in June. Like other bushy plants with many stems and masses of small flowers, catmints can be shorn with scissors after blooming. Seize the whole top of the clump and cut off handfuls, reducing the height of the plant by about half. Give baby's breath, threadleaf coreopsis, perennial candytuft, and creeping phlox the same treatment. Catmint, coreopsis, and baby's breath will rebloom. The candytuft and phlox won't. It is not in their nature.

The method of deadheading depends on the growth habit of the plant. Cut down the whole stalk of plants that bear their flowers on nearly leafless stems, like the Siberian and bearded irises. Other candidates include: daylilies, Shasta daisies, hostas, garden pinks, coral bells, and lilyturf.

Plants that have leafy stems have to be handled differently. With peonies, cut the faded flower and stem back to a set of healthy leaves. I recommend removing peony flowers as soon as they are past their prime. If you wait until the petals drop, they will make an awful mess all over the foliage.

Many summer-blooming perennials have leafy flower stalks. Cut the old flowers and stems of false sunflowers, rudbeckias, coneflowers, yarrows, salvias—there are many others—back to just above the foliage or to new side buds. Some perennials with leafy flowering stems get so unattractive after blooming that you may want to get rid of the whole stem. That's all right, too, as long as new growth is emerging at the base of the plant. Lady's-mantle and hardy geraniums are June bloomers that belong to this group.

As a rule of thumb, if you can see new basal foliage, you can cut the old flowering stems to the ground, leaves and all. Summer-flowering globe thistle falls into this category. First, cut the dead flowers back to the foliage or to new side buds. Then, when the side buds have flowered and faded, look at the base of the plant. If there are signs of new growth, cut the mature stem to the ground. Be advised that the new foliage is not going to reach the height of the old foliage. It will remain a low green mound until it succumbs to frost. So you will have a gap in your bed. In its prime, globe thistle is a big, bulky plant and belongs in the middle or back of the border.

Most deadheading is a matter of common sense. You don't want to snip off blossoms and leave behind a hedgehog of naked stems. Cut bare stems back to foliage or to side buds; shear bushy plants, and be respectful of leafy stems. If in doubt about leafy stems, wait until you see new basal foliage before cutting to the ground.

True lilies are a special case. Although their leafy stems become very ugly after the flowers have faded, *do not cut them down.* Cut off the dead flowers, but leave the stems. Those awful-looking things surrounded from top to bottom with short, ratty leaves are essential for food-making purposes. Only when the whole stalk has turned yellow may you cut it down to the ground. Lilies should be treated rather like daffodils. Find them a tall, leafy partner to hide behind after flowering.

Daylilies also present a minor foliage problem. Much as I love and appreciate these workhorses of the border, I am forced to admit their foliage looks unattractive after flowering. Many of the leaves turn yellow or brown, starting with the tips. But there are several things you can do about it.

You can live with it and plant daylilies in the middle of the border where their foliage won't show much; you can pull out the yellowing leaves by hand, which is time-consuming if you have a lot of daylilies; or if you are patient, you can wait until new leaves start coming from the base of the plant, and then cut off all the old foliage. Or you can do what Diane Campbell does to my daylilies—cut off the brown tips of the leaves. They look a bit odd, but they no longer stick out like sore thumbs.

Pinching back is an early season activity that can greatly improve the looks of naturally leggy perennials, like chrysanthemums, Montauk daisies, sunflowers, and asters. It can also save you work. By removing the end shoots, you can keep these plants shorter and more compact. The actual technique of pinching back is easy. If the stems are young and soft, you can use your fingers. Otherwise, use a pair of clippers, and cut each stem back to just above a set of leaves. The angle where the leaf meets the stem is called an axil. Cut to just above that point. New side buds sprout in the leaf axils.

Mike Ruggiero likened the technique of pinching back to pruning a hedge. "You cut a hedge, and it grows sideways. Removing the growing tip forces side growth," he explained. "In some cases, if you pinch back, it eliminates the need for staking." That hit a responsive chord! I have to stake almost everything, because the bed is on a slight slope and faces east. The tall plants lean downhill and toward the sun and would pitch forward without support.

Martha also has a staking problem, but for a different reason. In her rich, constantly moist soil, plants nearly double their normal height. One year, I gave her a clump of 'Gateway', a cultivar of our native joe-pye weed. In her garden, it soared to 10 feet. The next year, she pinched back every shoot by half and was delighted with a more compact clump and slightly smaller flowers.

Last year, I pinched back all the sedums in my garden. When the stems of *Sedum* 'Autumn Joy' were about 6 inches high, I cut them in half and found that the clumps remained lower and fuller. The flower heads were more numerous and a bit smaller, and I didn't have to support the clumps with a girdle of bamboo stakes. *Sedum* 'Vera Jameson' doesn't grow tall enough to need staking, but the stems are floppy. By the time it blooms, the clump has spread open, exposing a bald spot in the middle. Pinching the stems back by half when the clumps were young kept them much tighter and tidier. Late-blooming plants like mums and asters can be pinched back repeatedly until mid-July. After that, you run the risk of discouraging bud formation.

In addition to pinching back, Lynden, Martha, and I do a bit of pruning during the summer months. Pruning is to woody plants what pinching back is to herbaceous perennials: cutting or trimming for the looks and welfare of the plant. Martha prunes her roses after they have put on their June show. (Elsewhere, she will share her secrets for an easy-care rose garden.) She also trims the spiraeas in her perennial border.

After the flat, pink flower heads of *Spiraea japonica* 'Little Princess' fade, she clips the plants into tight domes. Repeated the length of the bed, they are an antidote to the frothy flowers and soft foliage of other perennials. Their tidy shapes attract the eye and give the whole bed a solid, purposeful appearance. A bigger spiraea called 'Anthony Waterer' provides a bit of form in a nearby island bed.

Lynden always has clippers at the ready in a holster on her belt. She prunes the barberries in her border into neat globes and doesn't hesitate to shape any perennial that lends itself to similar treatment. "I trim baptisias and amsonias into tight rounds, because it's terribly important to have geometry in a perennial garden," she says. "I want that round shape against the horizontals of the land-scape and the hedge."

To improve the natural shape of a perennial clump or a twiggy shrub, like spi-raea or barberry, cut back the twigs and stems to just above a set of leaves or a leaf axil. Barberries and spiraeas are singularly forgiving of inept pruning. You could even shear them with hedge clippers.

Staking. This is a subject dear to my heart. I used to be a terrible staker be-cause I took the view that staking was something I shouldn't have to do. Grit-ting my teeth, I inflicted my displeasure on hapless sunflowers, trumpet lilies, and ornamental grasses. I lashed the lilies to their stakes like martyrs and bun-dled sunflowers and grasses into corsets of string. They didn't fall over, but they looked artificial and unattractive. I *had* to do better than that.

Today, I am a willing and skillful staker. But this turnaround has taken time and understanding. First, you have to accept staking as the price to pay for grow-ing certain kinds of plants: garden giants, like sea kale; trumpet lilies over 4 feet; some of the ornamental grasses; tall rudbeckias; tall plants with hollow stems, like meadow rue and old-fashioned valerian; naturally floppy plants, like bush clematis; and plants with huge, heavy flowers, like double peonies. Are these plants worth it? You will have to decide for yourself. I wouldn't be without them.

Sometimes the fault, dear gardener, is not in the plant but in the site. If you grow sun-loving plants in partial shade, they will reach for the light and need support. If your soil is as rich and moist as Martha McKeon's, tall plants may put on an extra foot or two, in which case they will require a prop. If you allow clump-forming plants to get too big before dividing them, they will fall open in the middle and have to be encircled with stakes and string.

Try to look upon staking as an art form, not a boring garden chore. Properly staked, your plants will be more attractive and your garden more beautiful. The secret is unobtrusive staking that respects the integrity and natural carriage of each plant. You must understand its habit of growth and choose a suitable method of staking. Timing is important, too. It depends on the type of plant and the method of staking employed.

There are a number of new devices that make staking easier and less obvious than old-fashioned peony hoops and lurid peacock-green bamboo stakes. Steel mesh grids in circular frames are a great help with clump-forming plants, like pe-onies, grasses, globe thistles, asters, tall black-eyed Susans, hardy geraniums, and other large, bushy plants that have a tendency to flop. The grids, along with sets of detachable legs, are coated with green plastic, which makes them almost invisible against the foliage. There are several sizes, from a foot across to extra-large 30-inch grids intended for the big grasses. The circle of the 30-inch size is so big that it requires two sets of legs—three to a set. The legs come in different lengths, from 18 to 36 inches.

To use the grids to best advantage, set them in the ground before the plant's leaves have expanded. In the case of peonies, the best time is when the new shoots are about a foot high and the leaves are still tightly furled. The same timing applies to the bush clematis, and other plants with many lax stems. Catch them while the leaves are still either furled or youthful. Globe thistles open out their leaves early, so get the grid on as soon as possible. Large, mature leaves will suffer if they are forced through the mesh.

Position the grid at about half the ultimate height of the plant, and attach the legs one at a time. It isn't always easy to get them all the same height if your soil is rocky. But it won't matter if they are crooked; foliage will soon hide the whole contraption.

Plain old chicken wire is a cheap substitute for plastic-covered grids. It has the drawback of being flimsy, and the wire soon rusts, but that isn't all bad either. Rusty chicken wire is just about invisible. It can be used in two ways. You can lay a square or rectangle of wire on the ground and let bushy plants and grasses grow up through it. Martha McKeon has had great success with this technique. The plants lift the wire as they grow. When they are about half their mature height, she guides any trapped stems through the mesh and sticks bamboo stakes in the ground at an angle to hold the wire approximately horizontal.

The other way to use chicken wire is to fashion it into a cylinder for fine-stemmed plants like pink boltonia and the notoriously floppy bush clematis, *Clematis integrifolia*. The fine stems and leaves grow through the mesh so that the plant's soft silhouette is preserved, but the wire keeps the plant from falling over on its neighbors.

If you are already too late with your grids and wire, you'll have to resort to stakes set at intervals around the perimeter of the plant and a couple of courses of string—the number of courses depends on the height of the plant. A tall clump of asters might require a course of string a foot from the ground, another at 2 feet, and a third higher up. Set the stakes at a slight angle so that they make a vase-shaped enclosure to accommodate the spreading habit of the clump.

Plastic garden stakes in many sizes and two inoffensive shades of green—dark green and yellow-green—have revolutionized staking. One type has small projections overall that help hold the string in place. The other type has a bamboo pattern along its length with raised horizontal rings that serve the same purpose. They keep the string from slipping down. The plastic stakes are not cheap, but they last for years. I get a few more each season. They can be used to make enclosures for tall, bushy plants or they can be used to support single stems.

Using individual plastic stakes in the shade of green that most nearly matches the color of the stems is the best method of supporting lilies, delphiniums, meadow rues, hollyhocks, and other plants with tall, straight stalks. The trick is to let both the stake and the stem lean at a natural angle, instead of forcing them to stand at military attention. Wait until the plants are nearly full grown—in bud, even, but not yet in bloom—before setting the stakes in the ground. The effect should be graceful instead of rigid.

The only problem with waiting until the plant has achieved maturity is the danger of damaging its roots. Plants that have masses of wiry roots won't miss a few, but you could do irreparable harm to a lily by shoving a stake through the bulb. Be careful, and keep the stake several inches from the stem. If each stake is parallel to the stem it supports, it will hardly show.

With the stake safely installed, first loop string around the stem, then make a figure eight around the stake. The twist in the string will keep the soft, sensitive tissue of the stem from rubbing against the hard plastic of the support.

Watering is a sore subject around here. In the summer of 1995, we drilled a new well in the fond hope that we would have enough water to run the house and water the garden. Heretofore, the garden made do with a limited supply from an old hand-dug farm well. As soon as we have a drought, the dug well goes dry, so it isn't much use. Nor, alas, is our new well. We ran out of water while clearing the chlorine from the line. In time, the well recovered, and with extreme care I was able to selectively water enough to pull the shrubs through the worst drought in 35 years. The perennial garden looked dispirited but suffered comparatively little, thanks to the mulch of leaves.

Drought is a great lesson. It reminds you just how important moisture-retentive soil is. Water is more than just a thirst quencher to a plant. It dissolves nutrients and is, therefore, the means by which food is delivered. Mulch is almost as important as soil in preserving natural moisture. So before you start worrying about irrigation systems, *do* something to your soil and don't forget to mulch.

If you are lucky enough to be able to water, water deeply so that the soil is damp 6 inches down. A light sprinkle is just a waste of water. The recommended amount of moisture for most common garden perennials is 1 inch a week. Well, there can't be many places in this country where rainfall is delivered on cue. Here in Connecticut, we are likely to get 3 inches one week and none for the next three. Water if you can and when needed. The best way to find out if it is needed is to check the soil under the mulch. Stick your fingers in it or dig a little hole with a trowel and see if it's damp.

I water individual clumps or plants that look droopy with a hose and nozzle that produces a heavy but gentle flow of water. If you have good water pressure, an overhead sprinkler works well, covers a large area, but wastes water. I use one when water is abundant early in the season. A drip irrigation system with underground tubes is expensive to install but very efficient. In a perennial bed, the snag is the danger of damaging it during routine dividing and transplanting. As you have guessed, my experience with drip irrigation systems is limited. I have tried a soaker hose but found that too much water leaked out at the end nearest the source of supply and none reached the far end.

Water will become an escalating problem as the demand increases with every new housing development. Beefing up the humus content in your soil, husbanding the natural moisture with organic mulch, and choosing tough, adaptable plants are the best defenses against drought.

$\mathcal{TLC}$:
$\mathcal{F}$all and $\mathcal{W}$inter

⚜

There is always a moment during the growing season when what can go wrong has gone wrong. The weather is hot and humid, or chilly and overcast; there hasn't been enough rain or there's been too much; slugs have made holes in the hosta leaves; and the foliage of the remaining perennials is looking dreary.

Be prepared for this period of disenchantment. It usually doesn't last long, especially if you take action. The best thing is to *do something*. Get out there and cut down some spent stalks; pull off some of those yellow leaves; put a new edge on the border with the edging tool; deadhead everything in sight. Good housekeeping is not only a morale booster, it is the secret of a decent-looking garden in August.

By Labor Day, you and the garden should have cheered up. I hope you planted *Sedum* 'Autumn Joy', the blue mist shrub, and some ornamental grasses. You will enjoy them this fall. If you pulled yourself together in August, you should be able to sit around and admire your handiwork during the mellow month of September.

If you are going to include tulips and daffodils in your border for next spring, October is the best time to put them in. Plant the daffodils first. They need several weeks of above-freezing temperatures in order to develop a strong root system. Tulips develop roots more quickly and can be planted later. Indeed, they must be planted later—starting around the middle of October. Otherwise they may get ahead of themselves and suffer a setback when cold weather arrives.

A word of warning: If you are going to put bulbs in the border, place them intelligently. Don't put them in the front of the bed, because they will disfigure your garden for weeks with their dying foliage. Put them behind and among leafy plants, like daylilies, Siberian irises, and peonies. These perennials will not hide the bloom but will conceal the bulb foliage as their own leaves expand.

Do not fail to label the spot where you put your bulbs; otherwise you will dig into them when you are dividing perennials. I came around to labeling after many such unfortunate encounters. Decide whether you are going to put the label in front of the clump of bulbs or behind it, and *be consistent*.

Early October is a good time to plant dormant peony roots. Try to get them in the right place the first time, because they dislike being moved. However, if you must move or divide established clumps, fall is the only time to do it. Remember that peonies are as long-lived as many shrubs, so plant them with the same care. The holes should be 18 inches to 2 feet wide and deep. It is hard work, but the peonies will appreciate it. Prepare the soil well, and work in lots of compost. Tamp down the soft soil at the bottom of the hole, and be sure you don't plant the peony roots too deep. Those pink or white protuberant "eyes" should be only an inch or two below the soil surface. Check the depth by placing a yardstick or garden stake across the hole.

In southern New England, the growing season is still in full swing for most of October. The first frost usually comes early in the month, but most perennials laugh off cold snaps. Fall doesn't get serious around here until the end of the month. Then, it's all hands on deck. Being surrounded by a hardwood forest, we have great quantities of leaves to rake. Diane and I start by raking the heavy accumulation out of the beds and along the stone walls.

We use tarps to haul huge loads down the hillside to the flat lawn, where my husband shreds them with the rotary blades of the mower. In minutes, he reduces an enormous pile to a windrow of wonderful mulch. When he has finished, we collect our booty and dump it behind the barn until spring, when Diane and I return it to the perennial beds. This is one of the really big jobs of the year. Dealing with the autumn leaves takes several weekends, but it is worth every minute of the time we spend in order to have the mulch.

Meanwhile, the border begins to need tidying. There are two schools of thought about cutting down spent perennial foliage. One maintains that the collapsed leaves act as protection for the plants and can safely be left until spring. The other says, clean up everything to minimize rodent damage, prevent disease, and give no succor to insects. A thick layer of dead leaves is perfect habitat for mice, voles, insect eggs, and fungus spores. I belong to the second school and feel more strongly than ever after voles played havoc with my perennials in 1995. (See "Deer, Diseases, and Insect Damage.")

Cleaning up the border goes on for quite a long time, because some plants look attractive well into the fall. A few are perfect for winter decoration. The following are winter assets and should be left standing: any plant with dry, rigid stems; plants with flower heads that catch the snow; and plants that have interesting skeletons. I am very enamored of calamint's airy mound of threadlike stems and delight in the flower heads of *Sedum* 'Autumn Joy' and black-eyed Susans.

Lynden Miller is fond of the graceful gray skeletons of Russian sage, especially against a dark-twigged barberry bush hung with red fruits. She also loves tall, arching grasses. If these have fallen open during the growing season, discreetly prop them up with stakes and string so that the snow won't knock them down. You should, of course, have done that early in the season, but better late than never. The rest of the perennials in the borders get cut to the ground whenever their foliage finally dies.

Peony stems and leaves are among the first to go. They should *never* be added to the compost pile, because botrytis disease is carried over the winter in the stems. There, small, sinister black bodies called sclerotia lie in wait. In the spring, they turn the base of the new, young stems brown and mushy. Even stems that appear to have escaped often produce buds that turn brown and fail to open. I put peony stems and leaves into plastic bags and send them to the landfill. The stalks and foliage of true lilies and of bearded irises meet the same fate and for the same reason. Both harbor diseases and insect eggs.

It doesn't matter when you cut down the rest of the withered foliage. Many of my daylilies retain green leaves into December, while others are ready for the shears in October. All that matters is to get the job done before winter sets in and the weather makes working outside either unpleasant or impossible.

To mulch or not to mulch, that is the question. A winter mulch serves a somewhat different purpose than a summer mulch. The main objective is to prevent the alternate freezing and thawing that result from dramatic changes in soil temperature. The worst-case scenario often occurs in my primrose garden. The soil is wet, which primroses enjoy, but it expands as it freezes and drags their roots out of the ground. When the ice melts, their roots are left high and dry.

The pattern of freezing one day, thawing the next, has a particularly adverse effect on the following: shallow-rooted perennials, like primroses; recent transplants; divisions that have not yet taken hold; and young plants with tentative, adolescent root systems. All these would benefit from a winter mulch tucked around them, and even covering them completely.

Mulching a bed of mature perennials for the winter is unnecessary. But if I plant daylilies or divide perennials later than I should, I put the same chopped leaves I use in the summer around them, only more heavily—up to 4 inches.

If you mulch before the ground freezes, it will delay but not prevent freezing. Once the ground is frozen, the mulch will keep it frozen despite sudden warm days. The real enemy is a sunny day with unseasonably warm temperatures followed by a bitter night in the single digits. Living plant tissue can be damaged by such abrupt fluctuations. A winter mulch maintains a relatively consistent environment for the plant roots.

Suitable materials for a winter mulch include salt hay, evergreen branches, and dry leaves. Salt hay grows in coastal marshes and has stiff stems that don't rot easily. Decomposition is welcome in a summer mulch, but a winter mulch has to hold up against the elements, and should be light and airy.

For the primroses in the woodland garden, I use pine boughs. My neighbor's trees provide a ready source, and pine needles stay on the cut branches all winter. Cut hemlock boughs shed their needles almost immediately. Unfortunately, nothing prevents the wet soil from freezing and rising up in a honeycomb of ice that pulls the primrose roots out of the ground. But where the soil is drier, the boughs arching over the primroses shade the ground and keep it frozen, despite sunny days.

Like so much else in gardening, there is disagreement among gardeners about when to mulch for winter. There are prefreeze mulchers and the postfreeze mulchers. In the case of the primroses, I practice prefreeze mulching because the ground freezes more gradually under the pine boughs. Postfreeze types maintain that mulching before the ground freezes promotes late-season growth that can be damaged by cold. I've never had that problem.

Although the subject of this chapter is the perennial garden, it is worth noting that woody plants also need a bit of TLC before winter arrives. You might as well see to their needs while you are outside working in your border. Once the ground is frozen, shrub roots cannot draw up water to replace the moisture lost through the pores on their young twigs and branches. Mulch young trees and shrubs and continue to water—an inch a week—until the ground freezes.

Broad-leaved evergreens like rhododendron, pieris, and mountain laurel have a particularly hard time in the cold weather. Water is constantly being lost through those large leaves. When a rhododendron curls its leaves, it isn't because it is cold, it is in order to conserve water. Pores on the back of the leaves permit the escape of moisture. By curling in on themselves, the leaves reduce the surface area from which the moisture evaporates. Water broad-leaved evergreens until the ground freezes, and top up their year-round mulch.

In Connecticut, I tend to think of the first two weeks in March as the tail end of winter rather than the beginning of spring. It is another low point in the gardening year. The perennials you left for seasonal decoration are no longer decorative. The leaves you thought you had piled neatly have escaped and are littering the lawn and flower beds. Don't despair. An afternoon of vigorous raking will make all the difference to you and to the garden.

Next, tackle the perennial border. To cheer yourself up, cut down *Sedum* 'Autumn Joy' first. Your heart will leap as you come upon fresh, ice-blue rosettes of foliage at the base of the old stalks. Look around, and you will also see the emerging red thumbs of peonies; tiny new purplish-green leaves on the stems of catmint and pale gray ones on the Russian sage.

Cut down the grasses as soon as you can—before they shed all over the garden and before the new growth gets tangled up in last year's foliage. With scissors or sharp clippers, cut them down as low as possible. Wear gloves or you'll get splinters from the brittle stems. Blue oat grass is an exception. *Do not cut it down at all.* Just run your fingers through it, starting at the base of the clump and bringing them up through the foliage, like a comb.

If you planted the blue mist shrub, this is the time to prune it. It can be cut to a stubby, twiggy bush about a foot high. You are in no danger of cutting off flower buds, because it blooms on the shoots it will make during the coming season. Your aim is to make the plant shorter and more compact, and you do it in much the same way that you cut back a perennial. Even as early as March, you will find tiny pairs of gray-green leaves showing on the woody branches. Cut

Pruning

Vigorous shrubs, like buddleia, which bloom in mid-summer on new wood, can be pruned to stubs in early spring.

Shorten all the branches of twiggy, summer-blooming shrubs, like blue mist shrub, by about half every spring. Make the cut just above a pair of side buds.

Red twig dogwood can be allowed to mature 2 or 3 years before cutting one third of the oldest stems to the ground. Young growth has the best winter color.

back to just above a pair of new leaves. In subsequent years, you will cut back about half the previous year's growth. You can and should cut off deadwood at any time.

Buddleia is another summer-blooming shrub that is a great addition to the perennial border. It, too, should be cut back in late winter or early spring. I cut mine to within a few inches of the ground. It is an unbelievably vigorous shrub and puts on 6 feet or more in the course of a summer. You may cringe, but go ahead and cut it down to 6-inch stubs. I perform this heroic operation on the purple smoke bush, too.

The red twig dogwood is a candidate for early spring pruning. The usual recommendation is to cut it almost to the ground every year because the young twigs are the reddest, but I don't. I cut the oldest, least colorful stems flush with the ground, leaving the others for two or three years. Less pruning makes for a bigger shrub. If you have a smaller garden, go ahead and cut it down.

Shape and trim your spiraea into neat rounds now and again after they flower. After that, trim them any time you think they need it. They flower in the summer on the new shoots produced during the spring. Shrubs that form flower buds late in the summer and in the fall are described as blooming on "old wood."

Forsythia is one of these. By October, you will find the flower buds at the base of the leaves, all ready for spring. So prune it right after flowering. Cut to the ground a few of the oldest canes. New stems will come from the base to replace them. Forsythia is indestructible. If you have inherited huge overgrown plants, cut them to the ground and start all over again. They will soon return with more vigor than ever. Then, keep taking out a few of the heaviest, oldest stems each year after flowering. The rule of thumb is to prune most flowering shrubs right after flowering.

After pruning, your first garden chore is to fertilize your perennial garden. Some gardeners are suspicious of fertilizers these days, but they needn't be. All you are doing is replacing what the plants have already used up.

My most trusted authority on fertilizing is Rita Buchanan. She has advanced degrees in botany, a beautiful garden, and abundant common sense. She points out that you apply fertilizer for the use of the plants during the growing season. By fall, it is gone because they have turned it into roots, stems, leaves, flowers, and seeds. Over time, the fertilizer you put on the garden turns into material for your compost pile.

"People are concerned," she says, "because they have heard terrible things about overfertilization. Overfertilizing causes nitrate buildup in our drinking water and pollution in our lakes. But there is a big difference between fertilizing and overfertilizing. The correct amount may be as little as a couple of pounds per hundred square feet. The problems of overfertilization occur at places like golf courses."

For the first twenty-five years that I gardened, I fertilized the perennial beds every spring with an all-purpose 10-10-10 granular fertilizer. But since I began to mulch heavily, I have fertilized infrequently and have been unable to detect an appreciable difference in the growth rate of the plants. My theory has been that the mulch seemed to add enough of what the plants needed.

However, I grow a great many plants in containers every summer and fertilize them heavily. They need a well-drained soil so that they won't rot, but that means that they have to be watered often—daily in hot weather. The nutrients are washed away and have to be replaced. To this end, I apply weekly doses of Peter's 20-20-20 water-soluble fertilizer with the watering can. The results are spectacular.

Rita says that the best way to decide whether or not to fertilize is by looking at the plants. "In a lot of situations, the nutrients available to the plants from decomposed compost, mulch, or whatever organic matter you have worked into the soil are sufficient—especially with woody plants and perennials."

If your soil is sandy, the chances are it is short of nutrients, and your garden would benefit from a complete 5-10-5 fertilizer. If it is heavy clay and rich in organic matter, it probably contains enough nutrients for all normal purposes. This year, I am going to fertilize. After last summer's drought and the vole damage, the border needs all the help it can get.

Ideally, granular fertilizer should be applied to damp soil. The only way it can reach the plants is through their roots, and the only way the roots can absorb it is in solution, so moisture is critical. If you apply fertilizer to dry soil, water it in. As for the method of application, I fill a small bucket with granules and go around the bed making a circle of fertilizer around every plant. Each gets a small handful. Then, I scratch it in with a hand cultivator, and water, if necessary.

Keep fertilizer away from leaves. Those granules are a salt, and salt on plant foliage has the same effect as salt on a green salad. Salt draws water out of the leaves. People talk about fertilizer "burning" leaves, but what it is really doing is drawing the moisture out of them.

Compost:
Let It Rot

You were left a few chapters back with a pile of sod and no further instructions. I hope you thought ahead and added to it all the bits and pieces from
the border: the faded flower heads, spent stalks, and foliage from your August
housekeeping; any grass clippings from the lawn; the debris from your fall cleanup; and, finally, the grasses and perennials you cut down in March. The pile may
be rather a mess at the moment, but it will all be worth it in the end.

The word "compost" comes from the same root as "composite," meaning
something made up of diverse elements. It is derived from the Latin *ponere*, to
place, and the prefix *com*, together. Placing together the organic detritus from
kitchen and garden to improve the tilth of the soil has been going on since
Roman times. When Marcus Cato wasn't fighting wars, he wrote treatises on
rural management and was an early proponent of composting.

Thanks to Ruth Stout, Louise Marston, and my favorite English aunt, I feel
as passionately about composting as I do about good soil, and probably for the
same reason. I came to composting much later than I should have. It took a visit
from Aunt Joan to spur me into action.

I had been gardening for several years when she came to stay with us for a
few weeks in the late sixties. She was a wonderful gardener herself and took a
keen interest in all that we were doing, but she was scandalized when she discovered that I had no compost pile.

Even in her little walled garden in the Cathedral Close in Norwich, she had found a corner where she saved every vegetable peeling and apple core, along with garden debris. She made a wire mesh enclosure about 2 feet by 2 feet. As a seventeen-year-old visitor, I used to dump the tea leaves there myself. Every so often, she would fluff up the whole thing with a spading fork. A few weeks later, there would be a bucket or two of beautiful humus.

My first compost bin was constructed under Aunt Joan's watchful eye. She helped me find a suitable place down by our barn in the shade of an ash tree. At her behest, I made a square pen with four garden stakes and a length of 3-foot-high chicken wire. In it, I put every scrap from the kitchen (except bones, fat, and bits of meat), along with weeds, grass, and autumn leaves. That was before we took to shredding the leaves for mulch.

Aunt Joan died in the late seventies, but I think of her once a day, every day, as I ply the path to the new compost bins behind the garage. There are three of them in a row against the fence. The solid back is made of two 4-by-8-foot slabs of pressure-treated plywood. The sides and front are made of cement blocks that used to be part of the old garage wall. Each bin is about 4 feet square and 3 cement blocks high—about 2 feet.

I put rough debris in one—things like the heavy stalks of joe-pye weed and sunflowers. Coarse material takes about twice as long to rot as fine material. Both decompose more quickly if the piles are turned, but I find turning them too much work. I poke holes down through the debris with a spading fork instead. It is not as effective as turning, but the organic material all breaks down eventually.

The way I compost, the coarse pile takes two years to become humus; the other two piles each take a year. One is currently in service and one is resting. In the spring, I'll take the stuff that hasn't broken down off the top of the finished pile and add it to the rough pile. When I have used up all the humus during spring planting, the bin is empty, and I'll start filling it again.

By August or September, the resting pile is ready. I'll remove the top layer and add that to the working pile. When I have used up the humus, I'll start filling the empty bin, and leave the other to rest over the winter. And so it goes. It isn't the most efficient method or the fastest, but it doesn't take much work, and the dividends are enormous.

Ruth Stout never even bothered with a compost pile. She just spread her garden detritus where she wanted the compost and waited for it to rot. However, her vegetable garden did look as if she had put her compost piles between rows. I

Compost Bins

My compost bins were easy to assemble from used cement blocks and required no tools. The blocks are simply placed one on top of the other against the plywood back.

A wire enclosure is the easiest form of compost bin to construct. Use scrap lumber for the posts.

This composter is called a Bio-Orb and is designed to be rolled back and forth to aerate the contents.

love her book and believe implicitly in her methods but still prefer my garbage in a bin.

In the Neil Simon play *The Odd Couple*, ill-matched bachelor roommates find two kinds of meat sandwiches in their refrigerator: green and brown. Unpleasant for lunch, but perfect for a compost pile, green and brown layers are just what you are after. The green component is provided by weeds, vegetable peelings, grass clippings, and spent foliage; the brown from fallen leaves, twigs, wood chips, and straw. The microorganisms that do the work of breaking down this raw material into compost need nitrogen from the green materials and carbon from the brown materials. Be advised that the green layers break down quickly, and the dry brown materials take longer. So try to keep the balance right.

The microorganisms also require oxygen and moisture in order to live and do their work, so the pile should be moist but not sopping wet. The word "pile" is misleading in the context of a compost bin. The contents should be spread around, not heaped up. In fact, it helps if there is a depression in the middle to catch water. If it is very dry during the summer, it is beneficial to water the compost.

To incorporate air, most books suggest turning the pile, but partially decomposed organic material is heavy to lift. There are other ways of accomplishing the same thing. Start the pile on top of a really coarse layer of stalks or branches. Do what my aunt used to do, fluff it with a fork. Or what I do, drive the fork straight down into the pile and wiggle it around.

Temperature affects the speed of decomposition. The warmer the weather, the more quickly the raw materials will decompose. The microorganisms responsible for decomposition also create heat as they go about their business of eating and reproducing. As these activities accelerate, the temperature in the pile climbs. When the pile cools off to air temperature, the microorganisms have done their work and the compost is ready for the garden.

Ideally, you should shred everything that goes into the bin first. The smaller the pieces, the greater the surface area presented to the microorganisms, and the faster they can work. But not many gardeners have shredders. The next best thing is to cut up heavy stalks with the clippers and chop things like citrus and melon rinds, which have remarkable staying power. Another argument in favor of cutting up citrus and melon rinds is to discourage wildlife. Opossums, skunks, and raccoons all like to forage for tasty hunks of fruit rind, but they don't bother with small pieces.

If you haven't room in your backyard for compost bins as large as mine, look into one of the new composting devices advertised in many garden catalogs. I know they work because a meticulous gardening friend, who lives in New York City, made quantities of wonderful compost with one of the simplest—a tall plastic container with air holes in the sides and a plastic top. He followed the instructions that came with it with great success.

Composters come in more than a hundred different styles and makes. I am intrigued with the ones that look and work like little cement mixers. A turn of the handle aerates the contents and speeds decomposition. Try one. However large or small your garden, don't be without homemade compost. It's worth its weight in gold.

Because there is never enough of it, save your compost for preparing new planting holes. My idea of real luxury would be an unlimited supply to spread over the perennial garden as mulch, but that is an impossible dream.

Composting has everything to recommend it, practically and philosophically. It is thrifty, good for the environment, and satisfying to the soul. I draw profound comfort from knowing that what was once beautiful living plant material contributes to beauty again. Everything that was, is; everything that is, will be—ad infinitum—thanks to the miraculous process of composting.

Deer, Diseases, and Insect Damage

⚘

I want you to love gardening and not to get discouraged. Therefore, it is tempting to gloss over the problems of plant diseases, insect pests, and mammalian predators. But it certainly would be less than honest. The unhappy fact is that gardening is more difficult than it used to be. Deer are a relatively new problem, and dealing with diseases and insect pests is far more complex because we are increasingly aware of environmental hazards.

In 1962, when I found the leaves of my phlox "all curled up and filled with something that looks like spit," I went to the nursery where I got the plants and said, "What shall I do?" The answer was, "Spray with Lindane and Malathion." I did, and that was that. At the time, Rachel Carson was a voice crying in the wilderness. Her book *Silent Spring* had not yet alerted us to the dangers of pesticides, and ignorant gardeners like myself did what we were told by professionals.

Having belonged to that generation, I now feel ill at ease using or recommending anything. While I do believe that considerable research is being done to come up with safe insect controls, I still refrain from using anything stronger than insecticidal soap. Gardens are part of everyday life, which has its ups and downs. Gardens also have their ups and downs.

My advice is: Do all you can to protect your garden from predators; seek out disease-resistant cultivars of vigorous, easy-to-grow plants, and give them what they want. Try to identify insect pests accurately. I have recently read that 75 percent of all known kinds of living animals belong to the insect world. Learn all you can about these creatures who so greatly outnumber us. When you have done all of the above, take a tip from an old music hall song: "Stick a geranium in your hat and be happy."

There is good news on several fronts. Nowadays, disease resistance is an aspect of plant breeding that is being pursued with diligence. Many new cultivars of disease-prone species, like border phlox and bee balm, have been improved to the point of being able to shrug off powdery mildew. If I were starting a new garden, I would also look for disease-resistant peonies that can stand up to botrytis spores.

With the exception of the peonies, the bulk of my perennials are not bothered by insects or diseases. They are tough old babies, either adaptable foreigners that have taken to our climate like ducks to water—daylilies (from China, Japan, and Siberia) and Siberian irises (from Europe and Russia)—or natives already accustomed to our conditions: sunflowers, coneflowers, rudbeckia, boltonia, and coreopsis, to name a few.

Over the years, these plants have survived deer and woodchuck damage. They have risen above bouts with fungal disease and disfigurement by chewing and sucking insects. And they have all come through severe drought. I regret to say that the worst thing that has ever happened to my plants is still a work-in-progress. In 1995, the roots of nearly half my faithful old perennials were eaten by voles, and I have not yet found a satisfactory control.

Poisons, while effective against mice and voles, are too dangerous around pets and children. Mouse traps baited with peanut butter work, but larger mammalian visitors, usually skunks or opossums, often spring the traps. Nor are there enough traps in the state to cope with the number of voles—they breed every 21 days. Our cat is a valiant ally, but what is one among so many? The only thing we can do is ride out the population explosion. This summer, I plan to fill in with annuals, hoping that their comparatively insignificant root systems will be less appealing.

In most parts of the country, deer are garden enemy number one. Due to increased residential development, deer and homeowners have become painfully conscious of one another. Moreover, the number of deer has risen dramatically over the past two decades. In the modern world, they have only two predators—hunters and, in some parts of the country, coyotes. As neither is welcome in the suburbs, deer flourish there.

When their habitat is destroyed by development, they take up residence in backyards. When their source of wild food is taken away, they substitute nutrient-rich foundation plantings and flower gardens. Improved nutrition and a relatively safe environment favor these beautiful, destructive creatures.

Deer will eat almost anything—grass, twigs, bark, moss, mushrooms, and the foliage, flowers, and buds of virtually all herbaceous perennials. I used to see lists of deer-proof plants in gardening magazines. But the lists have disappeared as the deer population has increased. While they have definite food preferences—tulips, hostas, daylilies, roses, yews, junipers, and euonymus—deer will eat whatever is available if they are hungry enough.

A number of repellent sprays have been developed that work reasonably well, among them Hinder, Big Game Repellent, and Miller Hot Sauce. Some gardeners swear that spreading Milorganite, a sludge-based fertilizer, around plants protects them. Deer are said to find the smell offensive. Other gardeners are convinced that bars of soap hung from the branches of their shrubs work wonders. In my experience, these measures are successful only if the deer problem is minor.

The only 100 percent effective protection is a properly installed deer fence. For country properties, a slanted seven-wire electric fence is the best. Instead of being upright, this fence looks as if it had been pushed over at an angle. The rails, positioned at 10-foot intervals, slant from the ground upward and outward toward the enemy. The fence is relatively unobtrusive and only 4 feet high, but it is approximately 6 feet deep. The width discourages jumping. A vertical seven-wire electric fence takes up less room and is effective in situations where the deer problem is not too severe. Contact your Cooperative Extension Service and ask about deer fencing.

We have a section of slanted seven-wire electric fence around the woodland garden, and it has worked like a charm. The rest of our garden, about an acre and a half, is enclosed by a stone wall topped with a vertical woven wire fence—not electrified. The stone wall varies in height from 3½ to 6 feet.

We bought rolls of 6-foot-high turkey wire and stapled it to the trees and saplings that stand behind the wall. In places where there were no trees, we installed cedar posts. By raising the wire 2 feet from the ground, we achieved a height of 8 feet—enough to discourage all but the most athletic deer. However, I had to fill the 2-foot gap at the bottom with chicken wire after a doe and two fawns managed to squeeze underneath.

If having a garden is a high priority in your life, look into fencing. More and more people are turning to physical barriers for protection. Lynden Miller had an electric deer fence installed several years ago. Until recently, Martha McKeon had been using Hinder successfully. But applying it every few days was time-consuming. This year, she and Bill have started putting up a woven wire fence.

Working only on weekends, they have already finished a 150-foot stretch. For support, they are using a combination of existing trees and metal posts. Martha has ambitious plans to grow hedgerows all along the fence and is already making cuttings of suitable shrubs.

Much smaller, but almost as destructive as deer, woodchucks are familiar garden predators in the Northeast. While deer browse and tear, woodchucks chop and slice. It is small comfort that they do it neatly, but it is one way of identifying the culprits. Deer leave telltale footprints and more mess.

Anyway, you will probably catch your woodchuck in the act. Unlike deer, they feed in broad daylight, preferably in the early morning or late afternoon. But I've seen them munching away at all hours. I had no luck controlling them with repellent sprays, but trapping proved surprisingly easy. "Chucks" are stolid, unimaginative creatures, devoted to their little routines. If a Havahart trap baited with Red Delicious apples is located in the right place, they obligingly lumber in, showing no fear when the door snaps shut behind them. They often sit there calmly eating the apples.

Here are a few tips for would-be trappers. Havahart makes two models. One is a professional model that has a single opening and an improved triggering mechanism. This trap costs about $10 more than the homeowner's model, which is like a wire tunnel. If you have a tunnel-style trap, tie one end shut.

Study the habits of your chuck for a day or two. He or she will invariably return to the scene of the crime by the same route. Set the trap with the open end facing in that direction. Early morning is the best time.

Don't leave the trap baited all night. Skunks and opossums are nocturnal feeders and like Red Delicious apples almost as much as woodchucks do. Being shy, stubborn, and well equipped to retaliate, skunks are difficult to remove from the trap. Chucks, on the other hand, bear the trapper no ill will and will scurry off as soon as the coast is clear. I take them to a boat-launching area a mile away and release them by propping open the door and staying out of sight for a few minutes.

Fencing out woodchucks works well for a vegetable garden, but be sure to

A Harahart trap
baited with Red Delicious
apples lures even the most
cautious woodchuck. Use at least
two apples because smaller rodents, like chipmunks,
often steal part of the bait and escape through the
openings in the wire mesh.

136

sink the wire at least a foot deep. Chucks are good diggers. The best deterrent is a dog that spends a lot of time outside in the garden. No chuck ever darkened our landscape while our old Jack Russell terrier was on guard. When Abby no longer posed a threat, the woodchucks knew it.

Moles sometimes pose a problem, chiefly in the lawn, where they raise a network of ugly tunnels. Contrary to the fears of some gardeners, moles don't eat much plant material. They are basically carnivores, and they do get rid of grubs and insects. Unfortunately, they also eat earthworms. On the whole, it is hard to look upon moles with favor.

Antimole devices are a bit of a joke in our household. To no avail, I tried wooden windmills mounted on stakes driven into the ground. The vibration transmitted through the stakes was supposed to be anathema to the moles. When a pair of far more expensive battery-powered vibrators also failed, my spouse pointed out that they had served their purpose: making a buck for their creators.

Mole-Med, a product tested at Michigan State University, has been more successful. It is a castor oil–based liquid, approved by the EPA, and you spray it on lawns. It doesn't kill moles, but it drives them away. I have had it applied to the lawn twice, and the results are encouraging. It was applied in the spring of 1995. During the summer, the lawn was mole-free, but they returned in September. Another application was made at that time. We'll see.

Some users have proclaimed Mole-Med an all-purpose repellent effective against skunks, rabbits, squirrels, woodchucks, and raccoons. But I'm afraid that is wishful thinking. Here, woodchucks, squirrels, and chipmunks still abound.

So much for pests. Diseases are another dreary topic, but prevalent enough to warrant discussion. Like cold germs that afflict people, spores that cause plant diseases are ever-present. Whether or not they develop into a full-blown case of botrytis or powdery mildew depends on the constitution of the plant and on the weather. Disease spores flourish in heat and humidity.

Rita Buchanan looks at the situation this way: "The truth is that the plants either live through these plagues and diseases or they don't. You wonder how much difference you can make. If they don't live through it, there are other things you can grow."

Here are a few things you can do to ward off diseases: Read catalogs carefully and always choose disease-resistant cultivars of your favorite plants; give them soil that drains well; provide enough room between plants for good air circulation; pick off dead flowers and foliage during the season; and do a thorough fall cleanup. At that time, get rid of any foliage that might harbor fungus spores—peony and lily foliage, especially.

Insect damage is a fact of life in a garden. During the 1940s, 1950s, and 1960s, all-out war with lethal chemicals barely made a dent in the insect population, while the consequences for human beings and the environment were frightening. Although new, less dangerous insecticides are being developed, there are no long-term guarantees that these are safe either. Look at it this way: There is going to be insect damage in your garden, whether you spray with insecticides or not. You have to decide how much is tolerable. Raising our threshold of tolerance is the first step.

Integrated Pest Management, called IPM for short, is a relatively new approach to coping with insects (see Selected Further Reading). It focuses on studying their life cycles and figuring out when to intervene and with what, starting with the least toxic form of control. The first line of defense is physical intervention—pick it off and squash it. If that is out of the question, as in the case of thousands of tiny aphids, squirt them with a forceful jet of water from the hose. It is rough on the plants, but they can take it. Aphids are soft-bodied and can't survive that much abuse.

When handpicking and hosing fail, the next step is to determine when to spray and what to use. The object is to hit the insects at the weakest point in their life cycle. But first, you have to identify them. The manner in which they eat their food will tell you which tactic to use.

Beetles and caterpillars are chewing insects and can be killed with stomach poisons sprayed on the leaves. One of the safest methods of dealing with chewers is to spray with *Bacillus thuringiensis*. Commonly called "Bt," it is a disease-producing bacterium that affects caterpillars and beetles but not people and pets. Trade names for this insecticide are Biotrol, Biogard, Dipel, and Thuricide.

Sucking insects, like aphids and leafhoppers, have a tricky mechanism for probing under leaf surfaces. They draw out the plant juices from inside, so it is no use putting poisons all over the outside of the leaves. You have to spray the insects themselves with poisons that damage their bodies. These poisons are called contact sprays. Insecticidal soaps and horticultural oil sprays are considered safe and effective. I have used Safer brand insecticidal soap with moderate success. There is a caution on the bottle that says not to use it on plants exposed to full sun. It burns the foliage. It also burns immature leaves on some plants.

Improbable as it may seem, some insects are actually on our side. These are called beneficial predator insects, and the new, more cautious approach to pest management allows them to do their job. The most familiar and beloved insect benefactor is the lady beetle. Its bright orange back and neat black spots frequently appear as a decorative motif.

Welcome this little creature into your garden. Its larvae will consume many aphids. Actually, you won't recognize the immature lady beetles. The larvae (the stage before the cocoon forms in preparation for finally hatching the mature insect) have yellow and black jointed bodies, but rest assured that your aphid problem is in good hands. Lady beetles can be ordered by mail, but you must be able to provide them with aphids. Don't order them just as a precaution, or they may die.

Green lacewings are also eagerly recruited by environmentally conscious gardeners. As larvae, lacewings attack aphids, mealy bugs, and even caterpillars. Available through mail-order catalogs, the lacewings are usually shipped as eggs, along with a supply of food in case they hatch in transit.

You can buy the more expensive lacewing larvae, which arrive ready for work. At this stage, they have weird-looking pointed bodies. Tiny as they are, they will set about solving your aphid problem right away, but they require careful handling. You have to use the point of a pencil to put them where you want them.

By far the most appealing of the gardener's natural allies are the birds. With catholic tastes in food and hungry fledglings to feed, most of our common birds get rid of huge quantities of harmful insects during the summer. Even seed eaters, like grosbeaks and cardinals, do their fair share. A quarter of the cardinal's diet consists of insects, while rose-breasted grosbeaks are reported to feast on wood borers, leaf beetles, aphids, stinkbugs, tent caterpillars, and gypsy moth caterpillars. All that and beauty, too.

The charm of the birds notwithstanding, pest control today is one of the most frustrating and debatable aspects of gardening. There are no easy solutions, and gardeners have to learn more in order to deal with this situation intelligently. If you have specific questions, try contacting your local Cooperative Extension Service.

Taking Stock

⚜

Following a detailed account of the ills that befall a garden, I'm afraid to ask if you are having fun yet. But if you have had just one wonderful surprise in your garden and a few mornings when you couldn't wait to get outside, I'll be content. Making a garden isn't easy, but it is the most absorbing, deeply fulfilling activity I have ever engaged in. To make something beautiful is the dream, but the real point is just to be out there doing it.

I garden for the flowers, of course, but a more compelling reason is to experience the dizzying, delicious smell of spring and to be out-of-doors in October's bright blue weather. I garden so that I can lie on a bench in the dead of winter and look up at the bare trees catching the sky in a net.

I garden because it makes me feel alive. Everything else is a bonus: discovering that some far-out color scheme actually works; finding hundreds of perky green seedlings surrounding a favorite hellebore; coming upon the bloom of a spectacular daylily that I have never seen before and that I will have only for one day. This is what it's all about.

For me, gardening is first and foremost a sensual pleasure. However, it is also a stimulating intellectual puzzle. I delight in learning about plants and trying to find the right homes for them. I enjoy wrestling with design ideas and trying to make sense of the landscape. Most of all, I relish experimenting with ever-changing garden compositions. The essence of gardening is its ongoing nature. It is what I have learned to love best, but what beginners find difficult.

There was a time when I longed for our garden to be finished. Indeed, I believed that completion was the objective. In my earliest notebook, there are wistful references to this goal and numerous expressions of frustration: "I seem to spend an awful amount of time moving things hither and yon every year." That was written in April 1964. How horrified I would have been to know that thirty-two years later, I would still be at it—moving things from place to place.

When I began whacking down barberry bushes and planting perennials all those years ago, I had no idea that I was embarking on a lifelong journey. Gardening creeps up on you. But by the end of the first season, you will have some idea whether or not you enjoy the process. If you find yourself thinking in terms of "next year," you are hooked.

You will go through stages. The first involves learning how to grow things and expanding your repertoire of flowering plants. This stage is dominated by flowers. You have a nonselective yearning for color and, to this end, spend a great deal of time working out what blooms with what and trying to put them together effectively.

Next, you become a foliage freak. You can't get enough handsome leaves, variegated leaves, colored leaves. A further development is a sudden fondness for metallic foliage shades—silver, pewter, and steel. Soon, you will thrill to the architectural qualities of big leaves and develop a thirst for vertical accents. At that point, grasses are in your future.

Then one day you will find fault with your perennials for leaving you in the lurch in August, and you will begin to explore the possibilities of unusual annuals and tender perennials. This is the moment when you will discover Logee's Greenhouses in Danielson, Connecticut. It doesn't matter where you live. For better or for worse, Logee's is as near as your mailbox. You will have trouble with the unfamiliar botanical names in the catalog, but it is good practice, and there are so many tantalizing plants for terrace containers and to brighten up your August border.

Finally, your restless gardener's eye will demand more form, and you will begin to add woody material. Those dwarf evergreens that left you cold for the first few years will suddenly catch your attention, and you will curse yourself for not having started to plant evergreens, deciduous ornamental trees, and shrubs sooner.

In a recent conversation with Lynden Miller, I lamented not having planted more evergreens when I first began gardening. "I know," she said. "You can make all kinds of mistakes, as long as the bones go in first. Of course, I didn't put them in first, I put them in last. We all do." So fortify yourself with the comforting thought that no less a gardener than Lynden Miller made some of the same mistakes that you will make.

Though I doubt that you will take our advice about planting evergreens first, I hope one day you will remember it. But all this is down the road. If you have survived one season with your spirits high, you are already well on the way. Right now, get out your notebook. At this stage in your career, it is the most useful gardening tool you own. Ideally, you should have been making notes all along, but if you haven't, start now.

Make notes about your first season. What actually did bloom with what? You may not remember. That's the point of the notebook. Try to pin down blooming dates next year. No two gardens are alike. And the blooming dates given in this book may not match those in your garden. Your microclimate is unique.

Make notes about the behavior of your plants, including reservations. But don't get rid of a perennial out-of-hand. Early on, I cast aside balloon flower after growing it for a couple of years. In time, I regretted my haste, and a few years ago I reinstated this lovely perennial. From the first, I loved its buds, the shape of tiny hot-air balloons, and the starry blue flowers, but the stems were so floppy I chose not to deal with them. If I had waited another year, the plants would have become sturdier, and I would have learned how to stake them.

Over the years, I have developed the three-year rule for perennials. Give a new plant one year to recover from the shock of being plunged into a strange environment. It takes time to develop new roots and adjust to your soil and climate. Give your newcomer another year to get its act together. The second season, it should put on substantial growth and produce a few flowers. The third year, it's your turn. You deserve a good show. If the plant doesn't measure up, on to the compost pile with it.

The three-year rule works with most perennials, but there are some that take longer to reach their full potential. The big hostas tend to be slow starters. They grow easily, well, and *slowly*. It takes four or five years for some of those with mammoth leaves to produce the sort of clumps that you see in gardening books. Peonies eventually grow into impressive clumps, but it takes time. Gas plant is another worthwhile, long-lived perennial that calls for patience. I have had mine for three years, and finally, last summer, it began to look like a plant. But it will be a long time before I can expect many flowers.

Develop the habit of note taking. It requires discipline, but it will pay off. I

One of the gates in Lynden Miller's yew hedge leads to an allée of crab apple trees and an inviting garden bench.

The center section of Lynden's border, with its closely woven pastel color scheme. Major plants are identified below.

barberry 'Rose Glow'

variegated grass

false indigo

purple coneflower

Siberian iris

Russian sage

phlox

Salvia

knautia

annual

geranium

blue oat grass

annual

purple
smokebush

rose of
Sharon

maiden
grass

lamb's
ears

salvia

phlox

Siberian iris

sedum
'Autumn
Joy'

barberry

berian
iris

geranium

artemisia

catmint

A painterly composition employing subtle colors and textures

Architecture is an important element in Lynden's garden.

Well-chosen edging plants unify Martha McKeon's colorful summer perennial border.

The view across Martha's rose garden
and island bed toward the border

learned more from my notebooks than from any other single information source, including books, lectures, and classes. The notes were often sketchy. There were gaps of months, of a few years, even, but the education of a gardener and the history of an ever-changing garden is all there in these erratic jottings.

In the old days, I wrote down all sorts of things. I recorded successes and failures; penned diatribes against the weather and composed paeans in praise of favorite plants. I had a lot of questions, too. The phrase "I wonder . . ." appears often. Sometimes, the questions are answered eventually by another gardener's comment or observation, also duly written down.

I still take my notebook with me whenever I visit a garden or nursery. One autumn, I fell in love with a friend's ornamental grasses and made a note to that effect. The next spring, I came across the note and promptly bought *Miscanthus sinensis* 'Variegatus', which I planted with *Sedum* 'Autumn Joy' and the blue mist shrub that I already had. That fall, the garden appeared far more varied and satisfying than before, thanks to the grasses.

Nursery visits are bound to provide fodder for your notebook, because you will meet many new plants. After a recent winter jaunt to Twombly Nursery in Monroe, Connecticut, I decided that I had to have more evergreens for the perennial border and made notes of those that I liked. At the moment, I'm leaning toward a dwarf columnar blue spruce I saw on that occasion.

Looking back over my notebooks, it is obvious that I arrived at many of my plant combinations by observing them blooming in other gardens and writing it down. Seeing is believing. If you see a plant blooming on May 1 in a local garden, you know you can expect it to bloom at the same time in yours.

In 1962, a garden next door to the local supermarket precipitated me into an amorous fling with bearded irises. My notebook records the ultimately painful course of that affair. At first, I was swept off my feet by the "wonderful masses of yellow, light lavender and pink." Later, I had second thoughts about the pink: "I'm not wild about it. It's sort of flesh-pink and somehow wrong for an iris." In the end, I had second thoughts about all bearded irises. Today, only one—prophetically called 'Allegiance'—remains in my garden.

Color was an early preoccupation. I still find it one of the most enthralling aspects of perennial gardening. Notes like the following sharpened my awareness of gradations of color: "The daylily 'Apollo' is a pleasant soft orange, exactly the color of the Mid-Century lilies." The name Mid-Century identifies a popular strain of hybrid lilies.

Ten years later, this entry appeared: "In the first week of July, there are little spots of vivid color—purple lythrum, bright red bee balm, a huge patch of wild orange daylilies—all this at the same time the pink, white and red astilbe corner is in bloom. At first I thought it looked rather awful, but at least there are lots of flowers, and the bizarre colors are surrounded with so much green grass that it seems to work."

To digress briefly, the reference to the astilbe corner reminds me of another value of the notebook. Recording severe weather events and acts of God keeps you in your place. The astilbe planting was a great success until the untimely demise of the oak tree that shaded it. One summer, the oak was struck by lightning. It crashed to the ground, and what had been a shade bed became a full-sun bed. I never again found a good place to grow astilbe. The rest of the mature trees on the property are maples, and the soil beneath them is too dry for these moisture-loving perennials.

Thirty-five years of taking notes about the weather and related phenomena teaches you something about your climate. In the Northeast, it is realistic to expect the unexpected. I choose to remember the rare summer when rain is meted out an inch a week. I succeed in forgetting the far more usual summers featuring periods of drought. But the notebooks keep me honest.

From this accumulation of notes, I also know something about our micro-climate. In the fall, our garden is the last in the neighborhood to be hit by frost. The cold air rolls off the higher elevations, slipping over us and settling in the lower valleys. This means that the flowers of some late-blooming perennials, like the willow-leaved sunflower, are safe in my garden and not in my neighbor's.

Many of my notes are of a practical nature, reminders to do things: "Mid-Century lilies are hidden behind the lythrum and should be moved." There are innumerable references to plants that should be moved and endless something-should-be-done-about lists. Years ago, I knew that "something should be done with the bank by the garage—leveled, reduced in height, spread out?" It was the right idea but took nearly a quarter of a century to implement. The solution proved to be a retaining wall, which we could not have afforded any sooner, anyway.

The bulk of my notes were and are about plants and how they perform. Purple coneflowers were fairly new to me when I wrote: "Need more of this to have it show up from a distance." At the end of July, globe thistle was "still attractive and very blue, but the yellow daylilies have gone by so it isn't as effective as it should be." A much better companion was found in an orange daylily cultivar called 'Rocket City', which bloomed with the globe thistle.

My notes are always full of plants or bulbs that I want. In the spring of 1985, I noted holes in the bulb display in the border. "Need 'White Emperor' tulips in mid-section behind and to right of peony 'Scarlet O'Hara'." That year I was pleased with goat's beard. "Move it to far end of shady border—want more." "Must have" and "want more" are frequent refrains.

Notes about the form and behavior of new plants fill up pages of my notebooks. "Hosta from Lori has leaves 5 to 6 inches long and 3 to 4 inches wide; color is clear green with neat white edge a quarter of an inch wide, not splashed with white. The plant seems to wander, rather than clump-up." The last observation proved useful. That particular hosta is a very good ground cover because of its spreading habit.

Annuals get mentioned, too. In 1989, the winners were: "nicotianas—I cut back the Nickis [a named group of compact nicotianas], and they have looked good all season; nierembergia is a *very* nice tub plant and frost-resistant; lovely linear foliage and bright purple, cup-shaped flowers three quarters of an inch across, facing upward; nolana was a flop—pretty flowers open for a couple of days at a time, but ratty foliage." Down with nolana!

All the notebooks are crammed with descriptions of unfamiliar plants and little sketches to help me remember shapes and patterns. *Lespedeza* was a new one in 1987: "A dense-foliaged little bush three and a half feet high; white pea-flowers in small clusters from leaf axils; leaves bluish-green; many, many little branches, each with three leaflets." This description was accompanied by a rough sketch of the foliage, which was one of the plant's charms. Many gardeners would have taken a photograph instead, but I find it easier to concentrate on details if I describe them, instead of fussing with the camera.

These are the sorts of notes you should start making for yourself. I use my notebooks for everything to do with the garden. I write things down when I read and when I go to lectures. I remember a wonderful lecture Pamela Harper gave at the New York Botanical Garden. The title was "Easy Plants for Difficult Situations." When she talked about perennials for dry shade, I began scribbling frantically.

One of the plants she recommended was a shrub with handsome, sharply lobed foliage and white flower clusters: "Oakleaf hydrangea; very good for dry shade—look up. Surrounded by hosta 'Halcyon'—very pretty, blue-green

Good deciduous Shrubs for the Border

Oakleaf hydrangea
(_Hydrangea quercifolia_)

Recommended by
Pam Harper. Very
good for dry shade.

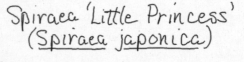

Spiraea 'Little Princess'
(_Spiraea japonica_)

Dainty foliage and
pink flowers; can
be sheared.

Threadleaf
Japanese maple
(_Acer palmatum_
'Dissectum')

Dissectum refers to the whole group of these gorgeous,
lacy trees. Stays 6 to 8 feet high with wide
spread.

leaves." I couldn't find the exact hosta cultivar, but within the year I had found a similar one and re-created this grouping beneath my maple trees.

Martha McKeon is also a firm believer in note taking. "I get forgetful," she says. "If I have an idea that I don't want to forget, I'll jot it down. That's important because a lot of gardening is the result of intuition and imagination, and that kind of stuff can leave you. You go outside, and you get a sudden thought or a little impression—I have to write those things down."

Later, she'll read over her notes and reconsider her inspirations of the moment. "I'll think, 'I'm not going to do that after all.' But a lot of the ideas that have worked best and that I am satisfied with came from my notes. I take notes all year long—in the winter, too. If something occurs to me, I just write it down and shove it in the gardening notebook. Sometimes I even copy notes over and organize them in categories. If there's something you get excited about, even for a second, you should capture it."

Although Martha is an expert needlewoman and talented with her hands, she finds drawing plans on graph paper difficult. "I did do a plan for the perennial border, and for the first couple of years, it helped me get things a little more organized, but I just take notes now. I write down mistakes, too. If I see something that is really wrong in terms of placement or size or whatever, I write it down so that I won't do it again."

That's one reason to keep a notebook—to avoid repetition of the same mistakes. Another is to increase your enjoyment of gardening. The garden is at its best in the early morning before "dawn goes down to day." In the soft, slanting light, it sometimes looks almost perfect. Wander around before breakfast at least every week or two, notebook in hand, and jot down things that please you.

Look at the lady's-mantle. The leaves still balance tiny crystal balls. Your new daylily 'Pearl Lewis' has just opened. It is the color of cantaloupe ice cream. What would complement that color? A lavender-blue partner like Russian sage? Quick! Write it down. If you start a notebook now, one day you will have the fun I've had—of recalling the special joys of a self-taught gardener.

Looking Ahead

❧

It takes about three years for a new perennial garden to mature. You will certainly have flowers the first year, but don't expect riotous bloom unless you start with large plants in gallon containers. The second year, the original plants should increase substantially in size and produce more blossoms, and the third year, you should be able to gaze with pride on your handiwork.

At that time, you may decide you want more of a favorite plant. This is one reason for dividing perennials. Another is that some perennials actually need dividing at the end of the third season in order to maintain their vigor. Phlox, asters, bearded iris, Shasta daisies, and coral bells are among those that require early and frequent division.

Although none of my perennials *demand* this attention so soon, some would benefit from it. Lusty daylily cultivars can multiply at an amazing rate. Waiting longer than three or four years can mean strenuous work on the part of the gardener. Although the clump may continue to flower well without intervention, it is in the gardener's best interest to get out the shovel sooner rather than later.

Dividing ornamental grasses becomes next to impossible if they remain in place too long. How long is "too long"? As long as it takes to grow into a large clump. I was given a husky division of fountain grass in 1991. In the spring of 1995, Martha and Bill McKeon came over to help me divide some of my grasses, including the fountain grass. Their method is to dig straight down all around the perimeter of the clump. Then, with the grass still in the ground, Bill quarters it with an ax. The four pieces have to be dug out with a shovel. In the case of the fountain grass, digging out the divisions resulted in one casualty—the handle of the shovel.

Martha took two chunks of the fountain grass and made numerous smaller divisions. I left one in place and replanted the remaining division. By the end of the summer, my two clumps were almost as big as the original. The moral of this tale is that most plants like to be divided, and if you grow ornamental grasses, you'd better have kind friends like the McKeons.

Division is a form of asexual or vegetative propagation, as opposed to sexual propagation by seeds. It means that pieces of the parent plant are removed and grown as new individuals, identical in genetic makeup to the original. The object is to dig up the crowded clump and separate it into several pieces, each with enough roots and stems to survive on its own.

There are other methods of vegetative propagation. Making additional plants of taprooted perennials is usually accomplished by root cuttings, a procedure that requires a bit of knowhow and is outside the realm of this book. But the idea is to slice up pieces of root 2 to 4 inches long, place them upright in pots filled with a growing medium, and keep them moist until new shoots appear.

The tricky part is that the cut ends of the root pieces look exactly alike to the novice. However, roots know which end is up. No shoots will grow unless each piece is oriented in its pot the same way the whole root was oriented in the ground—top upward, bottom downward.

A few perennials are difficult to divide because their roots are fleshy, brittle, and easily damaged. These include the otherwise easy-to-grow balloon flower, peonies, old-fashioned bleeding heart, gas plant, butterfly weed, and lupines. For the same reason, these plants dislike being moved. Mind you, I have moved all of the above without killing them. But don't try it unless it is really necessary.

No matter how it is done, dividing looks like cruel and unusual punishment. Some plants have to be torn apart or even assaulted with sharp instruments. Many gardeners are appalled at the thought of cutting up a perfectly healthy plant. A red-blooded male friend who had just become interested in gardening was offered hosta divisions by a neighbor, but when he saw her fall upon the clump with a butcher knife, he begged her to stop.

The truth is that most perennials thrive on division, and all but a few tolerate it with equanimity. The plants mentioned in the text are tough. They welcome division and won't take it amiss, even if you bungle the job. As you become more experienced, you will hack, slice, tease, and wiggle your plants apart with aplomb.

Daylilies and hostas have spreading masses of fleshy roots that put up with all manner of mangling. Hostas don't need to be divided at all. In fact, they con-

Dividing Grasses

Being prairie plants, grasses are equipped for drought with masses of deep roots. Dig out small clumps and split them with a stout knife.

Bill McKeon's techique for dividing a large clump is to cut back the foliage; quarter the clump with an ax while it is still in the ground, and dig out the separate pieces.

tinue to improve with age, becoming increasingly handsome. But if you want more of a certain cultivar, you can lift the whole clump and separate it into smaller pieces. Be forewarned, dividing a big hosta clump requires brute force.

The same is true of overgrown daylily clumps. At great physical cost to the gardener, ancient clumps can be rejuvenated by digging them up, hacking them apart, and replanting smaller divisions in enriched soil. Some books recommend dividing daylilies every three or four years as a matter of course, but many cultivars can be left much longer before they need division. It depends on the vitality of the individual cultivar.

Daylily clumps increase in size when new plants develop from buds on the "crown." When you first plant your daylilies, look very carefully at the point where the leaves join the roots. This junction is the crown. It is, in fact, a modified stem, and like any stem, it has points where new shoots emerge. These are called nodes. But this stem has been squeezed together like an accordion, and the nodes are only visible as very fine lines encircling the stem. Nevertheless, each ring is the site of a potential new daylily plant.

The more new plants that develop on top of the crown, the bigger the clump of daylilies grows. Eventually, old clumps have to be divided because the newer plants have been hoisted up in a sort of hummock, and their roots no longer get their fair share of moisture and nutrients. Some daylily cultivars make new plants hand over fist and have to be divided every four or five years. Others increase much more slowly.

Daylilies are the most forgiving of perennials and can be divided at any time of year. In the Northeast, the best time is in August, after flowering and before that fall spurt of new growth. The old foliage is looking shabby anyway. Cut it down to 6 or 8 inches so that you can see what you are doing. Then, dig up the whole clump; hose the earth off the roots; and try to pull the clump apart with your hands. Failing that, get a big screwdriver and force it straight down into the middle of the clump. Twist the screwdriver this way and that. The twisting motion usually works no matter how crowded the roots are. If that doesn't work, shove a couple of digging forks into the clump, back to back, and force the handles apart.

Dividing and replanting give you another chance to improve the soil by topping up the humus content. Take special care to add lots of compost to the hole before replanting divisions. For the quickest display, replant several small clumps in a group. And treat all divisions like new plants (see "Planting"). Be sure to keep them moist and shaded for a few days until they settle in.

On the whole, clump-forming perennials are easy to divide. Their roots fan out into the soil, like the spreading crown of a tree, branching again and again and making a tangled web of roots and rootlets. Because there are lots of them, the plant doesn't miss a few roots when you cut, pry, or wiggle the clump apart.

In all cases the method is roughly the same: Dig up the clump, shake off the soil, and pull the plant apart. A bald spot in the middle of a clump is common with older plants. When you have the clump out of the ground, save only the outer portions that have juicy, young roots and several stems attached. Throw away the dry, woody bits from the middle. Replant the divisions with care, adding organic matter to the hole. Spread out the roots, firm the soil around them with your hands, and water gently but thoroughly.

There is another way to handle daylilies and Siberian irises that have gotten really out of hand. First, cut the foliage back to a few inches. Then, instead of attempting to dig up the entire clump, take a sharp shovel, spade, or butcher knife and cut the clump in half. Leave half in the ground, undisturbed, and remove the other half. Get rid of the worn-out part in the middle and backfill the hole with enriched soil. You can subdivide the rest into smaller divisions.

The timing of your ministrations depends on the type of plant. The daylilies and Siberian irises are easiest to handle in late summer and early fall, while spring division is best for hostas. Like daylilies and Siberian irises, hostas can be divided in situ. Before the leaves expand, scrape some of the soil away from the clump, and look for a logical place to make an incision. There is often a natural sort of dividing line between groups of emerging leaves. With a heavy knife, cut through the crown and roots and lift out a wedge, complete with plenty of roots and several tightly furled leaves. Backfill the hole with humus-rich soil, and plant the new division or divisions as soon as possible.

Spring is the best time to divide plants that form dense colonies of shallow-rooted stems. With plants like phlox, asters, boltonia, and hardy chrysanthemums, dig up the mat of crowded stems and shake off the earth. They may fall into separate pieces. If not, pull them apart into small divisions with several robust green shoots and lots of roots. Replant. Consign the less vigorous roots and stems to the compost pile. Provide a bit of shade for the new divisions and keep them watered.

Some of my sunflowers send out underground stems that give rise to new plants at a distance from the parent. Spring is the best time to detach these, discard the weaker shoots, and replant the strong young plants in a group. They will immediately form a clump. Early in the season, vigorous, well-rooted shoots are rarin' to grow.

If you divide carefully and provide optimum growing conditions for the divisions, you can probably get away with dividing any time of year, but the following plants are fussy. Ornamental grasses must be divided in the spring only; peonies (see "TLC: Fall and Winter") in the fall; and bearded irises in midsummer, immediately after flowering.

Although I think you will ultimately be discouraged by disease and pest-prone irises, I can't imagine not trying them. The flower shape is unique, and the colors are glorious. So here's how to divide them. After they have flowered, cut the stalks down flush with the rhizomes. The rhizomes are those fat, bumpy structures from which the roots, stalks, and leaves emerge. They are, in fact, modified stems, complete with nodes that give rise to the aboveground parts of the plants. Roots do not have nodes and cannot produce new plants.

Cut the leaves to about 8 inches, and lift the mat of interlocking rhizomes out of the ground. The old rhizomes in the middle will be surrounded by short, plump, new-looking rhizomes. These are the ones you want to save. Chances are, the clump will fall apart of its own accord. If not, pull it apart and, with a sharp knife, cut the fresh, vigorous rhizomes off the old ones. These may be single divisions with one fan of leaves or a rhizome with two smaller "offsets" (new rhizomes, complete with roots and leaves). Replant the divisions in enriched soil. Set the rhizomes just beneath the surface of the soil, about 9 inches apart, and all facing in the same direction.

Get rid of the cut leaves and old rhizomes in the trash. Iris borers enter through the leaves as minuscule caterpillars and work their destructive way down into the rhizome by late June or early July. If their presence goes unnoticed at the time of division, their life cycle will continue uninterrupted, and the vicious circle will be completed the following spring.

If you have never divided perennials before, be bold and resolute. Even clumsily done, division is good for plants. Replant the divisions in soil well laced with organic matter; and provide moisture and shade. Remember that a division is the equivalent of a new plant. It will take a year to settle in. After that, you can expect lush growth and an abundance of flowers.

Part Four

Landscape Design

❋❋❋❋❋❋❋❋❋❋❋❋❋❋❋❋❋❋❋❋❋❋❋❋❋

Looking Around: The Bigger Picture

*

After three seasons, you will feel reasonably confident about growing easy plants and putting them together. If you are not pleased with your flower bed, I will be very much surprised and disappointed. By now, it should have some beautiful big clumps of daylilies, a couple of grasses, some stout-hearted *Sedum* 'Autumn Joy', and a few things you just couldn't resist at the local nursery. On the whole, you should be enjoying it. But getting through the first year can be rough.

I keep thinking back to my own struggles and wondering if you were horrified by how small a 1-quart perennial looks in the garden. Were pests and predators a problem? Was the weather cooperative or frustrating? Did you make it to September without throwing up your hands? Or was the month of August the last straw?

The final entry in my garden notebook for the 1964 season was dated July 22, and it read: "I quit! We've had a frightful drought which has wrecked great hunks of lawn, and everything is just too depressing to write about." Many of the early notebooks ended on a note of despair. But my mood was always jubilant by the following spring.

March 11, 1965. "Hurray! The first robin! I started cleaning up the perennial bed and raking the lawn." A month later: "A heavenly real spring day with temperatures in the sixties. Fourteen crocuses in bloom. Leveled the pile of topsoil and seeded over the old driveway." The day after that: "Good old New

157

England! It snowed and sleeted most of the morning, though there is no accumulation. Actually, it was perfect for the grass seed."

Gardening is like a roller-coaster ride. There will be times when you want to get off, but I hope you won't. The feeling passes, and bit by bit, gardening becomes part of your life. A flower bed is just the beginning. When you have a season or two under your belt, you start looking around. You may discover, as I did, that your perennial border is not in the best of all possible places. At this point, you begin to seriously consider the rest of your property.

Making your garden into a pleasurable, manageable place has a lot to do with creating relationships and organizing space. What most of us find disturbing is that we are confronted with too much of a good thing or too little. Our properties have either too many separate entities—a flower bed here, a tree there, a shrub somewhere else—or they are a blank slate.

In the first instance, try to think of ways to reduce the number of unrelated elements. Link separate plantings together. If you have an isolated tree and a couple of shrubs nearby, make an island bed to contain all three. If too little definition is the problem, try to organize your space by planting trees and shrubs all along the perimeter of your property. Make divisions within. If you have a long, narrow lot, put a hedge or fence crosswise to make two spaces and connect them with a ready-made arbor.

Consciously or unconsciously, the eye seeks a target on which to alight. Try to find or create focal points. In a small garden, the focal point could be a birdbath or a sundial. In a larger garden, it might be a wooden fence with a flower bed in front of it or a bench backed by a planting of evergreen shrubs. In our garden, the focal point is a vista.

If you cling to three themes—creating relationships, dividing space, and providing something to look at—you will find your own solutions. In the meantime, take inspiration from other gardens.

I arrived at solutions to common landscape problems by a combination of intuition and serendipity. I divided the pool lawn from the lower lawn with a juniper hedge; joined beds together; made paths back and forth across the east-facing hillside; and cleared brush to open up the view.

My garden is defined by a strong linear axis. An axis is nothing more than a straight line. In landscape design, it serves as a sort of backbone around which other elements can be arranged. Construction of our ill-fated swimming pool determined the axis of our property and catapulted me, prematurely, into the design phase of my gardening life.

The pool shape we had chosen was rectangular—32 feet long and 16 feet wide. In order to make sense in terms of the rectilinear house and terrace, it had to be centered on and perpendicular to these man-made features. To that end, we took stakes and string, stretched a line from the center of the terrace due north, located the middle of the pool about 30 feet from the terrace, and told the contractor to put 'er there.

The pool site was leveled by a gouge-and-fill operation. Soil from the hole was used to support the long side of the rectangular basin. This resulted in a raw earthwork that ran parallel to the pool for a hundred feet or so, halting the downward drift of the land. Instead of a slope, we now had a level plane supported by a bank. It divided the lawn into an upper and a lower level. Above the bank, the sweep of uncluttered space was arresting. Moreover, it drew my attention to the potential view.

At that time, we couldn't even see the stone walls that bounded our garden. They were smothered in vines and hidden by shrubby growth. Beyond them, trees closed ranks on every side except to the north, where a hint of the land's agricultural past was still evident. Woodland had not yet claimed one small field. Instead, it was dotted with native cedar trees, gray twig dogwood, blackberry canes, and barberry bushes. I suddenly realized that cutting down the brush would create a vista.

In 1965, we cleared the field. Heretofore, we had been surrounded by uniform greenery. You did not know where to look because it all looked the same. Now, we found our gaze directed onward and upward through the clearing between walls of forest trees. The narrow, controlled view up into the field reinforced the linear axis already established by the orientation of the pool.

The field cries out for a rustic "folly" or a group of tall evergreen trees at the far end, but even without that focal point, the field draws the whole garden in that direction and gives our landscape purpose. When the brush was gone, I finally saw the possibilities inherent in our property.

However, order was a long time in coming. At the same time we put in the pool, we abandoned fiscal common sense and added an attached garage to the house. The impact on both our finances and our immediate surroundings was negative. There were great stretches of naked earth and piles of dirt everywhere.

It was difficult, therefore, to see much potential in the east-facing hillside above the pool.

The lower part of the slope was covered with rocks and subsoil from the garage excavation. The rest was a jungle of trees and saplings roped together by sinuous grapevines and poison ivy. This whole mess was in full view of the terrace and the pool.

In desperation, I graded the pile of debris and arranged some of the bigger rocks at the foot of the slope as a retaining wall. With scant soil preparation, I then stuck in some daylilies—an old cultivar called 'Marionette' with golden-yellow flower segments and a dark-red eye zone.

Meanwhile, it was not lost on me that the perennial garden was in the wrong place. The site had been a second choice, hastily made after my encounter with the septic tank. Its virtues were relatively level ground and full sun. Also, you could see it from the terrace. Now, the pool bank obstructed the view. I made a gloomy observation to this effect in my notebook and was still fussing about it the following spring: "This year, I want to move the flower bed to someplace at pool level, but I don't know where to put it!"

Then, in July, the daylilies on the hillside bloomed for the first time. Dozens of flaring red and gold trumpets leaned gracefully toward the sun, like performers taking their curtain call. The incline was good for drainage; the eastern exposure was perfect for sun-loving plants; the flowers were visible from the terrace, and the angle was flattering. At last, I had found a suitable home for the peripatetic perennial border.

It would be years before the hillside behind the border was cleared of brush. But in my mind's eye, I saw a long, straight flower bed supported by a handsome fieldstone retaining wall. It was the obvious design solution, effecting a satisfactory union between the garden and the geometry of the house. But we had already shot our modest wad, and hiring a stonemason was out of the question. If I wanted a retaining wall, I would have to build it myself.

Little by little, I began laying a course or two of large rocks at the foot of the slope. As the perennial border lengthened, so did the wall. But instead of making the wall straight, I let it follow the contours of the hillside. The result has been photographed many times—the perennial bed, the homemade wall, and the broad band of silver lamb's ears at its feet, curving in and out at the base of the slope.

The pool has long since gone. It was fun for a few years but never a thing of beauty. When the sides collapsed, we were relieved to have an excuse to fill it in. Now, lawn unrolls northward unimpeded. The edges are defined on one side by the wavy ribbon of lamb's ears; on the other by the straight line of the juniper hedge.

Originally, the pool bank had been planted with vinca. The vinca flourished for a couple of years, then died. We replaced it with spreading junipers—not the ground-hugging kind but a compact form of the old-fashioned pfitzer juniper with long arching branches. These tough evergreen shrubs not only covered the bank, they grew tall enough to create a feathery dark green wall between the upper and lower lawn. We keep the edge along the upper lawn trimmed and let the lower edge grow naturally.

Lynden Miller's garden departs from the simple linear axis with a much more interesting and complex layout based on European models. The magnificent semicircular yew hedge establishes a hub scheme from which paths radiate into the surrounding field like the spokes of a wheel. This elegant arrangement divides space and links together all parts of the garden.

When Lynden and her husband, Leigh, bought their Connecticut farmhouse, there was no garden, just a half-moon of mowed grass at the back, which gave Lynden the idea for a semicircular perennial bed. Beyond the lawn lay a swimming pool, and close by, the ubiquitous woodland threaded through with honeysuckle and poison ivy.

Right away, the Millers started pushing back the wall of undergrowth and clearing the surrounding fields. In 1980, they planted the yew hedge to hide the pool from the house and to provide an evergreen background for the perennial border. Not long afterwards, Lynden wrapped a handsome white wooden fence around the *outside* of the hedge "so that it would look attractive from the pool side."

"I love fences and enclosures," she explains. "And I wanted it to look as if the hedge was there because the fence was there. A lot of the time, I've added the bones afterwards." In the early days, even Lynden had to feel her way around her landscape.

The year after the hedge was planted, the Millers put in the main arbor, and later they added the gate that frames the major axial path into the field. "Even after the installation of the arch and gate, we were left with the field and no focus," says Lynden. "That's when I put in the first path."

A few years later, she was still dissatisfied with the view. The path led out

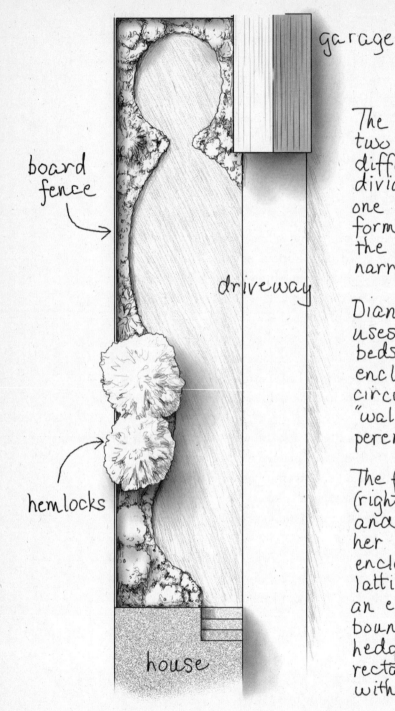

garage

board
fence

driveway

hemlocks

house

The gardens on these
two pages illustrate
different ways of
dividing space —
one informal, one
formal. Both make
the most of long,
narrow city lots.

Diane's garden (left)
uses the planting
beds as structure,
enclosing a small,
circular lawn with
"walls" of shrubs and
perennials.

The formal garden
(right) that Betty Ajay
and I designed for
her client has three
enclosures: the
lattice-covered deck,
an ellipse of lawn
bounded by yew
hedges; and a
rectangle edged
with boxwood.

Board fencing separates this garden from neighboring properties on either side.

The arbors are employed as room dividers.

The gazebo provides a focal point.

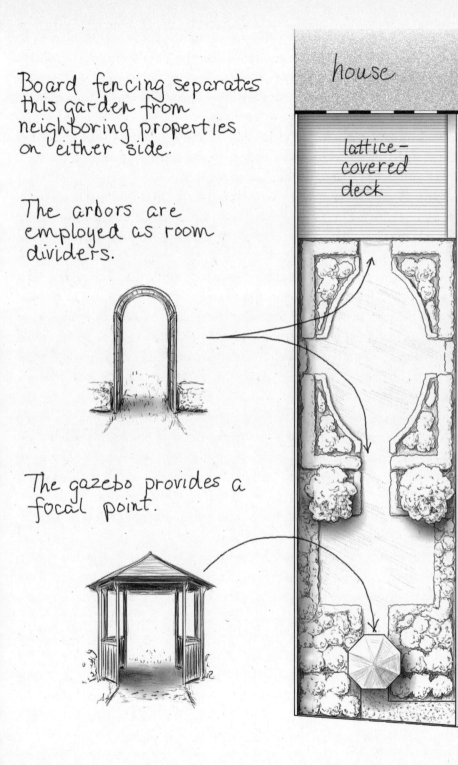

house

lattice-covered deck

163

into the field and to the edge of the woods, but there was nothing to see. To remedy the situation, she built a white wooden arbor and placed a bench beneath it. Meanwhile, she added two secondary openings in the hedge. One leads down an allée of crabapple trees to another bench. The other opening establishes a link with the swimming pool enclosure.

Lynden's garden has formal elements, like the wooden archways and arbors and the immaculately clipped yew hedge. But her hand lies gently on the land, and the garden blends into the surrounding countryside.

Ragna Goddard's approach to a similar landscape situation was different. She took the field that came with her eighteenth-century Connecticut farmhouse and made the crooked straight and the rough places plain. Her garden is laid out on a grid pattern.

When Ragna and her husband bought their property, there was no trace of a garden. "All we had was the house and a grape arbor," she recalls. The rest was field fringed with woodland. "I looked at the grounds and felt that since there was one architectural feature in the yard—the grape arbor—the garden should be linked to it. The arbor repeated the north–south axis of the house and had a very nice relationship to it. So I built this garden, and connected it to the house."

If she had chosen a spot for that first garden at random, as I did, she would have wound up with my problem—a floating island of flowers in a sea of grass. As a graphic designer, she knew better. In an article she wrote for *Fine Gardening* in 1990, she explains her modus: "All I had to do when I started my garden was to establish the north–south and east–west axes, both aligned with the house. This gave me two lines of reference from which I could lay out square- or rectangular-shaped gardens."

Ragna, who came to the United States from Germany, believes that American homeowners with a new property make one basic mistake. They parcel out areas for different activities—garden, play area, utility yard, activity center—then discover that they are stuck with a series of isolated units. So they try to connect them to the house, which by this time is very difficult. She recommends instead starting with the house and working away from it.

Hers is an architectural garden, connected to the house, but separate from the surrounding wilderness. Untamed nature is kept at a distance. "When you view your property from the house," she says. "You view it like a landscape painting. It should have a foreground, middle ground, and background."

There are three different gardens now, all aligned with and linked to the house and to each other by pathways, trellises, arbors, and fences. The man-made structures divide the space into pleasing enclosures, and each boasts a focal point. In the main garden, the centerpiece is a sundial that gives the Goddards' property and herb business its name—The Sundial Herb Garden. In the knot garden, a stone ornament presides over geometrical patterns traced by miniature hedges of clipped herbs. A fountain graces the third garden.

If your property is relatively level, the lessons from Ragna's garden can easily be put to use in your own backyard. Strike out a line from the center of the house; find a spot along it and draw another line at right angles to it. Make this the center of your garden. Put a sundial there to mark the spot. Enclose a square with sections of picket fence, and you have created a separate garden space and related it to the house.

If you live anywhere in Connecticut, you will enjoy and learn a great deal from a visit to The Sundial Herb Garden in Higganum. Once a year, Ragna gives a lecture there that provides homeowners with a formula for developing their property. "Your garden does not have to be enormous in size," she says. "You can create a garden or an outdoor room with four planters on a terrace—if you place those planters in certain locations."

The McKeons' garden is like mine, open and informal. Their broad front lawn slopes down to the pond. On the other side, Bill has thinned the trees and cleared the underbrush. The focal point of this peaceful, parklike view is a bench. The bench consists of two stout tree stumps and a fine, thick slab of oak that Bill salvaged from the landfill. Not all focal points have to be elaborate.

Nor does creating relationships have to be a major undertaking. On my first visit to her garden, Martha and I used the hose to outline a small island bed. We wanted to incorporate a dogwood tree and a nearby rock outcrop into a single unit. Out of two items, we made one. It was as easy as that.

Her island bed also serves as a partition. Its long dimension lies in the same direction as the perennial border and creates a wide grass path between the two, inviting visitors to venture down to the pond. "I love that bed," says Martha. "After you helped me lay it out that day, I dug it up. Then, you came over and said it should be wider. So that fall, I widened it. I redid the planting last year, but basically, it has stayed the same shape."

On another occasion, we got out the hose and forged a link between the far end of her perennial border and the pond. There had been a maddening little hiatus where the border met the saturated soil of the swamp. Weeds filled the void and made the border look unfinished.

To fill that gap, we curved the end of the border around to join the shoreline of the pond. Bill strong-armed large rocks into place at the water's edge, and Martha filled the hiatus with huge clumps of water-tolerant grasses, red twig dogwoods, and, to tie the tall plants to the ground and to the pond, several clumps of sweetspire (*Itea virginica* 'Henry's Garnet'). Soon the sweetspire will form solid, weed-defying mounds of arching stems and handsome foliage.

If you live in town and feel that none of the above applies to you and your garden, see if you can get a few ideas from these two city gardens.

Not every gardener would have seen the potential in a lot 75 feet long, 17 feet wide, and densely shaded at one end by two immense hemlocks. But Diane Campbell did. "Well, not at first," she says. "I just jumped in because I wanted to hide the ugly spots where no grass would grow, so I started underneath the hemlocks and made a little crescent bed."

Gradually, she extended the bed until it reached the far end of the property. It follows the shade pattern of the hemlocks, curving in and out along the weathered wooden boundary fence. In the deepest shade, the bed glows with light borrowed from the chartreuse leaves of *Hosta* 'Sum and Substance'. Because Diane likes "wake-up colors and lots of yellow," 'Stella de Oro' daylilies, true lilies, and other sun-loving perennials fill a little cul-de-sac at the far end.

Here, the border bulges out to form a peninsula embracing a small circular lawn. A matching bed encloses the cul-de-sac, dividing the garden into two areas: the shady open stretch near the house, and the sunny, flower-filled enclosure at the other end. Skillful placement of a birdbath provides a focal point.

The other city garden was designed, with my help, by Betty Ajay. Betty's client had just acquired a wonderful old brownstone house with a long, narrow backyard. Our first sight of this 22-foot-by-82-foot space was daunting. It was strewn with building debris and rusty oil drums and bounded by a sagging chain-link fence. The view featured a garage with a corrugated-iron roof.

Breaking up the space and hiding the garage were high priorities. To accomplish the first, we designed a deck next to the house. Leading off it and through an arbor, we drew an elliptical lawn within a rectangle of yew hedges and filled the corners with shrub roses edged with Korean boxwood. At the far end of the ellipse, we added another arbor leading to a small rectangular lawn set crosswise to create a feeling of breadth.

The client wanted to grow vegetables and flowers, so we surrounded the rectangular lawn with narrow beds. At the bottom of the garden, we set a Victorian gazebo against a background of tall evergreen arborvitae and rhododendron that blocked out the garage.

It was gratifying to watch this garden take shape. In the end, the client was pleased and so were we. Small as it was, the garden had everything: enclosures, interrelated spaces, a focal point, and an abundance of trees, flowers, and shrubs.

Naturally, I wish you could visit all these gardens. Looking at other gardens and analyzing what you see is one of the best ways of learning about design. The only trouble is that you are usually invited to see gardens in their prime, and mature gardens awe new gardeners.

Instead of succumbing to a hopeless longing for big trees and perennial borders filled with massive clumps of peonies, try to strip away the verdure and see the bones of the garden. Think in terms of the spaces and how they are divided. What did this gardener use to create a sense of enclosure? To hide the compost pile? How are the various parts of the garden linked together? By paths or with beds of a single ground cover? How has your eye been guided to see what the gardener wants you to see?

Learning to look may seem a roundabout way to study garden design, but it works.

Backgrounds, Enclosures, and Edges

❦

At the time I relocated the perennial border, the hillside behind it was still more or less jungle. Believing that the perennials would look better when the brush was gone, I set to with loppers and Swedish saw. But when I stood back to enjoy the improved view, I was dismayed.

Without the solid wall of greenery, the flowers seemed to disappear against the busy background of tree trunks and understory shrubs. From this experience, I learned that a uniform green background, even a wild and weedy one, shows off flowers to advantage.

From then on, whenever I cleared a section of the hillside, I planted a rhododendron. I had fallen in love with these magnificent broadleaf evergreens on my 1949 visit to England. At first, you could hardly see the new shrubs behind the tall perennials in the border, but within a few years, 'Scintillation', 'Janet Blair', and 'Roseum Elegans' began to provide a background for the flowers.

They add color, character, and form to the hillside all year. In the winter, their dark bulk sets off the blond grasses and the bright stems of red twig dogwood in the border. If the weather has not been too sunny and bitter during January and February, their spring display is breathtaking. In the summer, the perennial border depends upon them for a flattering deep-green backdrop. As foliage plants, the rhododendrons are at their best in the fall, when autumn rains have plumped every cell with moisture and washed the dust of summer from their gleaming, elliptical leaves.

It is hard to overemphasize the value of a green—preferably evergreen—background for a perennial garden. Whether the greenery is provided by a hill-side of rhododendrons or a hedge, it creates unity and fills the negative spaces between plants. Flower shapes and details show up against it, like jewelry displayed against dark velvet. All colors, from the palest to the brightest, are favorably affected. In a cottage garden, a hodgepodge of unrelated colors can be unified by a preponderance of green foliage. A hedge renders the same service to a mixed perennial border. If the plant material is evergreen, the hedge also furnishes winter decoration in the absence of flowers.

Listen to Lynden Miller on the subject of her hedge. "The yew hedge is the glory of our garden all year long. Leigh prunes it and makes this beautiful angled cut that gives it another plane. In the winter, Mary Scranton, who helps me in the garden, comes up and shakes off the snow. My heart would be eternally broken if I lost that hedge. Look what it does for me. It makes secrets of all the other parts of the garden."

With her book *The Secret Garden,* Frances Hodgson Burnett struck a responsive chord in every gardener's heart. We love secluded places, and seclusion is achieved by enclosure. I have always been more than a little envious of the ancient flint and mortar walls 10 feet high that surrounded my aunt's garden in Norwich. Climbing pink roses shimmered against the textured gray surface and carried the garden upward. The walls not only furnished a backdrop for the flowers, they shut out the rest of the world and made the garden a private retreat.

The modest height of our New England stone walls—only 3 or 4 feet—does not give you that feeling of enclosure. But the walls do divide space, establish boundaries, and provide a background for flowers. When I was young, local stone walls were still serving their original purpose. Topped with strands of barbed wire strung between posts, they kept the cows where they belonged. Now the wire has rusted away and the posts have rotted, leaving only the rocks, elephant-gray in color and encrusted with medallions of gray-green lichen. Along with green, the color gray is a great unifier in the garden.

Siting borders against stone walls has one drawback. Our walls are alive with mice and voles. If you use a fieldstone wall as a backdrop, leave a grass path between the wall and the bed. The visual effect will be the same, but the grass barrier will discourage rodents from invading the garden.

An attractive foundation planting provides an almost instant backdrop for

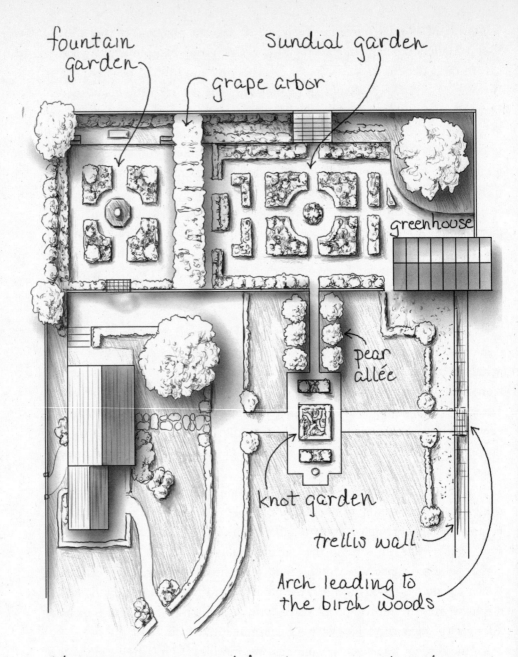

fountain garden

Sundial garden

grape arbor

greenhouse

pear allée

knot garden

trellis wall

Arch leading to the birch woods

Ragna Goddard's garden is laid out on a grid pattern. The grape arbor repeats the north-south axis of the house, while the east-west axis runs from the front door through the center of the knot garden.

colorful flowers. In Maureen and Dick McLachlan's garden, junipers, azaleas,
and rhododendrons set off the flowers of sedum, yarrow, asters, and other perennials.

There is nothing wrong with a wall of the house as a background for a flower
garden, either. Wonderful effects are achieved in England, where houses are usually made of durable materials. There, vines and climbing roses unite house,
garden, and setting. If your house wall is made of wood, a trellis might be a safer
means of supporting climbing plants. I have to exercise vigilance to confine an
evergreen euonymus to the foundation of our house. It threatens to grow up
under the clapboards.

The color of your house should be a major consideration if you are contemplating its walls as a background for a garden. I love hot colors, but even to my
heat-tolerant eye, there is something garish about a magenta-purple azalea
against a modern red brick wall. Old brick is a different story. Often hazed over
with a bit of moss and bleached to dusty salmon, old brick complements any
color.

White walls also require careful handling. Far from being a good blender,
white is an arresting color. It is the most reflective of all colors and a real attention getter. A white New England farmhouse would dominate a mixed perennial
border, while a house painted barn-siding-gray would unite a multicolored
flower bed. More about color later.

A split-rail fence, a stockade fence, or a picket fence can support a climbing
rose and provide a setting for a perennial border. Again, think about the color of
your fence. If it is made of lattice panels with large openings, white is fine, but a
solid fence of white boards would be a more difficult background unless it was
covered with vines. A large expanse of white would detract from all but the
brightest flowers.

Many of the devices that gardeners employ to divide space can double as
backgrounds and boundaries. I am very partial to lattice and trellis partitions in
a garden, with or without vines and climbers. No one has made better use of
these airy wooden structures than Ragna Goddard. She designed hers with great
care, and they were made to order, but ready-made sections of trellis and lattice
can be purchased at lumberyards.

From Ragna's doorstep, you look down across the knot garden to a trellis
wall. "The trellis forms the background of the courtyard area," she explains.
"Then, the property drops down, and you have this meadowlike area which we

trim now and then. I call it the semicontrolled area. Beyond that, you have the woods, where nature is doing its own thing."

Through an arch in the trellis wall, a grassy path seems to disappear into the birch forest in the distance, but it is all sleight of hand. The path is the entrance to an imaginary trail. "In a garden, no matter how precise, there should be an element of surprise," says Ragna with a sly smile.

It is fascinating to see photographs of this part of her garden before the installation of the trellis wall. Everything was wide open—the area of mowed grass stretching to the edge of the woods. A single tree with a bench beneath it provided the focal point. The view was pleasant, open, and unmysterious. The trellis completely changes the onlooker's perception of this space. While the landscape is clearly visible through the square openings of the trellis, the suggestion of a visual barrier creates a feeling of sanctuary within and mystery without.

Even in less skillful hands than Ragna's, partitions and fences will give your garden structure and an air of stability. They can be used along property lines as boundaries or in the garden to separate one area from another. If you use ready-made panels of fence and lattice, you can have a dress rehearsal. Prop up the 4-by-8-foot sheets and see how they look before installing posts.

Edges are to the flat plane of the ground what partitions and fences are to the three-dimensional landscape. They outline, contain, and define space. The edge of a flower bed, for instance, not only shows the shape of the bed, it defines the shape of the path or lawn that adjoins it. Look at edges in a garden as if they were pencil lines in a drawing. Notice not only the line but the volume it contains.

A crisp edge between a flower bed and the lawn goes a long way toward making a garden look orderly. Cutting through the sod with a long-handled crescent-shaped edging tool is relatively easy. Unfortunately, maintaining a clean line is not. The edge has two dimensions. There is the flat pattern of the line itself and the vertical cut into the sod. As the lawn grows, the flat pattern loses its definition and has to be trimmed with shears. Meanwhile, the roots of the sod begin to grow into the garden soil, blurring the vertical edge.

There is no ideal solution to maintaining well-defined edges between beds and lawns. Various kinds of plastic edging strips are available from garden centers. These are installed by digging a trench along the bed, setting the plastic edging in the trench, and pressing it firmly against the sod. Short stakes can

be driven into the ground to hold the edging while you backfill the trench
with soil.

I am not sure these edgings are worth the trouble. They are ugly and a curse to install. Because the strips coil up when you try to straighten them, they are difficult to keep neat and level with the lawn. Even if you manage to get the edging properly installed, it often heaves when the soil freezes. I have given up on these devices, finding it easier to cut a new edge than to fight with the plastic strips.

Mowing strips are another way of treating the edge between a flower bed and the lawn. A band of durable material, such as flagstone, brick, or cement, is set flush with the lawn at the edge of the bed. If the band is wide enough to accommodate one wheel of the lawn mower, no further trimming will be necessary. On a level site, a mowing strip works well and looks attractive. It should be made of an appropriate material that blends in with the rest of the garden.

The most ingenious mowing strip I have ever seen was used to edge matching borders in an elegant country garden. The layout was based on an English model, but the use of indigenous materials preserved the garden's American flavor. The mowing strips were fashioned from flat fieldstones laid flush with the lawn. Each one had been handpicked because it had one straight edge. The straight edge was placed next to the garden and the irregular edge set into the lawn. The effect was the best of both worlds—formal on the garden side, and informal on the grassy side.

Low hedges are another way to outline the margins of a garden. Be sure you choose plants that are cast-iron hardy and easy to grow in your area. A hedge full of holes and deadwood is worse than no hedge. However you treat the edges in your garden, keep them crisp and neat. Look to the edges, and the rest of the garden will give the appearance of serenity and order.

Paths and Steps

Everybody loves paths. One of my earliest memories is of grass paths winding through scrubby seaside vegetation down to the shore in Jamestown, Rhode Island. My parents had taken my older brother and me there to visit friends. I was four and do not remember the people with whom we stayed, but I recall the mystery and excitement of the paths and the sweetness of the summer air redolent with the scent of rugosa roses.

Quite apart from luring children on adventures, paths deliver guests to your front door and provide access to different parts of your property. In 1970, our garden designer friend Betty Ajay wrote her guide to home landscaping. Too late for me, she addressed many common landscape problems and suggested solutions. One of her soundest recommendations was to establish a system of walkways all the way around the house.

It had never occurred to me that one might want to walk around the house dry-shod. But I think of this advice regularly as I slog through the mud to the compost pile, to the lath house, and to our outside cellar doors. In addition to these practical considerations, paths and steps play an important role in the ongoing quest for a well-organized, harmonious garden. Paths are excellent devices for dividing space and creating relationships.

In a New England country garden like mine, grass paths are the easiest to make. My most successful paths evolved in the course of clearing the slope above the perennial border. Under the vines and brush, I discovered huge boulders and outcrops of bedrock. Around each one and at the foot of the old maples, I planted ground covers and, wherever possible, rhododendrons.

By the time all the brush had been removed, there were half a dozen isolated beds. Because I had to use the small mower—the hillside is too steep for the tractor—cutting the grass between the beds was tedious and time-consuming. So I started joining them together. They followed the lay of the land and eventually formed ribbons of planting separated from each other by grassy paths.

The path behind the perennial bed is the widest and very nearly level. This is fortunate because it is a wheelbarrow route between the lath house, compost pile, and the rest of the garden. Another path running roughly parallel to it leads behind a hedge of forsythia and along the stone wall boundary at the top of the slope. The rhododendrons, as big as bushel baskets when I planted them, now hide the perennial garden below. From the lawn, the upper path is hidden from view, except for a few teasing glimpses between rhododendrons.

Deemed hopeless by me thirty years ago, the shady, east-facing slope is almost my favorite part of the garden. In an alcove off the upper path made by the foundation of an old ice house, there is a wooden bench. You catch glimpses of it from the lawn and immediately want to find a way to it. Thus the paths have a purpose. How can so simple a ploy work so well? When you set out toward the bench, it disappears from view behind the shrubs, then reappears farther on. En route to the bench, there are things to look at—ferns, hostas, epimediums, Solomon's seal, wild ginger, and spring bulbs.

For many years, there was one highly unsatisfactory spot on the hillside, where the upper path plunged down the steepest part of the slope. Mowing it was a nightmare. The lawn mower always tried to run away, dragging me behind it. I knew that a flight of stone steps would solve the problem and have romantic charm. But building stone steps seemed beyond my skills. Then I hit upon a compromise. Instead of steps overlapping each other, I made small, sloping terraces between single low steps.

The steps themselves are fashioned out of three or four large, squarish rocks set firmly in the ground next to each other, like a retaining wall. I covered the sloping platforms between steps with wood chips. Now there is no need to mow there at all. Making terraces is one way that an amateur gardener can reduce the grade of a hillside. Terracing a gentle slope with low retaining walls is relatively easy. Retaining walls over 3 feet high require foundations and are best left to the pros.

In the woodland garden, the paths are narrow—about 3 feet wide and covered with finely shredded pine bark that makes a lovely, springy surface and dries out quickly after a rain. The paths are edged with old fence posts. When the underground part of the posts rotted, I sawed off the bottoms and salvaged the upper part. Set into the soil a couple of inches and held in place with short stakes, the erstwhile fence posts keep the shredded pine bark in place.

Besides containing the path, the logs hold back the soil where I have built up planting areas. However, I wish I had taken the trouble to excavate the paths a few inches. The log edging would have stayed put better, and the stakes would have been unnecessary.

Deer tracks are a good start for woodland paths. Or else use a lawn rake to sweep a path through the fallen leaves. If you don't like the shape, play with it until you do. I love the woodland paths. They are not intended for speed or efficiency; they are meant for a slow, solitary, looking-and-listening kind of stroll.

The centerpiece of my little woodland garden is a pond encircled by a very narrow pine bark path. "Pond" sounds rather grand for what it is. Swamps at higher elevations up in the state forest overflow in the spring and fill this hollow behind our barn. It dries up in June, but for a few poignant weeks, it is home to peepers and wood frogs; marsh marigolds and Japanese candelabra primroses.

The terrain is uneven, and the path descends to the water's edge in places. Where the change in grade is steep, a few big rocks set into the slope serve as steps. Where the slope is gradual, cedar logs make adequate risers for mulch-covered platforms. The logs are easy to handle and not too heavy. I laid them myself quite recently. They are held in place by stakes made from lengths of steel pipe about an inch in diameter.

Using a similar technique and 8-foot cedar logs, I made quite a successful retaining wall. Cedar is durable and should last several years. By the time it rots, the bank it is supporting will be planted so closely with ferns that it will no longer need propping up. The logs are stepped back into the slope and held with steel pipes driven into the ground.

Grass paths organize and define Lynden Miller's garden. The main axial path to the white wooden arbor was of prime importance to her. "I kept mowing and remowing that path to get it the right width," she says. "Then, I'd run back up to the second floor to see if it looked right." So that's how you do it. Get out the lawn mower and carve space by mowing paths. Then, run indoors and study the line of the path and the space it describes from an upstairs window.

Lynden's garden is organized by the radial scheme
of paths that both divide and also connect parts
of the garden.

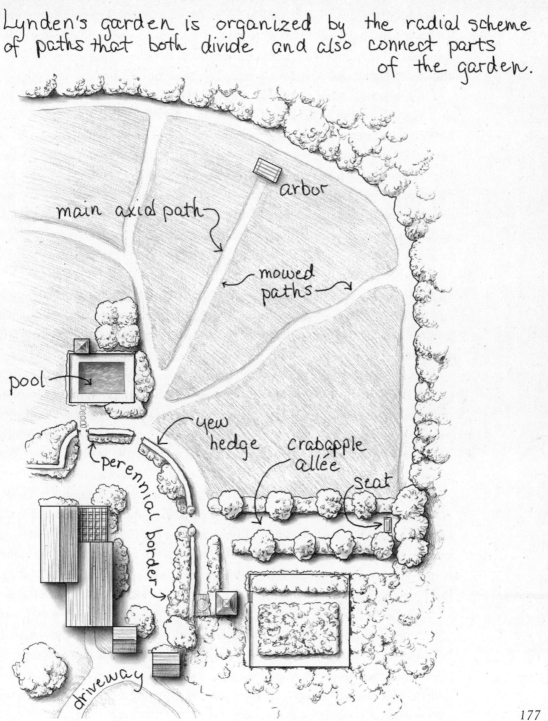

main axial path

arbor

mowed
paths

pool

yew
hedge

crabapple
allée

seat

perennial border

driveway

Even in the winter, Lynden tends the paths, keeping them closely shorn until the snow flies. Lightly covered with snow, you see the smooth surface clearly delineated by the taller field grasses on either side. Rough and smooth work as architectural elements in the design.

For ten years, Ragna Goddard collected old bricks. When she had enough, she began to lay the paths in her garden. She figures that she must personally have laid between 16,000 and 18,000 bricks—sometimes more than once. To her chagrin, she discovered that there is a right way and a wrong way to lay brick. For instructions on how to prepare a proper base for brick paths, Gordon Hayward is your man. Hayward's wonderful book *Garden Paths: Inspiring Designs and Practical Projects* (see Selected Further Reading) is full of excellent practical advice for prospective path and step makers.

If you live in a cold climate like ours, preparation is critical for successful brick paths. They have to be excavated to a depth of several inches and laid on a base of sand from 2 to 4 inches deep for drainage. The deeper the excavation and thicker the layer of drainage material, the less your brick path will shift in the winter. Pitch is important, too. You want excess water to run off as quickly as possible.

We have a little bit of brick paving leading from the terrace onto the lawn. It goes with the low brick seating wall that encloses the terrace. While it looks attractive, the path is not a success. It is very slippery in the winter. The reason may be that the wrong sort of bricks were used. There are two kinds, paving bricks and facing bricks. Pavers have a dense texture that makes them water-resistant. Facing bricks are more porous and made of softer clay.

For an informal effect, paths can be surfaced with hard, loose material, like gravel and crushed stone, or soft, loose material, like pine bark mulch and wood chips. The most formal, elegant paths are made of cut stone laid with mortar or in stone dust. Concrete is a durable, utilitarian material that can—in the right-hands—be rendered agreeable-looking by embedding pebbles in the surface. Fieldstone is beautiful and has its place, but not for a front walk. It's too uneven.

When we built our attached garage and opened up a driveway to the south, we felt the need of an entryway. A lovely man who worked with my husband had been a landscaper in another life. Seeing us floundering around with our property, he offered to help us out by designing an entryway. Bowled over with gratitude and desperate for order, I accepted. So Herb Achtmeyer made us a very attractive plan of curving beds on either side of a fieldstone walk to the front door.

We dug the beds in the shape he designed and did the planting. So far, so good. Then we found a couple of college kids to lay the walk—not so good. By now, we should have realized two things: that the path, as drawn, was too narrow, and that fieldstone was not a suitable material for the main entrance.

As a rule of thumb, entryway paths should be 5 or 6 feet wide. Ours is only 4 feet. A front walk is intended to convey guests to the door in one piece. Ours is a deathtrap. Fieldstone is appropriate for our house in terms of period and style, but it gets poor marks for safety. The sight of my husband's ancient cousin teetering along that path on a walker nearly stopped my heart. Moral: The function of a path should determine its design and surfacing material. A final note about our front walk. No one ever uses it anyway.

Don't be discouraged from path making by our example. Many kinds of paths can be designed and laid successfully by amateurs. Others require more expertise. You will find all kinds of paths beautifully described and illustrated in Gordon Hayward's book.

Covering the Ground

❧

Willy-nilly, a mysterious, powerful agency covers the earth's surface with *something*—water, rock, sand, or plants. As homeowners, we are constantly modifying these ground covers to suit our own purposes. If we refrain, nature prevails. So to maintain our tenuous hold on the landscape, we pave driveways, lay terraces, put in lawns, and plant trees, shrubs, and flowers. In short, we surface our properties with ground covers of our choosing.

This being the age of the auto, a depressingly large area must be devoted to a ground cover suitable for cars. Of necessity, driveway and parking space occupy a substantial proportion of a suburban property. Even on a sprawling country property like ours, these amenities take up a lot of room.

Our driveway and parking space should have taken up even more room. The turnaround is too small, and it gets smaller every year. Soil from the slope above washes downhill and builds up on top of the asphalt. While it was the driveway contractor's business to solve water problems, last-minute changes made it difficult. Having received a zoning variance to build the garage, we were already too close to our boundaries.

Building codes were less stringent in those days. At the time we added our attached garage and the driveway, we made a little sketch, presented it at the town hall, and somebody said, "Fine." Then, somebody else had second thoughts, and we made arbitrary changes in the plan. As a result of haste, the driveway has always been a disaster, but driveways don't have to look like ours.

On property after property, Betty Ajay has proved that a driveway and parking area can look like a handsome paved courtyard, as welcoming as it is utilitarian. "The conventional shape, a single lane with a turnaround at right angles to it, announces its function, but you don't have to make it that obvious. A driveway and parking area can be any shape you like, as long as there is enough room for a couple of cars to turn easily."

Before the contractor shows up at your door, take stakes and string and experiment with different shapes. If there is a practical reason why the shape you have chosen is unsuitable, he will be the first to let you know.

The Ajays' own drive is an ample circle surfaced with gray crushed stone in oil, which costs less than asphalt and is infinitely more appealing to the eye. It is edged with good-looking granite blocks, about 10 inches long by 4 inches high and 4 inches wide, set in mortar. Green lawn, low-growing Japanese holly, and pachysandra soften the perimeter of the parking area.

If you want a paved driveway, you really need to find either an experienced landscape designer who will direct operations or a skillful, landscape-sensitive contractor who specializes in paving. Either way, you should get estimates and ask questions. These people should be familiar with building codes and have solutions to drainage problems. Ask what happens to the water when there is a torrential thunderstorm and where the plow will put snow in the winter.

In addition to these technical questions, ask about the impact on nearby trees. Tree roots extend far beyond the perimeter of the crown. Disturbing the soil with heavy equipment can damage enough roots to kill a tree even at a distance of 12 feet from the trunk. Nor is it advisable to raise the soil level within the perimeter of the crown. If more than a few inches is added, its weight will compact air spaces and drive out the oxygen required by tree roots.

On a level site, a crushed stone or gravel driveway poses fewer problems and can be installed by amateurs. Bill and Martha McKeon put in their crushed stone driveway themselves. "Fools that we were!" says Martha with a laugh. "It was a lot of work, which we had to do in bits and pieces. And for a long time, it was very ugly. But I like the way it turned out. Originally, it was a dirt driveway, and for years, there was a brook running across it. We covered the dirt with a few inches of trap rock, and after Bill installed the drainpipe, we added more trap rock."

As the drive abuts their lawn, they used pressure-treated 6-by-6 landscape ties to contain the loose stone. "You do have to trim the edges with the weed

Martha McKeon built this trellis from saplings in a couple of hours. She secured them with black plastic cable ties. Festooned with climbing hyacinth bean, the ties are virtually invisible.

whacker," says Martha. "It takes Bill about five minutes every couple of weeks."
In the winter, the snowplow throws a certain amount of trap rock onto the lawn, and in the spring, Martha hires Libby, their older daughter, to throw it back.

"I don't think of the driveway as high-maintenance, by any means," she says. "But we did make mistakes. The six-by-sixes should have been flush with the lawn, and the finished surface of the driveway a few inches lower. We should also have bolted down the landscape ties and mitered the corners."

Whatever the driveway's shortcomings, they don't show, and in the summer, Martha transforms part of the parking area into a little outdoor café, complete with white wire chairs and tables among potted plants. Overhead, a homemade sapling trellis covered with luxuriant annual vines provides a bit of shade. Bill picked up the furniture at the landfill, a source of many McKeon treasures, and Martha painted it and made cushions for the chairs. It shows what can be done with a few props and a bit of imagination.

The inspiration for this unusual seating area came from photographs of Dutch gardens. A mutual friend returned from a visit to Holland and showed us slides of his trip. Martha was struck by the fact that no matter how small the yard, there was always somewhere to sit and have breakfast or just look at the garden. "I suddenly remembered all this furniture that I had refinished. I love it, and I thought, I've really got to use this stuff. That was the summer you made the trellis and showed me how to do that, and so the next year I added the trellis."

Our favorite outdoor seating area came about by necessity. A few years ago, we were giving a summer luncheon party. The day was hot enough to fry eggs on the terrace, and we were driven to the shade of an apple tree on the lower lawn. Separated from the upper lawn and perennial border by the green bulk of the juniper hedge, it was like being in a different garden. You couldn't see the hot summer colors of the daylilies. Everything was just cool, green, and restful. It was so pleasant that we decided to make a permanent place for our old wooden furniture and the picnic table.

The apple tree has a beautiful, symmetrical crown. We cut out a matching circle of lawn beneath it and covered it with wood chips. Every year we top up the wood chips and clip off any apple suckers that grow from the base of the tree. My husband no longer has to duck under the branches to mow, and the tree much prefers the mulch of wood chips to the ministrations of the lawn mower. Maintenance consists of picking up apples and raking leaves in the fall. You have to exercise a bit of care not to remove too many wood chips in the process.

We regard eliminating the lawn under our apple tree as a step forward. As you may have gathered, I am less interested in lawn grasses than in other plants. Our lawn is a potpourri. It consists of commercial grass seed mixes where we have patched bald spots, the original field grasses, clover, creeping Charlie, mazus, and other annual and perennial weeds. When it is green, it looks quite respectable. When it has been stressed by drought, some of it goes dormant; some of it stays green; the weeds thrive; and crabgrass abounds. But it doesn't look that much worse than other lawns.

The trouble is that American homeowners have an image of immaculate green velvet lawns that is entirely inappropriate to many areas of the United States. We simply don't have the cool, moist, overcast weather that favors fine-textured perennial grasses. We envy British lawns but not the British climate. You can't have it all.

It is possible, of course, to have a beautiful, smooth, uniform green lawn, but it requires considerable expense and effort. Your first task is to do research in order to select the right grass for your climate. You have to prepare the soil with as much care as you would lavish on a flower bed and take proper care of your grass garden once it is planted.

Lawn is only one of many possible ground covers. In the desert, cacti and other drought-tolerant perennials are a better choice than aristocratic bent grasses and Kentucky bluegrass. Meadows make sense in nonwooded areas. You don't have to have tall weeds right up to your front door, but you might want a wilder area beyond the boundaries of your cultivated garden.

My friend Mary Stambaugh turned a vast, rolling lawn at the back of her house into a meadow with a grassy path sweeping through the center. An apron of mowed lawn overlooks the waving grasses and clumps of yellow sunflowers (*Helianthus mollis*), yellow spires of Carolina lupine (*Thermopsis caroliniana*), blue spires of false indigo (*Baptisia australis*), rosy joe-pye weed (*Eupatorium purpureum*), and dainty purple meadow rue (*Thalictrum rochebrunianum*).

In the spring, Mary's meadow is full of daffodils. "The tough old Dutch bulbs are the best for naturalizing," she says. "Look for cultivars like 'Unsurpassable', 'King Alfred', 'Ice Follies', and the later-blooming pheasant's-eye narcissus [*Narcissus poeticus*]."

The herbaceous perennials were introduced into the field as husky, full-grown plants capable of fending for themselves. However, Mary is still protective of her favorites. They can compete with the wild grasses, but she digs out poison ivy and shrubs like the invasive multiflora rose. She also spot-kills thistles with a judicious squirt of herbicide. A meadow, once established, is low-maintenance, but *not* no-maintenance. The whole field is mowed once a year in October, after the perennials have dispersed their seed.

At the front of her house, Mary transformed the lawn into a rock garden. No doubt, generations of farmers turned in their graves as she hauled in tons of rock to clutter up the land they had labored to clear. Now, the rocks look at home once again among dwarf evergreens, grasses, and all the mats, tufts, and "buns" of her alpine plants.

In heavily wooded sections of the country, why not substitute understory plants and wildflowers for lawn somewhere on your property? Copy nature's landscaping technique and create an intermediate layer of flowering shrubs. Carpet the ground with ferns, hostas, and other plants mentioned in the chapter on "Some Easy Perennials for Shade."

Reducing the amount of lawn on your property is ecologically and economically sound. I have read recently that more than 24 million acres of lawn stretches across suburban America from sea to shining sea. That's a lot of lawn. To keep it green requires tremendous amounts of water and fertilizer; to keep it mowed, gallons and gallons of gasoline. Green grass is beautiful, but so are trees, shrubs, wildflowers, herbs, moss, garden perennials, and different kinds of paving—brick laid in patterns, stepping-stones, raked gravel, rocks, and pebbles.

Part Five

Finishing Touches

Roses

I t is unthinkable to write a gardening book and not mention roses. In the genus *Rosa*, to which all true roses belong, there are over a hundred species, but to most people a rose means only one plant—the hybrid tea rose. Its flowers are beyond compare. As the long, pointed buds open, silken outer petals roll back to reveal those still furled at the heart of the blossom.

This classic form and the habit of continual bloom are what modern hybrids are all about. They are the result of crosses made between ancient species of hardy European roses and equally ancient roses imported from Asia. *Rosa odorata* from China contributed refinement of flower, its tea-scented perfume, and its delicate constitution. Another Chinese rose, *Rosa chinensis*, is responsible for the habit of continual bloom.

"Traditionally, hybrid teas give you long stems with a large terminal bud at the end and a beautiful flower," says rosarian Donna Fuss, of the Elizabeth Park Rose Garden, in Hartford, Connecticut. "The origin of hybrid tea roses is complex, but if you start modern and work backwards, it is easier. In 1876, French hybridizer Jean-Baptiste Guillot crossed a 'hybrid perpetual', which is a European rose, with a China tea, which is an Eastern rose, and came up with a rose called 'La France', the first hybrid tea. From that come all our modern hybrid teas."

Although there are hundreds of named hybrid tea roses, 'Peace' is probably the most famous descendant of 'La France'. And like many of its forebears, it has a story. When the Nazi invasion of France brought World War II to the doorstep of hybridizer Francis Meilland, he was determined to save one very special rose. Despite close scrutiny, he was able to smuggle out three packages of this plant. While two were confiscated, the third arrived safely in the hands of American rose grower Robert Pyle. Pyle was awed not only by the beauty of the flower but also by the performance of this plant. He called it "the greatest rose of our time." On April 29, 1945—the day that Berlin fell—the rose was named 'Peace'.

The history of the charismatic rose is laced with war and violence. In the twelfth century, Henry II of England was so enamored of the pink and red Gallica rose that he named it for his mistress, the fair Rosamund. His wife, Queen Eleanor, did not relish playing second fiddle to 'Rosa Mundi', in the flesh or on the bush. To get back at the king, she set her sons against their father and dispatched Rosamund with poison.

In the fifteenth century, another family feud precipitated the War of the Roses between supporters of the House of Lancaster and the House of York. Both sides chose roses for their standards. The House of Lancaster rallied around the red, semi-double *Rosa officinalis*, while the House of York fought under the banner of white *Rosa alba semi-plena*.

The squabble was finally straightened out when Lancastrian Henry VII married Elizabeth of York in 1485. About that time, a particolored red-and-white damask rose (*R. damascena* 'Versicolor') was discovered in a monastery garden and diplomatically called 'York and Lancaster'.

War continues to be waged in the name of the rose, especially the hybrid tea rose. Unfortunately for gardeners, its enemies are legion: subfreezing temperatures, mildew, black spot, and Japanese beetles, to name a few. Unless you live in the Pacific Northwest, California, or Texas, you will have limited success with this beautiful prima donna.

Michael Ruggiero works with roses of all kinds. He says of the hybrid tea rose, "It really is *not* a hardy plant. That's what disappoints everybody. If you get five years out of a modern rose, you're almost a genius. Under the very best conditions, you might get ten years. If you plant a rhododendron, you expect it to be there when you're gone. Not with roses, at least not hybrid teas. Shrub roses, yes. You might find an old foundation and an old shrub rose still there."

He holds out hope that the new roses hybridized by David Austin in England will prove to be the roses of the future. "Austin has succeeded in combining the constant-flowering habit of the modern rose with a plant that looks like an old garden rose." Old garden roses are graceful shrubs with good foliage. The same cannot be said of hybrid teas. No matter how wonderful the flowers, the armature that supports them is leggy, and the foliage susceptible to disfiguring ailments and pest damage.

Cold tolerance is another issue with hybrid teas. In the colder parts of Zone 6, they cannot be considered reliably winter-hardy. According to Mike, what happens to most roses is that their roots freeze. Freezing breaks down the cell tissues, and the plants die. The solution to this problem is very deeply prepared soil and good drainage. "In the Rockefeller Rose Garden, we have almost two and a half feet of good soil," he says. "That's the secret—deep, deep, well-drained soil. If you only prepare the top foot of soil, and there is any lingering moisture, it freezes solid. That's what kills the roots."

In addition to excavating at least two feet and providing the best possible soil, you need to protect the aboveground part of the plants from desiccating winter winds. When more moisture is lost through exposed canes than can be replaced by the roots, they shrivel up. To prevent this problem, Mike covers dormant plants, canes and all, with 12 inches of good, humus-rich topsoil.

For all his knowledge and experience, there are roses that Mike can't grow—even with winter protection, deeply prepared soil, and perfect drainage. "One of my favorites is called 'Sheer Bliss'," he says wistfully. "It's beautiful, and I love it, but no matter how much I cover it and protect it, it dies. That's in the bloodlines. Some hybrid teas are better than others. 'Chrysler Imperial' has been around forever and does well most places. We have others in the rose garden that are wonderful. But the best thing to tell people is to visit public gardens in their area and see which cultivars do best over a period of time."

My own experience with hybrid tea roses was brief and dismal. I adored them and failed utterly. 'Helen Traubel', which was pink and, according to my notes, "smelled heavenly," lingered two seasons in the garden. 'Love Song', which won rave reviews in 1964—"a beautiful deep, clear pink with yellow on the underside of the petals"—was gone the following year. The last entry mentioning roses was dated June 9, 1965: "Roses out [in bloom]; badly eaten and diseased."

Fortunately for rose lovers, a new breed of "landscape rose" is evolving. In an article in the 1991 *American Rose Annual*, a publication of the American Rose Society, William J. Radler describes this paragon. "These new roses will exhibit a variety of forms that will grow equally well in all areas of the country. Plants will be vigorous with a compact habit needing a minimum of pruning." In addition, we are promised large quantities of bloom in quick succession. The flowers will be weather-tolerant and will not need deadheading. Best of all, the foliage will be dense, glossy, and resistant to black spot. Black spot is a fungal disease that can quickly defoliate a rose.

While this laudable goal has not yet been reached, hybridizers have made strides in the right direction. The Meilland family introduced a trio of shrub roses that Martha McKeon swears by: 'Pink Meidiland', 'White Meidiland', and 'Bonica'. "You simply can't goof with the Meidilands," she says. I can vouch for all three, having watched their performance in her garden for the last five years. In fact, I am about to take the plunge and plant a few Meidilands myself.

'Carefree Beauty' is another of Martha's favorites and one that Mike Ruggiero likes, along with the newer 'Carefree Wonder' and newest 'Carefree Delight'. Mike is especially enthusiastic about 'Carefree Wonder': "It's even prettier than 'Carefree Beauty'—a nice, true pink—and really tough. We have a big hedge of 'Carefree Wonder' down in the rose garden. It's great. We've had it for four years, and not once have we protected it. For the first three years, we just let it ramble. It only got to about 6 feet high and flowered from spring to Thanksgiving. That's what I like."

'Carefree Delight' came out in 1996 and has a neat habit, very hardy constitution, and good-looking foliage that turns deep maroon in September. Mike describes the flowers as "lavender-pink with single petals and white centers." Another single he recommends is 'Escapade', which has bigger flowers. Developed in Canada, it also is very hardy.

'William Baffin' is a big, beautiful shrub rose with the blood of the *Rosa rugosa* coursing through its canes. Mike has the highest praise for this vigorous, pink-flowered rose. "It reblooms and can be used as a climber because it grows to about 10 feet. It's the one we have on those post-and-chain structures in the rose garden. We don't spray it; we don't protect it; it's out in the open and doesn't die. It was developed in central Canada, and, boy, is it hardy!"

Hybrids of the wild species *Rosa rugosa* are hardy to Zone 3, and all are good garden plants. They have crinkled, shiny leaves, fragrant red, pink, or white flowers, and fat, tomato-red hips. 'Blanc Double de Coubert' is white with semi-double flowers; 'Frau Dagmar Hartopp' is a single pink with 2- to 3-inch blossoms; and 'Sarah Van Fleet', also pink, has semi-double flowers 4 or 5 inches across. So even if you live in the Northeast, you can have a rose garden that looks attractive all season—once you have weaned yourself from hybrid teas. In

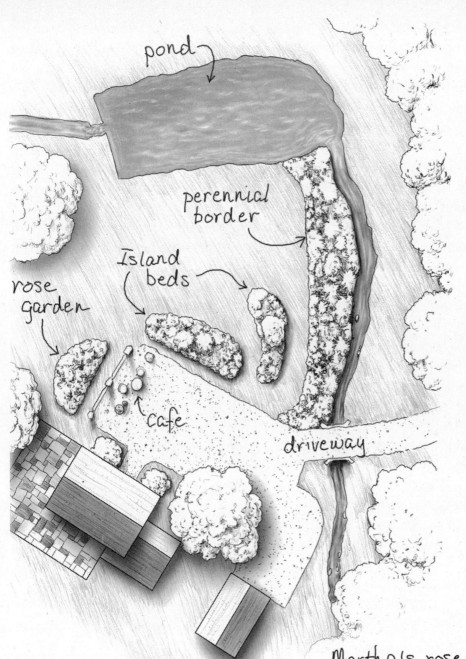

pond

perennial
border

Island
beds

rose
garden

cafe

driveway

Martha's rose garden
and one of the island beds are aligned with the
house. The perennial border conforms to the natural
line of the stream.

Self-
Taught
Gardener*

ℒ

mid-June, when very little is in bloom in my garden, the McKeon roses are a billowy sea of pink and white. Martha's 9-foot-by-18-foot semicircular bed is edged with silver lamb's ears and interspersed with sprays of lavender-blue catmint and little purple Johnny-jump-ups. I first saw the garden when the roses had only been in the ground two months. Having arrived bare-rooted in April, they had already sent up strong canes bearing clusters of beautifully formed flowers.

Bill McKeon, manning the borrowed rototiller, had prepared the bed the previous year. At that time, Martha added large quantities of old cow manure and worked it into the soil. That year, she planted herbs and a few roses. Then, in 1991, she ordered the pink and white Meidilands.

Martha makes light work of her rose garden. She top-dresses the bed with well-aged cow manure in the spring, and applies a summer mulch of wood chips. In the fall, she scratches away the chips and "plops more manure in a circle around each plant." Pruning is easy. When the flower clusters fade in the summer, she cuts each cane back to a leaf axil where a tiny reddish growth bud is visible. "You want that little bud facing away from the center of the plant," she explains. "So that the interior won't get crowded with twiggy growth." In the spring, she cuts the whole plant back to 12 to 18 inches and removes any dead wood.

As for spraying, Martha has stopped using chemical pesticides altogether. "The roses got black spot when I sprayed, and they got black spot when I didn't," she says. Japanese beetles are a trial, and they do a certain amount of damage, but Bill and the children pick them off and feed them to the frogs in their pond. The roses are happy; the frogs are happy; and the McKeons are happy.

Color

✿

Color—natural and man-made—is so much a part of our lives that we take it for granted. We live in a kaleidoscopic Technicolor world surrounded by color TV sets at home and color copiers at the office. Our actions are ruled by color. Colored lights control traffic, send messages, and issue warnings.

The printing on the screen of my word processor is yellow for high visibility, and "blackboards" nowadays are green because experts have determined that green, not black, is the most soothing color to the human eye. Red, on the other hand, excites the senses. Patrons may not notice the color of table linen, but restaurant designers know that red and pink create an atmosphere of warmth and stimulate the appetite. Innumerable restaurants employ these colors in their decor.

People have been fascinated by color for thousands of years. Seneca, a Roman philosopher with an interest in physics, used a prism to split white light into its component colors—red, orange, yellow, green, blue, and violet. But Seneca wrongly assumed that some action of the prism had created the rainbow. Fifteen hundred years later, Isaac Newton performed similar experiments with a prism and correctly deduced that the colors were not produced by the prism but exist as properties of sunlight.

Color theory is a complex subject that involves the study of light, optics, and electricity. But for years, painters and gardeners have been employing color to move and delight the eye without mastering these disciplines. Some gardeners are instinctively at ease experimenting with strong colors and enjoy taking risks. Others prefer to err on the safe side with soft pastel shades. Either way, I hope you will get some ideas from this chapter.

Playing with color should be the most carefree, lighthearted aspect of gardening, because color preferences are entirely personal. If someone doesn't like your color scheme, he or she may not even be seeing the same colors that you are. No two pairs of eyes are alike. It has been hypothesized that Gertrude Jekyll's failing eyesight accounted in part for the soft, blurry gray-blue-pink-mauve schemes for which she is best known in this country. In her prime, she was also a revolutionary colorist who used hot reds and oranges with a flourish.

My advice is don't be too cautious. Don't agonize over whether this color goes with that; try it. If you like it, it's a success. If you don't, it's a failure. It's as simple as that. You know what colors you like. You make decisions about color every time you buy clothes, furniture, sheets, towels, even groceries. Sweet bell peppers all taste pretty much the same but they come in red, orange, yellow, green, and purple. The brightly colored ones cost twice as much as the green, but who cares? They are irresistible.

Keep in mind as you garden that putting colors together should be unadulterated pleasure, and proceed accordingly. That being said, here are a few ideas that may be helpful. The two most useful and reliable methods of combining colors in the garden are based either on contrasts or harmonies. When you gasp at the brilliance of orange autumn leaves against a blue sky, you are responding to a vivid effect produced by the juxtaposition of complementary colors. The hard, enamel-blue of the October sky sets off the orange foliage in a classic color contrast. Placed side by side, complementary colors intensify each other. Of course, to the tree, it's just business as usual. The longer nights have warned it to divert nutrients into the stems and buds before discarding its leaves. But to the onlooker, fall foliage is a glorious spectacle of dazzling color.

On a small scale, we get pleasure from another seasonal contrast. What would Christmas be without sprays of red-berried holly, swags of pine, and wreaths of balsam fir bound with red ribbons? Red and green are complementary colors and, therefore, mutually enhancing, a fact not lost on greeting card designers. Easter affords commercial artists another opportunity to exploit the phenomenon of complementary colors. Purple and yellow are found opposite each other on the color wheel and side by side in every basket of foil-wrapped Easter eggs. Sharp contrasts like this are lively and dynamic.

Used full strength, paired complementary colors have a cheerful, forthright appeal, while tints or tones of the same colors have a completely different kind of charm. Tint and tone are useful words in the color lexicon. A tint is any hue mixed with white; a tone, any hue mixed with black. Thus, pink is a tint of red, and navy is a tone of blue.

Tints of complementary color schemes are staples in Laura Ashley fabrics and English chintz. Here, you have lilac and primrose instead of purple and yellow; dusty rose and olive instead of red and green; misty blue and a soft shade of apricot instead of cobalt and orange.

These gentle color combinations are restful and agreeable, but they are still contrasts, not harmonies. Harmonies consist of from three to six colors adjacent to one another on the color wheel, with one color in common. Red plays a part in five other colors: violet, red-violet, red-orange, orange, and yellow-orange. Any combination of these hues is a color harmony.

These are, in fact, the colors in my summer perennial border. The daylilies come in shades of red, red-orange, orange, yellow-orange, and yellow. Spikes of lythrum and gayfeather provide exclamation points of red-violet. The only color missing is violet. Instead, there are shades of steel-blue from globe thistles. But, basically, the main border is a jazzy symphony in hot color harmonies.

Don't think for a minute that this combination of colors was calculated. It evolved because daylilies come in that warm color range, and they were my favorite summer-blooming perennials. I arrived at the startling addition of red-violet because I wanted the vertical form of the lythrum and could see that the color worked with the other hues. I didn't analyze why, but there is a reason: Red-violet is in the same family as primary red, the common denominator in my hot color scheme.

While I can't imagine plotting out my entire garden with a color wheel, experimenting with one is an intriguing way of learning what goes with what. You can't fail to get a few ideas for color schemes to try. Available at art stores, color wheels cost only a few dollars.

I love all colors—warm and cool, industrial strength and pastel, light and dark. I love color harmonies in the mauve, lavender, purple, and pink range, and color contrasts like red and green, blue and orange, purple and yellow. I also enjoy fiddling with dangerous combinations of sooty purple and mahogany-red, the colors you find in coleus leaves, and contrasting them with sharp, cool colors like pale yellow-green. And I get a kick out of color games, like playing with the whole range of a single hue, from the palest tints to the deepest tones.

Betty Graubaum, a young friend who is an estate gardener, is a hands-down winner at this game. An innovative colorist, she tries out many of her combinations with annuals. One year, she planted a series of cutting gardens, each devoted to a single color. Her red garden had cosmos in every shade from deep magenta-red to true pink; nicotianas in chalky-pink and rose-pink; shell-pink snapdragons, hot pink asters, and middle-of-the-road pink dahlias. In another bed, she combined sunny colors: marmalade-orange snapdragons, creamy yellow chrysanthemums, and chrome-yellow marigolds.

For her own amusement and her parents' pleasure, Betty also plants a garden of annuals at their home every year. The garden is huge and always has a different theme. One season, it was planted in the arc of the rainbow, with each band of color subtly shading into the next. Another year, the plot was divided into four major sections by diagonal paths intersecting in the middle of the garden. The major sections were subdivided by narrower paths, and each wedge was devoted to a separate color. Instead of being arranged in the order of the solar spectrum, she set off shock waves by putting blue next to orange. Red separated blue and purple, and the pink bed lay between orange and yellow. She didn't want soothing color harmonies, she was after "something more sudden and startling."

Betty chooses the motif of the season during the winter, after she has received dozens of catalogs and seed lists. "I wait until I have them all together, because you never know what is going to strike you in the catalogs. If there is something wonderful, you might want to feature that."

There was the year she had designs on a nasturtium called 'Peach Melba'. "I'm also having ideas about shades of peach next to intense blues with creams on the other side—that might be nice. It's hard to get a lot of flowers in those intense blues, but it's doable with larkspurs and Chinese forget-me-nots."

In trying to describe her methods, she alludes to a book by Betty Edwards about the creative process. "You collect all this information—I go through the catalogs and gardening books and visit other people's gardens, taking notes about which annuals look interesting. You come up with all these different possibilities. Then, you turn your brain loose on it, and eventually, it comes up with something. I don't really think about the design. All of a sudden, it just pops out."

I admire Betty's inventiveness and love her audacity. Who else would combine red geraniums with orange zinnias, scarlet poppies and purple salvia? Of course, the poppies self-sow and come up in unexpected places every year, adding a piquant touch to even her best-laid color schemes. And what schemes! Her gardens are always beautiful, uninhibited, and, best of all, fun. That is what using color in the garden is all about.

If you want practice in combining colors, annuals are the way to go, especially if you plant them in pots on your terrace. Unlike perennials, they give you a chance to play with color without making a permanent commitment, and the scale is manageable.

I do a lot of container gardening, mixing different annuals and colored foliage plants in large containers. You can confine yourself to a single color per pot and arrange a number of pots together to achieve the same effect. The virtue of the second method is that if you don't like your combination, you can move the pots around. Either way, the whole works will be killed by frost, so you're never stuck with your failures.

Because my perennial border is devoted to hot colors during the summer, I use the containers to try different schemes. One year, I put a whole range of cool grays together in an old wooden box and added a bit of zing by throwing in magenta petunias. In 1995, I experimented with a lot of dark, richly colored foliage plants.

An annual from the West Indies called Joseph's coat (*Alternathera dentata* 'Rubiginosa') was new to me that year. It has long, lax stems covered with handsome red-purple foliage, shiny underneath and matte-finished on the upper surface. Its companions in the half whiskey barrel were the purple-leaved houseplant *Tradescantia pallida* 'Purple Heart' and a vivid pink verbena. The three colors are closely situated on the color wheel: blue-purple tradescantia 'Purple Heart'; red-violet Joseph's coat; and a tint of that color in the intense but cool pink of the verbena.

A much less successful combination resulted when I added a gorgeous mahogany-red coleus to this collection. The idea was a close color harmony within the red-purple range, but the color of the coleus was off by a mile. It was a deep tone of red, but it just didn't work. Strong, closely related colors, like reds and purples, can be exciting but hard to manage effectively.

What did work was a half whiskey barrel planted with black sweet potato vine, a decorative pepper plant with black leaves and tiny purple fruit, and a cool yellow-green coleus, inappropriately named 'Golden Wizard'. To this group I added hot magenta petunias.

The color of the black sweet potato is hard to describe. The undersides of the leaves are red-purple, but the upper surface is much darker, the deepest possible tone of black-purple. The foliage of the pepper plant was even darker. And the contrast with the light, bright, abrasive tint of yellow-green from the coleus was dynamite. These colors, by the way, are almost complements—the dark tone of purple opposing the light tint of yellow.

While it invariably works, it isn't necessary to stick slavishly to complementary colors in order to create contrast. Pairing any warm color with a cool color sets off vibrations. Monet was partial to warm yellows combined with cool blues and whites. He even designed china for his family using these colors.

Gertrude Jekyll employed the same scheme in her Munstead Wood garden. "In the yellow border is one patch of clear, pale pure blue, the Dropmore Anchusa Opal (Chinese forget-me-not), grouped with pale yellows and white." Elsewhere, she employed color to achieve an invigorating sauna effect—extreme heat followed by a brisk plunge into the sea. She planted whole beds of red, yellow, and gold flowers next to cooling expanses of blue, gray, green, and white.

Miss Jekyll played color in her long border like keyboard music, constructing rippling harmonies: silver-gray, pure blue, and gray-blue, modulating into white with palest pink and yellow, leading into stronger colors—yellows to orange and red—then receding into cool pastel tints of purple and lilac. "Looked at from a little way forward, for a wide space of grass allows this point of view, the whole border can be seen as one picture, the cool colouring at the ends enhancing the brilliant warmth of the middle."

I have an ongoing color experiment in the new perennial border, where there are a lot of pink daylilies. Thereby hangs a tale. In the sixties, the color pink was mostly in the eye of optimistic daylily hybridizers. The pinks I could afford were not the most modern and all bore a close relationship to orange. The shades could best be described as melon and peach. Today, hybridizers have succeeded in creating clear pink daylilies that really are pink. There are also lavender-pinks and salmon-pinks. The new bed is devoted to salmon-pinks.

The challenge is to find other perennials in deeper shades of warm salmon, coral, apricot, and yellow and to oppose them with perennials in cool lavender-blues. I've found that balloon flower gives me the perfect shade, and they bloom at the same time as the daylilies.

For the desired coral color, I am delighted with a penstemon called 'Prairie

Fire'. The snag is that it is almost finished blooming before the daylilies really get started, which goes to show that no matter how long you have been gardening, you don't always get it right. I expect to be moving plants around to my dying day. Martha McKeon, who loves daylilies almost as much as I do, has arrived at various color schemes by breaking off flowers and wandering around the garden with them until she finds a color partner that strikes her fancy. What could be easier?

Being an artist, Lynden Miller is light-years ahead of us all when it comes to combining colors, but one of the techniques she uses might be adapted by the average gardener. "When I do a design presentation," she says, "I always make collages with cutouts from catalogs. I don't paint. I cut out the actual plant." I think this technique could be fun and helpful. At the very least, you can push colored cutouts of flowers around on the kitchen table and see what you like together.

Lynden's advice to aspiring young landscape designers also has something to teach the average gardener. Here is what she tells young people who ask how to get started. "I think you should study history of art," she says. "You should go and look in museums to see how people put paintings together. It's just the same in garden design. You are working with line, form, texture, and color. You stand back and say, 'Now, have I got the right proportion of colors? Are the textures right? Should I move that a little bit to the left? Should there be a little more of this?' It's exactly the same as painting."

A wonderful painting by Monet, *Terrace at Ste. Adresse,* is a lesson in color all by itself. It shows hot color harmonies—a garden full of nasturtiums in red, yellow, and orange; and complementary color contrasts—flamboyant spikes of scarlet gladioli against a brilliant blue-green sea. In the center of the painting, a white parasol and woman in a white dress rivet the eye.

Do not underestimate the power of white in the garden. It is the most demanding of all colors, capable of drawing the eye from even the brightest neighbors. White is not a blender. Gray is the blender and green the peacemaker. Conciliatory green takes the edge off clashing colors and weaves the garden together. Take heart in the knowledge that if you have enough green foliage, you can get away with any color scheme. When it comes to color, nature is bold and painters are bold. Gardeners should be bold, too.

The Ever-Changing Garden

❧

I hope that the previous chapters have been useful and have set you on the road to a gardening life. If you can accept the fact that a garden is never finished, you will be way ahead of me when I was starting out. I look back at my young self with a certain amount of embarrassment—that impatient, ignorant, energetic twenty-nine-year-old, discouraged by the smallest setback but stubbornly determined to change the landscape.

A garden is in a constant state of flux. From hour to hour, day to day, season to season, and year to year, it is always changing. That is the nature of nature; the nature of life; and the nature of both the garden and the gardener. Changes come about by design, accident, and necessity, and as a result of time passing. Change is the least-talked-about aspect of gardening.

In thirty-five years, my garden has gone through innumerable changes. During the early days, it was wild, disorganized, and overwhelming—an irregular two-acre patchwork of field grass and rock outcrops, woodland and brushy pasture, stone walls swamped by vines, straggly shrubs, spring-flowering bulbs, old peonies, big trees and small trees. I longed for a plan—any plan, a bit of law and order.

Then there was the pool phase and more chaos, but also a glimmer of understanding and a growing desire for accommodation with the surrounding countryside. Clearing went on for twenty years—clearing, clearing, clearing. I remember the thrill of finally conquering the far northwest corner that had

Sedum 'Autumn Joy' through the Seasons

By mid-May, the blue-green foliage forms a neat globe.

Beautiful even without flowers, the stems and expanding leaves make a substantial contribution to the early summer garden.

Pink, fuzzy flower heads, gradually turning rose-red, enliven the perennial border for six weeks or more, beginning in late August.

When each dry flower head supports a cone of snow, there is nothing handsomer in the winter garden.

been a dump. Rusty wire still pokes up through the ferns and few remaining hostas. There used to be masses of hosta, but last year the voles wiped out most of it.

For a few brief seasons, I had wonderful delphiniums that I had grown from seed. They were part of my vegetable-gardening phase. In the vegetable garden, where they had good air circulation and no competition, the delphiniums were magnificent—huge spires of blue and lavender, just like the picture on the seed packet. Moved to the new perennial border, they were a goner in a single season.

My bearded-iris phase lasted perhaps three years—an intense, tumultuous love affair ending in much disillusionment. Their names haunt me still: 'Frost and Flame', 'Dark Fury', 'Solid Gold', 'Eleanor's Pride', 'Wintertime', 'Pacific Panorama', 'Cherie', 'Quick Silver', 'Extravaganza', and 'Allegiance'. All are long gone—except 'Allegiance'.

Once the evergreen garden was laughable. The bird's-nest spruce was no bigger than its name suggests, and the mugo pines were tufts of needles a foot tall. The foliage of the bearded irises towered over them. Among the rocks and junipers, I grew masses of pinks and dwarf irises. At some forgotten moment, the evergreens finally began to swamp the perennials, and for many wonderful years, the evergreen garden was my pride and joy.

The junipers grew together in a soft waterfall of green, lapping over the rocks. The mugo pines filled in, and the bird's-nest spruce outgrew its dimpled cushion shape. The beautiful dwarf blue spruce stood out against the dark green mugos, and the golden false cypress waxed handsomer by the year, growing into a graceful shower of dependent gold and green branches.

While my mind and eyes were elsewhere, a subtle shift took place. The plants grew into each other, and the evergreen garden evolved into a still-splendid-looking frieze of green and blue and gold. But the writing was on the wall. One year quite recently, I realized that if a single plant died, the entire composition would be destroyed. Sunrise, sunset. It happens so quickly. The evergreen garden is on its way out. This year, I will have to do something.

For a few years, the field that we cleared in 1965 looked like an English park—deer and all. My husband was young enough to get up there once a month with the Gravely tractor and mow the tough grasses and insistent woody invaders. But the time came when such work was too hard. The slope is steep. There are rocks and woodchuck holes. It is dangerous, and you become more cautious with age. The woody invaders moved in along the verges, and the field became narrower and narrower. We still mow what we can, and in the spring, it is golden with daffodils.

The perennial border was more beautiful last summer than it has been in its long life. I finally got the daylilies just where I wanted them in a rippling multi-color ribbon running the length of the bed. I've got good edgers, enough variegated foliage to stand in for flowers between peaks of bloom, the purple smoke bush to hold down one end, and the wonderful threadleaf Japanese maple to hold down the other. The lamb's ears never looked better. Then came drought, voles, and huge losses.

But spring has come. Maybe this will be the year of the annual. There are hundreds of interesting annuals I have never grown. There have been other changes in the past year. While I mourn the passing of our beloved old Jack Russell terrier, I have my new ally in the ongoing war against garden predators—the nine-month-old puppy. Rodents beware!

If you have come this far, you are well on your way to making a quirky, beloved garden of your own. By night, you dream the impossible dream garden; on stolen days, weekends, and long summer evenings, you trim, tailor, and tend the real garden. As you travel farther down the garden path, you become more and more involved. You want more, expect more, know more. You discover that the possibilities are endless.

Just around the bend, some overweening plant obsession is waiting to claim you for its own. Give in to it, as I have joyfully abandoned myself to primroses and daylilies. Wherever your gardening life leads, follow it, follow the gleam.

Appendix A
Help in Planning Your Garden

❧

PROFESSIONAL HELP

While this is a book intended primarily to help you help yourself, there are situations that call for professional know-how. The following come immediately to mind:

1. Dealing with dramatic changes in grade.
2. Siting swimming pools.
3. Designing driveways and parking areas.
4. Installing drainage systems.
5. Constructing retaining walls over 3 feet in height.
6. Laying terraces in mortar.

If you are contemplating one of these or any other large-scale project resulting in a permanent structure and a considerable outlay of money, you should consult a professional. But it is not always easy to determine who is qualified to do the work. Here is a quick rundown of who does what.

Landscape Architect

A landscape architect has the training to do all of the above and more. You have to graduate from a college or university program accredited by the American Society of Landscape Architects (ASLA) or have 10 years of experience in the field and pass an examination in order to call yourself a landscape architect. There are about 50 college and university programs that offer degrees in landscape architecture.

I have a gifted niece who is both an ardent gardener and a landscape architect. Her training began with a bachelor's degree in horticulture and concluded with a three-year stint at the University of California in Berkeley. She loves working on small properties and often lures clients into the gardening life. But she is unusual. Many landscape architects are more knowledgeable about hardscape than about garden plants. That's all right, too. Plants and planting are your department. Hardscape is the department of qualified pros.

In an article for *Fine Gardening* magazine, Frank Edgerton Martin, Associate ASLA, described the landscape architect's work as "shaping the outdoor environment."

There are chapters of the American Society of Landscape Architects in every state. Call the office in Washington, DC, for a list of members in your state.

American Society of Landscape Architects
4401 Connecticut Avenue NW, 5th floor
Washington, DC 20008-2302
(202) 686-2752

Landscape Designer

The Association of Professional Landscape Designers (APLD) is a fairly youthful organization of professionals. The expertise of its members falls into the following categories: "planning, design and/or construction of exterior spaces by utilizing plant materials and incidental paving and building materials." About 150 colleges and universities offer two-year programs and associate bachelor's degrees in landscape design. Some botanical gardens also offer in-depth design programs, among them the New York Botanical Garden and Longwood Gardens in Pennsylvania.

While landscape architects have degrees to back up their professional knowledge, there are many talented landscape designers who are neither licensed members of APLD nor holders of degrees. So how are you to know how good they are? *Ask to see examples of their work.*

When it comes to choosing a landscape designer, Betty Ajay has this to say: "I would hire a stonemason only if I had seen his work. The same goes for a landscape designer or a landscape architect. It is very embarrassing to fire someone, so be sure to do your homework. Visit properties they have designed."

Association of Professional Landscape Designers
Suite 1400, 11 S. LaSalle Street
Chicago, IL 60603
(312) 201-0101

Landscape Design Students and Alumni Association
New York Botanical Garden
c/o Continuing Education Department
Bronx, NY 10458-5126
(718) 817-8747

Garden Designer

There does not seem to be an association for gardeners who are so artistic and skillful with their own gardens that friends prevail on them for help. Most garden designers arrive at their profession in this way. They start out as home gardeners and augment their experience with classes and workshops. I hope you will become one of these artistic, skillful gardeners yourself, so I am rather opposed to sending you out to find a garden designer. However, their numbers are legion and their backgrounds varied. As one professional designer puts it, "My own garden is my best reference."

Landscaper

The title "landscaper" has no exact meaning and can be used by anyone who fancies it. As always, look at examples of the work. If the planting has just been installed, come back in a year and see if it is still alive and well.

Design Services

NURSERIES

Nurseries often provide design services. Again, do not settle for any nursery design service unless you have investigated the work they do. Remember that their major business is to sell plants, so you will probably be limited to their stock. It stands to reason that they will recommend plants they have on hand and in quantity.

SWIMMING POOL COMPANIES

Pool companies usually offer design services. By all means, look into them. Visit several pools the company has installed. If the work seems efficient but uninspired, you might want to hire a landscape designer who will work with the pool company.

HOW TO MAKE A BASE PLAN

To sketch out a base plan, you will need graph paper lined with ¼-inch squares. If you allow each square to represent 1 square foot, an 18-by-24-inch sheet will be big enough to accommodate a 72-by-96-foot lot or backyard. For a larger property, you may want to draw only the portion of it immediately surrounding the house.

Remember that plans are about relative sizes and shapes; distances and spatial relationships. To be useful, measurements do not have to be absolutely accurate, and you don't have to put in every detail. The purpose of this exercise is to show you where stone walls, fences, outbuildings, and major trees are in relation to the house. With this information on paper, you can begin sketching in possible planting areas, proposed decks and terraces, and any other additions.

Before you start, see if you can find a survey map of your property. The former owners may have one or you can contact the city building department. Where we live, survey maps are kept on file at the town clerk's office. These maps show your boundaries, complete with measurements that can be transferred to the graph paper. Our survey map included the "footprint" of the house and barn, and the McKeons' showed the house, detached garage, and their pond.

If you have to draw in the footprint of the house yourself, do that first. Measure the outside walls. It is useful to have a 100-foot reel tape measure for long dimensions and a 12-foot pocket tape measure for short distances. Measuring is much faster and easier

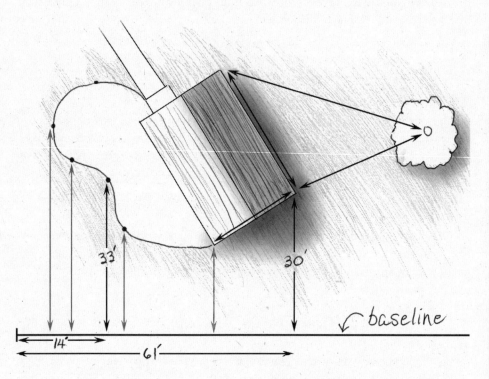

33'   30'

baseline

14'   61'

You can locate landscape features by measuring from the baseline or by triangulation.

with two people. Make a very rough sketch of the house and write in the measurement of each wall as you go along. It doesn't matter what your sketch looks like, just get down the necessary measurements.

Now that you have the dimensions of the house, you need to establish its location in relation to your boundary lines. You will need stakes and a ball of twine. Run a length of twine between two stakes along one fairly straight edge of your property. This is your baseline. Using additional stakes and string, stretch twine from the baseline—and perpendicular to it—to one corner of the house. Measure the string, and note the measurement on your sketch. Do the same with the next corner. Draw in that wall of the house, and compare the distance between pegs against the measurements you have already taken of the house. They should, of course, be the same. Lay out the rest of the walls on your plan.

Triangulation is a method of establishing the placement of landscape features by measuring from two fixed points on the house. To find the location of a tree in the lawn, take string and tack one end to a corner of the house; stretch it out to the tree and measure the length of the string. Note that dimension on the plan. Select another point on the same wall of the house, and do the same again. Tack string to that point and stretch it out to the tree. Jot down the dimension. The wall of the house forms the third side of a triangle, and you now know the length of all three sides, which establishes the location of that particular tree in relation to the house.

Curving beds or paths can be laid out on the plan using the same technique. At intervals along the baseline, take measurements perpendicular to it, and outline the curving shape using these points as a guide.

When I was mapping out our property, rock outcrops were a significant part of the landscape, so I included these on the plan. Put in any important surface feature of your landscape. Now study your plan. See if you can spot ways of relating separate elements to the whole by linking them with paths or ground covers.

Cover your finished plan with a piece of transparent tracing paper and try making new patterns over those that exist. Change the shapes of beds; add or subtract trees. Study and play with your plan. Even if you don't see how to use it now, your time won't have been wasted. Keep in mind that making a plan is a way of getting to know your land.

Appendix B
Common-to-Latin-Name Index and Recommended Plants

❧

COMMON-TO-LATIN-NAME INDEX

Recommended Perennials

COMMON NAME	LATIN NAME
Adam's needle	*Yucca filamentosa*
Astilbe	*Astilbe × arendsii*
Barrenwort	*Epimedium*
Black snakeroot	*Cimicifuga racemosa*
Black-eyed Susan	*Rudbeckia fulgida*
Blazing star or Gayfeather	*Liatris spicata*
Bleeding heart	*Dicentra*
Blue star	*Amsonia tabernaemontana*
Boltonia	*Boltonia asteroides*
Border phlox	*Phlox paniculata*
Bugleweed	*Ajuga reptans*
Calamint	*Calamintha*
Catmint	*Nepeta*
Christmas fern	*Polystichum acrostichoides*
Christmas rose	*Helleborus niger*
Cinnamon fern	*Osmunda cinnamomea*
Coralbells	*Heuchera × brizoides*
Creeping phlox	*Phlox stolonifera*
Daylily	*Hemerocallis*

COMMON NAME	LATIN NAME
Double sunflower	*Helianthus × multiflorus*
European ginger	*Asarum europeum*
False indigo	*Baptisia australis*
False sunflower	*Heliopsis helianthoides*
Fumitory	*Corydalis lutea*
Gayfeather or Blazing star	*Liatris spicata*
Globe thistle	*Echinops*
Goat's beard	*Aruncus dioicus*
Green and Gold or Goldenstar	*Chrysogonum virginianum*
Helen's flower or Sneezeweed	*Helenium autumnale*
Hosta or Plantain lily	*Hosta*
Interrupted fern	*Osmunda claytoniana*
Joe-pye weed	*Eupatorium purpureum*
Lady's-mantle	*Alchemilla mollis*
Lamb's ears	*Stachys byzantina*
Lenten rose	*Helleborus orientalis*
Lilyturf	*Liriope muscari*
Lungwort	*Pulmonaria*
Maidenhair fern	*Adiantum pedatum*
Meadow rue	*Thalictrum rochebrunianum*
Mugwort	*Artemisia lactiflora*
Mullein	*Verbascum*
New England aster	*Aster novae-angliae*
New York aster	*Aster novi-belgii*
Ornamental onion	*Allium*
Ostrich fern	*Matteuccia struthiopteris*
Peony	*Paeonia lactiflora*
Plantain lily	*Hosta*
Primrose	*Primula*
Purple coneflower	*Echinacea purpurea*
Royal fern	*Osmunda regalis*
Russian sage	*Perovskia atriplicifolia*
Sage	*Salvia*
Sedum or Stonecrop	*Sedum*
Siberian bugloss	*Brunnera macrophylla*
Siberian iris	*Iris sibirica*
Sneezeweed	*Helenium autumnale*
Solomon's seal	*Polygonatum*
Speedwell	*Veronica*
Spotted dead nettle	*Lamium maculatum*

Stonecrop or Sedum	*Sedum*
Threadleaf coreopsis	*Coreopsis verticillata*
Wild sweet William	*Phlox divaricarta*
Willow-leaf sunflower	*Helianthus salicifolius*
Yarrow	*Achillea*
Yellow archangel	*Lamiastrum galeobdolon*
Yellow foxglove	*Digitalis grandiflora*

Recommended Shrubs and Small Trees

COMMON NAME	LATIN NAME
Arborvitae	*Thuja occidentalis*
Blue mist shrub	*Caryopteris × clandonensis*
Boxwood	*Buxus*
Bumalda spirea	*Spiraea × bumalda*
Butterfly bush	*Buddleia davidii*
Dwarf Alberta spruce	*Picea glauca* 'Conica'
Dwarf Colorado blue spruce	*Picea pungens* 'Glauca globosa'
Japanese barberry	*Berberis thunbergii* var. *atropurpurea*
Japanese holly	*Ilex crenata*
Juniper	*Juniperus*
Miniature mountain laurel	*Kalmia latifolia* form *myrtifolia*
Oakleaf hydrangea	*Hydrangea quercifolia*
Purple smokebush	*Cotinus coggygria* 'Royal Purple'
Rhododendron	*Rhododendron*
Rose-of-Sharon	*Hibiscus syriacus*
Shrub rose	*Rosa*
Spirea	*Spiraea japonica* 'Little Princess'
Sweet pepperbush	*Clethra alnifolia*
Threadleaf Japanese maple	*Acer palmatum* 'Dissectum'
Thunberg spirea	*Spiraea thunbergii*
Variegated euonymus	*Euonymus fortunei* 'Emerald Gaiety'
Variegated red twig dogwood	*Cornus alba* 'Elegantissima'
Variegated yellow twig dogwood	*Cornus sericea* 'Silver and Gold'

Recommended Perennials for Sun

Achillea / Yarrow / Zones 3–10

Given full sun, good drainage, and adequate air circulation, yarrows are drought-resistant, long-blooming additions to the border. The delicate ferny foliage is either green or gray-green. Flat flower heads are made up of many little daisylike blossoms crowded together and come in shades of yellow, white, and cerise. Several new cultivars are particularly appealing: 'Salmon Beauty', pink 'Appleblossom', and cream-colored 'Hope'.

Alchemilla mollis / Lady's-mantle / Zones 4–8

Pleated, scalloped, gray-green leaves; frothy chartreuse flowers in early summer. Needs moisture-retentive soil and prefers some shade at midday. If the soil is moist enough, can take full sun.

Allium / Ornamental onion / Zones 4–8

Although they grow from bulbs, these ornamental onions form clumps. They can be planted and divided like any other clump-forming perennial. *Allium tuberosum* has upright blue-green blades of foliage and domes of starry white flowers in late summer. Be sure to remove dead heads or you will have hundreds of unwanted plants. *Allium senescens* 'Glaucum' produces a low, swirling mat of blue-green leaves and small pink pom-pom flowers late in the season. Doesn't self-sow.

Amsonia tabernaemontana / Blue star / Zones 3–10

A fine all-around perennial with excellent willowlike foliage on 2-foot stems; pale, sky-blue flower clusters in mid-May (Zone 6). Upright clump of leafy stems looks handsome all season and turns a clear yellow in fall. Tough native plant.

Artemisia lactiflora / Mugwort / Zones 4–10

This artemisia has divided dark-green leaves. Artemisias with silver foliage are beautiful, but *only if they have perfect drainage*. They cannot, therefore, be recommended without reservation. *Artemisia lactiflora*, on the other hand, is a tolerant plant. Though it would prefer moist soil, it isn't fussy. Can take some shade. A 4- to 5-foot sheaf of upright stems produces airy masses of minute white flowers. Use as a filler between other tall perennials.

Aster novae-angliae / New England aster / Zones 4–9

Many cultivars have been developed from the native species, but most have foliage problems. The leaves drop off the bottom third of the stem. Authority Joseph Hudak recommends heavy mulching to help retain moisture, which improves foliage performance. August-blooming 'Alma Potschke' has reasonably good foliage and long-lasting, shocking-pink flowers on 3-foot stems. Eddison favorite.

Aster novi-belgii / New York aster / Zones 4–9

The same foliage problems. 'Hella Lacy' is an exception, a 4-foot-tall winner with gorgeous masses of rich purple flowers in September and October.

Baptisia australis / False indigo / Zones 3–9

Attractive native perennial with handsome blue-green foliage divided into leaflets. This 4-foot early-summer bloomer has flower spikes resembling a loose head of blue lupine.

Boltonia asteroides / Boltonia / Zones 4–9

"Asteroides" means starlike, which is a perfect description of the masses of white daisy-type flowers. Blooms in September in the author's Connecticut garden. Excellent upright blue-green willowlike foliage.

Calamintha / Calamint / Zones 5–9

Calamintha grandiflora is a mound-shaped plant with little mauve-pink, lipped flowers. Nice edger. More colorful than C. *nepeta nepeta* but not quite as neat with regard to habit.

Calamintha nepeta nepeta (See page 49.)

Coreopsis verticillata / Threadleaf coreopsis / Zones 3–10
(See page 50.)

> Recommended cultivars: 'Zagreb'—egg-yolk yellow, dense foliage habit; 'Golden Shower'—similar to 'Zagreb'; 'Moonbeam'—pale yellow, looser foliage habit, and less permanent in the garden.

Echinacea purpurea / Purple coneflower / Zones 3–10
(See page 50.)

> Recommended cultivars: 'Bright Star'—orange cone surrounded by slightly drooping, crushed, raspberry-colored petals (rays); 'Magnus'—same color scheme but larger flower with petals that don't droop; 'White Luster'—creamy white petals; 'White Swan'—pure white petals.

Echinops ritro / Globe thistle / Zones 3–10

A large clump-forming perennial, 3 feet tall, with thistle-like foliage and prickly-looking, silver-blue flower heads as round as large marbles. Wonderful foil for daylilies. Recommended cultivar: 'Taplow Blue'.

Eupatorium purpureum / Joe-pye weed / Zones 3–10

For a large garden only. This imposing native is gorgeous as structure and handsome in flower. Can rise to 8 feet (more in wet soil). The cultivar 'Gateway' has an extended season of bloom from the last week in July until mid- to late September, the flowers changing color from rose to russet.

Helenium autumnale / Sneezeweed / Zones 3–10
(See page 50.)

Recommended cultivars: 'Butterpat'—all yellow; 'Riverton Beauty'—yellow with brown central knob; 'Bruno'—shades of red and rust.

Helianthus × multiflorus 'Flore Pleno' / Double sunflower / Zones 3–10
(See pages 50–51.)

Helianthus salicifolius / Willow-leaf sunflower / Zones 4–10

This sunflower has very good-looking foliage. The shiny dark-green leaves are long, narrow, and pointed—hence, willow-leaf. While the plant is cold-hardy, it blooms too late for the colder zones (Zone 4 and possibly Zone 5). The flowers are bright yellow with small, dark centers.

Heliopsis helianthoides / False sunflower / Zones 4–9
(See page 51.)

Recommended cultivars: 'Golden Greenheart'—double yellow with greenish tinge at center; 'Light of Lodden'—semi-double, bright yellow; 'Karat'—single yellow flowers.

Hemerocallis × hybrida / Daylily / Zones 3–10
(See pages 44–46.)

Note: For a list of daylily display gardens approved by the American Hemerocallis Society, contact AHS Executive Secretary Elly Launius, 1454 Rebel Drive, Jackson, Mississippi 39211. Phone: (601) 366-4362.

The following recommended cultivars are Eddison favorites for the Northeast and other cold climates. RED: 'Ed Murray'—very dark, velvety red; 'Chicago Ruby'—rich crimson-red; 'Ruby Throat'—color similar to 'Chicago Ruby'; 'Pardon Me'—small bright red. PALE YELLOW: 'Renee'—very floriferous, small flowers; 'Brocaded Gown'—huge, crepe-textured flowers; 'Wynnson'—lovely rounded flowers; 'Butterpat'—masses of little starry flowers. GOLDEN YELLOW: 'Stella De Oro'—only re-bloomer in my garden, many small, neat flowers; 'Condilla'—a beautiful double flower; 'Bengaleer'—huge, handsome gold. PINK: 'Lullaby Baby'—creamy pink; 'Becky Lynn'—rose-pink; 'Chorus Line'—medium pink with rose band in center; 'Delightsome'—true pink with ruffles; 'Jolyene Nichole'—rose-pink. NEAR WHITE: 'Joan Senior'—the best! ORANGE: 'Rocket City'—marmalade with darker eye; 'Hot

Ember'—fiery red-orange, well named; 'Paprika Velvet'—big, handsome red-orange. PURPLE: 'Little Grapette'—vigorous, small flowers, the color of "red flame" grapes.

Heuchera × brizoides / Coralbells / Zones 3–10

The ivy-shaped leaves can be blunt or pointed and form neat mounds from which wiry stalks of tiny red, pink, or white flowers arise. Long-blooming and attractive as a foliage plant if you provide humus-rich, well-drained soil.

Recommended cultivars of *H. × brizoides:* 'Chatterbox'—pink; 'June Bride'—white; 'Firebird'—red.

Recommended species: *Heuchera americana* 'Pewter Veil' is a beautiful foliage plant, dark-red leaves overlaid with pewter-gray; *Heuchera micrantha* 'Palace Purple'— valued for its foliage, which is deep purple-red.

Iris sibirica / Siberian iris / Zones 4–10
(See page 47.)

Recommended cultivars: 'Caesar's Brother'—purple velvet blossoms; 'Gatineau'— sky-blue; 'Ego'—rich sea-blue; 'Navy Brass'—dark blue-purple; 'White Swirl'— white, wavy falls; 'Butter and Sugar'—yellow and white; 'Harpswell Haze'—light blue, dark veins.

Liatris spicata / Gayfeather or Blazing star / Zones 3–9

Narrow leaves form a grassy tussock from which the flower spikes rise to 2 or 3 feet. Tuft-like flowers start opening at the tip and continue in descending order. Mauve-pink 'Kobold' is the most popular cultivar.

Nepeta / Catmint / Zones 3–10

Note: Most available nepetas belong to one of two species: *N. × faassenii* or *N. mussinii.* They are very similar, and either is fine. One-foot mounds of gray-green foliage and sprays of lavender-blue flowers are common to both. The mounds have a spread of about 18 inches. The cultivar 'Six Hills Giant' is twice that size.

Paeonia lactiflora / Peony / Zones 2–8
(See pages 46–47.)

Recommended cultivars: PINK: 'Mrs. F.D.R.'—huge double, early; 'Sea Shell'—single, mid-season. WHITE: 'Festiva Maxima'—double, early, has scarlet flecks among petals; 'Ann Cousins'—double, mid-season; 'Krinkled White'—single, early. RED: 'Jaycee'— disease-resistant, double, early; 'America'—single, early, good habit; 'Burma Ruby'— not always disease-resistant, but the most glorious color, single, early. CORAL PINK—a new color in peonies: 'Coral Charm'—semi-double, early, lovely color.

Perovskia atriplicifolia / Russian sage / Zones 5–9

A charming, most useful perennial with small, ferny, gray-green leaves and tall gray stems supporting long-blooming sprays of lavender-blue flowers. Good drainage is important to this plant from Turkey and Iran. Attractive curving gray stems in winter.

Phlox paniculata / Border phlox / Zones 4–8

Note: Every gardener loves phlox for its huge cumulus clouds of pink, red, white, or lavender flowers. But humus-rich, moisture-retentive soil is *essential*. Otherwise, the leaves get mildew and look awful. The clumps of leafy stalks should be thinned to a few sturdy stems every spring and divided every third year, at least. Border phlox is included in this list of recommended perennials, not because it is bulletproof, but because both Martha McKeon and Lynden Miller grow it beautifully—which proves it can be done. Alas, in the dry Eddison garden, it has never been a great success. Any named cultivar is beautiful.

Rudbeckia fulgida / Black-eyed Susan / Zones 3–9
(See page 51.)

Salvia × superba / Sage / Zones 5–10

Narrow, dense spikes of blue-purple flowers rise from clumps of pebbly-textured gray-green leaves to a height of 2 feet. Bloom early summer and continue blooming for several weeks. Cut back the flowering stems for another flush of bloom. Needs good drainage. Recommended cultivar 'May Night'.

Sedum / Stonecrop / Zones 3–10

There are several sedums that furnish the garden with long-season appeal. *Sedum* 'Autumn Joy' is an all-time Eddison favorite. (See pages 48–49.)

> Recommended species and cultivars: *Sedum kamtschaticum*—clumps of smooth green leaves topped with chrome-yellow flowers in starry clusters; *Sedum* 'Vera Jameson'—plum-gray foliage, pink flowers; *Sedum* 'Ruby Glow'—gray foliage with red edge, carmine flowers.

Stachys byzantina / Lamb's ears / Zones 4–8

Rarely does a common name so perfectly describe its subject. The leaves are the shape of lamb's or goat's ears and covered with soft, silver-white fur. The flower stalks are whitish and furry also, with tiny maroon blossoms tucked into the dense pile. Grown chiefly for the leaves, which form low mats. Hates wet sites but otherwise is very tough and handsome from spring through early winter. Rake vigorously in the spring to remove rotted leaves.

ꝏ

Thalictrum rochebrunianum / Meadow rue / Zones 5–10

Tall stems tinted purple rise from clumps of lacy, blue-green foliage to as much as 7 feet and bear large sprays of dainty lavender-pink flowers. The hollow stems must be staked—one stake per stem. Can take some shade. Exceptionally long season of bloom.

Verbascum chaixii / Mullein / Zones 5–10

Mullein is a spiky, useful plant for well-drained soil. Blooms early summer and adds height to the garden. Narrow spires of pale yellow flowers with purple-pink anthers. There is also a white form.

Veronica longifolia / Speedwell / Zones 4–10

A desirable plant with narrow, tapering flower spikes. 'Sunny Border Blue' is the pick of the crop. Beautiful, deep blue-purple color.

Yucca filamentosa / Adam's needle / Zones 4–10

A big clump of stiff, sword-shaped leaves gives rise to a tall, rather ungainly flower spike of whitish bells. The beauty of the plant is in the outstanding and unusual form of the foliage. The variegated cultivars are especially handsome year-round. My favorite is 'Golden Sword', with glowing yellow leaves striped in green.

Recommended Perennials for Shade

Ajuga reptans / Bugleweed / Zones 3–10

Ground-covering rosettes of leaves spreading by means of runners. Deep-blue flowers. Some cultivars have colored foliage. 'Variegata' is white and green. Large-leaved 'Catlin's Giant' has foliage that turns bronze in winter.

Aruncus dioicus / Goat's beard / Zones 3–9
(See page 58.)

Asarum europeum / European ginger / Zones 4–8

Beautiful low-growing foliage plant with polished kidney-shaped leaves. Insignificant spring flowers blooming close to the ground.

Astilbe × *arendsii* / Astilbe / Zones 4–8
(See pages 57–58.)

Recommended hybrids and species: 'Bressingham Beauty'—rich pink plumes; 'Bridal Veil'—loose, graceful white sprays; 'Etna'—deep-red spikes; *A. taquetii* 'Superba'—tall, late-blooming lavender-pink flower spikes.

Brunnera macrophylla / Siberian bugloss / Zones 3–10

Spring bloomer with sprays of vivid blue forget-me-not flowers, lasting for weeks. Cut flowering stems to the ground and a mound of large, handsome, heart-shaped leaves will fill in. Tolerates dry shade.

Chrysogonum virginianum / Green and Gold, Goldenstar / Zones 5–10

Low mats of coarse green leaves covered for a very long period with yellow, five-petaled, daisylike flowers. Spring bloomer that reblooms in fall. Adaptable, but grows best with some sun and can take full sun.

Cimicifuga racemosa / Black snakeroot / Zones 3–10
(See page 58.)

Corydalis lutea / Fumitory / Zones 5–10
(See page 59.)

Dicentra / Bleeding heart / Zones 3–10
(See pages 58–59.)

Digitalis grandiflora / Yellow foxglove / Zones 3–10

A true perennial with one-sided flower spikes. It has the typical finger-fitting, tubular flowers in pale yellow with brown markings inside. Blooms early summer. Rosettes of long, pointed leaves. Three feet tall.

Epimedium / Barrenwort / Zones 4–8
(See page 57.)

> Recommended species and cultivars: *E. grandiflorum* 'Rose Queen'—rosy-pink flowers; *E. g.* 'White Queen'—very showy, large white flowers; *E.* × *versicolor*—yellow-and-white flowers; *E.* × *rubrum*—crimson-and-cream flowers and foliage veined in red.

Ferns / Zones 5–8
(See pages 55–56.)

> Recommended species: *Adiantum pedatum*—maidenhair fern; *Matteuccia struthiopteris*—ostrich fern; *Osmunda cinnamomea*—cinnamon fern; *O. claytoniana*—interrupted fern; *O. regalis*—royal fern; *Polystichum acrostichoides*—Christmas fern.

Helleborus niger and *H. orientalis* / Christmas rose and Lenten rose, respectively
(See pages 56–57.)

Hosta / Plantain lily / Zones 3–9
(See pages 53–55.)

Note: Where snails are a significant garden pest, try growing hostas as container plants.

Recommended cultivars: BLUE: 'Blue Angel'—mature leaves are huge, as much as a foot wide; 'Hadspen Blue'—small, neat blue leaves; 'Blue Umbrellas'—very large blue-green leaves; 'Krossa Regal'—unusual vase-shaped plant with tall, gray-blue leaves. GOLD: 'Piedmont Gold'—large, handsome gold leaves with puckered texture; 'Gold Edger'—neat, heart-shaped leaves 3 inches wide, rapid grower; 'Sum and Substance'—huge chartreuse leaves of heavy substance, feels thick and satiny. VARIEGATED: 'Frances Williams'—large blue-green leaves with wide gold edging; 'Gold Standard'—large golden leaves with narrow dark-green margin; 'Francee'— dark green with white edges, large leaves. GREEN: 'Royal Standard'—large, rather narrow leaves, very shiny, flowers are white and fragrant; 'Green Fountain'—good ground cover; long, pointed leaves, rich green.

Lamiastrum galeobdolon / Yellow archangel / Zones 3–9

The cultivar 'Herman's Pride' is an Eddison favorite. Clump of upright stems to 1 foot tall surrounded by green leaves netted with silver. Tiers of pale-yellow flowers appear in late spring, encircling the stem for a few inches at the top; attractive all season.

Lamium maculatum / Spotted dead nettle / Zones 3–10

Good as groups or ground cover. Easy to grow and tolerant of dry shade. *L. maculatum* 'Beacon Silver' has pewter-gray leaves narrowly edged in green and pink, mintlike flowers. 'White Nancy' is similar but has white flowers.

Liriope muscari / Lilyturf / Zones 5–10

A truly indestructible plant of great value in the front of either a shady or a sunny border. Clumps of broad, grasslike leaves remain attractive all season. Small, narrow spikes of violet-blue flowers appear in late summer. The variegated-foliage forms are the most appealing.

Recommended cultivars: 'Silvery Sunproof'—yellow-white-and-green leaves; as name suggests, can take full sun; 'Variegata'—cream-and-green foliage.

Phlox divaricata and *Phlox stolonifera* / Wild Sweet William and creeping phlox / Zones 4–9

P. divaricata has lavender-blue or white flowers in clusters at the top of stalks a foot high. A native of the northeastern and north-central United States. Very pretty in late spring. Forms colonies of spreading stems from which the flowers arise. Cut back after flowering.

P. stolonifera has leafy runners that cling to the ground and send up 6-inch stems bearing clusters of blue, mauve, pink, or white flowers.

> Recommended cultivars: 'Home Fires'—hot pink; 'Pink Ridge'—medium mauve-pink; 'Blue Ridge'—lavender-blue; 'Bruce's White'.

Polygonatum / Solomon's seal / Zones 4–9

An elegant woodland plant at home in shade anywhere. Arching stems clad in elliptical leaves sport narrow, dangling greenish bells in late spring. *P. biflorum* is 3 feet tall; *P. commutatum* soars upward to 6 feet tall. Grow them in groups as a ground cover or among hostas and ferns. The most beautiful of all is a Japanese variety: *P. odoratum thunbergii* 'Variegatum', which has reddish stems and gorgeous leaves edged and tipped in white.

Primula / Primrose / Zones 5–9
(See pages 52–53.)

> Recommended species: *P. denticulata*—drumstick primrose; *P. acaulis* or *P. vulgaris*—common primrose; *P. polyanthus*—polyanthus primrose; *P. japonica*—Japanese candelabra primrose.

Pulmonaria / Lungwort / Zones 3–10

P. officinalis has clumps of elongated, heart-shaped leaves splattered with silver dots. Flowers arrive very early in spring and last a long time. The pink buds turn into lavender-blue flowers. Both colors appear on the plant at once. *P. rubra* has solid-green leaves and terra-cotta-red flowers. There are several cultivars of *P. saccharata*, including 'Mrs. Moon', with large, irregular silver spots. All need good, humus-rich soil and are not tolerant of dry shade.

Deciduous Shrubs and Small Trees for the Perennial Garden

Acer palmatum 'Dissectum' / Threadleaf Japanese maple / Zones 5–8

'Dissectum' is a name given to a whole group of beautiful small maples with finely cut leaves. Most are between 6 and 12 feet high at maturity. My 'Crimson Queen' is 25 years old, only 4 feet high and 10 to 12 feet across. 'Viridis' and 'Green Filigree Lace' have dainty green foliage and a similar mounding habit.

Berberis thunbergii var. *atropurpurea* / Japanese barberry / Zones 4–8

For colorful foliage, neat habit, ease of culture, you can't beat barberries. Cultivars of variety *atropurpurea* offer deep reddish-bronze leaf color. The plants can be sheared into neat forms and in the winter look solid and handsome hung with small, oval fruits. For the best color, plant in full sun. A Miller favorite for the border.

223

Recommended cultivars: 'Rose Glow' grows to about 5 feet. In spring, the new red-purple foliage is spattered with bright pink; 'Crimson Pygmy' is smaller, lower-growing—only 2 feet tall and 3 feet wide, without the pink variegation.

Buddleia davidii / Butterfly bush / Zones 5–9

A tall, wonderful addition to the perennial border that blooms from midsummer to hard frost. Well named, the narrow, gracefully drooping flower clusters in shades of lavender-pink, purple, and white attract flocks of butterflies. Long, wandlike branches grow 6 feet or more in a season but usually die back to the ground in northern gardens. Cut to stubs in the spring.

Caryopteris × *clandonensis* / Blue mist shrub / Zones 5–9

Compact, twiggy shrub with a rounded outline. The attractive foliage is aromatic and blue-green in color. Fuzzy blue flowers appear in every leaf axil in the late summer.

Clethra alnifolia / Sweet pepperbush / Zones 3–9

A native shrub that flourishes in wet places and tolerates most soil conditions. Forms a dense clump 6 to 8 feet tall, covered with small, upright pink or white flowers in mid-summer. Very fragrant. Foliage turns brilliant yellow in the fall.

Cornus alba 'Elegantissima' / Variegated red twig dogwood / Zones 2–8

An Eddison, Miller, McKeon favorite for its lovely variegated green-and-white leaves in summer and handsome red stems in winter. Grows to 8 feet. Cut old stems to the ground every few years. According to Michael Dirr, this is not a good performer south of Zone 8.

Cornus sericea 'Silver and Gold' / Variegated yellow twig dogwood / Zones 3–8

Very similar to *C. alba* 'Elegantissima'. Leaves edged in creamy-white, but with bright yellow stems for the winter garden. Again, this is not the plant for southern gardens.

Cotinus coggygria 'Royal Purple' / Purple smokebush / Zones 5–8

Gorgeous, rich red-purple foliage makes purple smokebush a dramatic accent plant for the perennial garden, but it *must* be contained by pruning. Cut it down to between 18 inches and 2 feet in the spring. Otherwise, it will become the huge shrub it wants to be. The hard pruning robs it of the fluffy puffs of sterile hairs that give it its common name. Easy to grow.

Hibiscus syriacus / Rose-of-Sharon / Zones 5–8

Upright, fan-shaped growth habit; can be grown as a multistemmed shrub or small tree. Its great charm is the large, hollyhock-type flowers that come in pure white, white with a dark red eye, and soft lavender-blue. It blooms heavily in midsummer and continues to produce a few flowers until frost. Unfortunately, the flowers are favored by Japanese beetles.

Hydrangea quercifolia / Oakleaf hydrangea / Zones 5–9

Large, handsome lobed leaves turn mahogany-red in the fall and persist until Christmas. In July, white conical flower heads. Grows well in shade.

Rosa / Shrub roses for the perennial garden / Zones 5–8
(See page 192.)

Recommended species and cultivars: 'Carefree Beauty'—semi-double pink, 3 to 4 feet; 'Carefree Delight'—upright, rounded shrub, 4 to 6 feet tall with pink flowers; 'Carefree Wonder'—low-maintenance, grows 3 to 4 feet, lavender-pink, single flowers; 'Bonica'—a tallish, upright shrub rose with good foliage and small pink flowers with buds like miniature hybrid tea roses; 4 feet by 5 feet; 'The Fairy'—excellent, bushy 4-foot plant covered all season with sprays of little pink flowers. ALL MEIDILAND VARIETIES—'White Meidiland' is low-growing, 2 feet high but spreading to 4 feet, with pure white flowers. Easy to grow. Look for the name Meidiland in the cultivar designation. These satisfactory shrub roses come in shades of red and pink. RUGOSA HYBRIDS: 'Sarah Van Fleet'—double pink flowers on a vigorous shrub; 'Blanc Double de Coubert'—semi-double white on large, disease-resistant shrub; 'William Baffin'—deep-pink flowers on canes 12 to 14 feet; 'Frau Dagmar Hartopp'—single pink, very fragrant.

Spiraea × *bumalda* / Bumalda spirea / Zones 3–8

Fine, twiggy growth habit makes this tidy shrub a favorite in Martha McKeon's border; 2 to 4 feet high, but can be kept trimmed into a neat round bush that produces flat, fuzzy, deep-pink flower heads from June to August. Shear in the spring and again after the first flush of flowers.

Spiraea japonica 'Little Princess' / Zones 3–8

A cultivar of low-growing Japanese spirea that makes a lovely, low mound of dainty leaves 2 feet high and 3 feet wide topped with pink flowers. Shear in the spring and again after flowering.

Compact Evergreen Shrubs for the Perennial Garden

Buxus / Boxwood / Zones 5–9

Recommended species and cultivars:
Buxus microphylla var. *koreana* / Korean boxwood / Zones 5–9

Hardier and more compact than the common boxwood of English gardens (*B. sempervirens*), this variety can survive −20°F. It does discolor somewhat in the winter, but otherwise is a beautiful disease- and insect-resistant plant with small, shiny evergreen leaves suitable for the perennial border or to plant as a hedge. 'Wintergreen' is an improved cultivar with superior winter foliage. Its natural shape is tidy and globular, and it can be pruned into a tight ball. 'Green Velvet' is a cross between Korean boxwood and common boxwood and reputed to remain evergreen in the winter. About 3 feet tall and 3 feet wide at maturity.

Buxus sempervirens 'Graham Blandy' is a very upright, narrow form of common boxwood that can be used as an accent. Height 6 feet, but only a foot wide.

Euonymus fortunei 'Emerald Gaiety' / Variegated euonymus / Zones 5–8

If you don't have reliable snow cover, growing variegated euonymus in Zone 5 may be pushing it a little. Otherwise, this is an invaluable, indestructible plant. As a ground cover, it will sweep over a bank 8 feet in all directions. It can also climb by means of rootlike projections, or it can be pruned into a ball. The leaves are dark green edged in white and turn pinkish in winter.

Ilex crenata / Japanese holly / Zones 5–8

Similar to boxwood, this holly has little evergreen leaves and a neat, dense, rounded habit. Can be clipped into formal shapes and used in the border, planted as a hedge, or included in foundation plantings. Quite shade-tolerant. 'Helleri' is a favorite with Betty Ajay, planted in quantity as a choice ground cover.

Juniperus communis 'Pencil Point' / Juniper / Zones 5–8

A well-named cultivar with a narrow, upright habit. Grows to 6 feet. Silver-blue in color.

Kalmia latifolia form *myrtifolia* / Miniature mountain laurel / Zones 5–8

While mountain laurel (*K. latifolium*) is a lovely, widely familiar native broadleaf evergreen, the miniature form is relatively new to the horticultural trade. Connecticut resident Richard A. Jaynes, Ph.D., has introduced some enchanting cultivars of this diminutive, 3-foot-tall form of mountain laurel. 'Little Linda' has very small leaves, fluted red buds and pink flowers; 'Tiddlywinks' has medium-pink flowers; and 'Minuet' has white flowers decorated with a maroon band. All are small in stature and leaf.

Picea glauca 'Conica' / Dwarf Alberta spruce / Zones 4–8

A familiar evergreen with very fine needles and a neat conical shape that answers the need for geometry in a perennial bed. My 25-year-old plant is about 8 feet tall. Spiral shapes and tiers are available from specialty nurseries.

Picea pungens 'Glauca Globosa' / Dwarf Colorado blue spruce / Zones 4–8

A great plant for structure in the border and elsewhere. Stiff powder-blue needles and dense, rounded shape—not a tight globe, but a bumpy, attractive round mound. 'Hunnewelliana' is neat and pyramidal with outstandingly blue needles. Grows to 3 feet in 10 years.

Rhododendron / Zones 5–8

Rhododendrons need no introduction. They are regularly included in foundation plantings and soon outgrow their allotted space. However, look for a group of small, compact rhododendrons called "yakusimanum hybrids." These were developed from the species *Rhododendron yakusimanum*, from the island of Yakusima in Japan. They rarely exceed 3 feet in height and width. Look for 'Yaku Angel', 'Yaku Duchess', 'Yaku Princess'. All have pink to white flower trusses and beautiful leaves lined with a feltlike coating called "indumentum."

Thuja occidentalis / Arborvitae / Zones 4–8

An attractive evergreen with flat fans of close-fitting, scalelike leaves. Unfortunately, they are the favorite food of deer, so choose spruce instead if you have a deer problem. Elsewhere, the cultivars 'Degroot's Emerald Spire' and 'Smaragd' are highly valued as narrow, pointed accents in the garden. Lynden Miller uses them at the openings in her hedge as "bookends" on either side of the gates.

Selected Further Reading

❧

Experience has taught me that gardeners buy more books than they have time to read. With this in mind, I have made a short list of indispensable books for self-taught gardeners.

The first three are large reference books. You really should have at least one of these, preferably all three. What makes these volumes outstanding is the people who wrote or worked on them. They know about plants and garden making from years of personal experience and from sound horticultural training. In addition, they write clear, readable English.

All three books are heavily illustrated, which makes them expensive. But color photographs are important if you are starting out and need to know what plants look like. Think of these books as a long-term investment. When you consider the cost of equipping yourself to ski or play golf, $150 is not outlandish.

BASIC REFERENCE WORKS IN A SINGLE VOLUME

Perennials for American Gardens, by Ruth Rogers Clausen and Nicolas H. Ekkstrom (New York: Random House, 1989).

All my favorite plants are among the 400 genera described. The most important genera have a substantial paragraph of general information followed by individual entries that give details about good garden species and cultivars.

Gardening with Perennials Month by Month, by Joseph Hudak. 2d ed., rev. and exp. (Portland, OR: Timber Press, 1993).

In the end, we all want flowers, and we want them to make pictures. The only way to make pictures is to assemble plants that bloom together. The month-by-month approach of this book is extremely helpful. It takes experience to combine flowering plants by blooming season. Mr. Hudak can save you years of trial and error. He is a teacher and landscape architect who has spent 40 years gardening in the vicinity of Boston.

Taylor's Master Guide to Gardening. Editor in chief: Frances Tenenbaum; editors: Rita Buchanan and Roger Holmes; illustrator: Steve Buchanan (Boston: Houghton Mifflin, 1994).

This splendid volume has a 200-page plant encyclopedia written by Rita Buchanan, and every entry is filled with the kind of I-have-grown-it-myself information that is priceless. In addition, there are excellent essays and dozens of high-quality photographs— garden scenes to illustrate design ideas, color schemes, and plant combinations; and individual portraits of trees, shrubs, vines, annuals, perennials, and grasses. I can't help mentioning that there are numerous photos of my own garden.

THE AMERICAN GARDEN GUIDES SERIES

These books are first-rate. Who better to advise home gardeners than experts from botanical gardens around the country? Each book in this series (there will eventually be 12 volumes) is compiled at the botanical garden or arboretum known for that particular type of plant.

The longest and most important section of each book is a plant encyclopedia called the "Plant Selector." So far, the volumes include *Perennial Gardening*; *Shrubs and Vines*; *Vegetable Gardening*; and *Herb Gardening*. *Perennial Gardening* was the work of Michael Ruggiero, who has been at the New York Botanical Garden since he was sixteen and is now senior curator of special gardens. Lynden B. Miller was a consultant on the project.

Each volume is full of excellent color photographs, but the guides are reasonable in price, around $25 each. They have soft covers that are flexible, but very tough, and just the right size to use and peruse.

ONE OF A KIND

Gardening by Mail: A Source Book, by Barbara J. Barton. 4th ed., rev. and updated (Boston: Houghton Mifflin, 1994).

No matter what you want for your garden, you'll find a source here. If you don't know what you want, you'll get ideas from *Gardening by Mail*.

The Gardener's Guide to Common-Sense Pest Control, by William Olkowski, Sheila Daar, and Helga Olkowski (Newton, Conn.: Taunton Press, 1995). As yet, I have not found an easy, accessible book about pest management. But this one is on the right track. It includes everything from weeds to mammalian pests.

PERENNIAL GARDENING I

To expand your repertory of building-block plants, get *Easy Care Perennials* and *Easy Care Shade Flowers*, by Patricia A. Taylor (New York: Simon and Schuster, 1989 and 1993). Modest in price, they are user-friendly, intelligently written, and smack of first-hand knowledge. Patricia Taylor's newest book is *Easy Care Native Plants* (New York: Henry Holt, 1996), which covers trees and shrubs as well as herbaceous plants.

PERENNIAL GARDENING II

Take the next step in perennial gardening under the guidance of Pamela J. Harper and Frederick McGourty, two wonderful gardeners.

Designing with Perennials, by Pamela J. Harper (New York: Macmillan, 1991), has it all: beautiful photographs by the author, literate prose, and inspiring advice about weaving a herbaceous tapestry. The author's forte is unusual plant combinations in subtle color harmonies.

The Perennial Gardener, by Frederick McGourty (Boston: Houghton Mifflin, 1989). The author's lighthearted, humorous tone makes the valuable information in his book easy to digest and fun to read. You will find plans for perennial borders; and useful plant groupings, such as long-flowering perennials and annuals for the perennial border.

WILDFLOWERS

Wildflowers in Your Garden: A Gardener's Guide, by Viki Ferreniea (New York: Random House, 1993). If you have a shady place or want a woodland garden, this book provides superb, step-by-step advice and lovely photographs by the author. It includes in-depth discussions of basic gardening techniques like soil preparation and plant care, in addition to garden plans and designs.

GRASSES

One inspirational and educational book stands out: *Ornamental Grasses: The Amber Wave,* by Carole Ottesen (New York: McGraw-Hill, 1989). A chapter entitled "A Few Good Combinations" is especially helpful, even to a rank beginner. Ditto a section on the care of grasses.

SHRUBS AND TREES

You'll need *Shrubs and Vines* from the American Garden Guides to look up plants that appeal to you. Take the next step with Michael A. Dirr's *Manual of Woody Landscape Plants* (Champaign, IL: Stipes Publishing, 1975). It is the self-taught gardener's shrub bible. Because the line drawings are of leaves and twigs only, some familiarity with the plants is necessary to appreciate the wealth of the information in this book.

ROSES

Reliable Roses, from the Serious Gardener Series, The New York Botanical Garden; co-author, Michael Ruggiero; series editor, Thomas Christopher (New York: Clarkson Potter, 1997). An authority you can trust.

COLOR

I highly recommend two next-step books for self-taught gardeners who become obsessed with color.

Color Echoes: Harmonizing Color in the Garden, by Pamela J. Harper (New York: Macmillan, 1994), is a beautiful book. The title refers to the repetition of a hue or a tint of that hue in two or more plants, a wonderful way to create unity. You will get all sorts of ideas for harmonious plant associations.

Color in Your Garden, by Penelope Hobhouse (Boston: Little, Brown, 1984), is not easy bedtime reading, but if you are really interested in how color works in the garden, it is a must. The photographs are numerous and excellent.

GARDEN PATHS AND STEPS

Garden Paths: Inspiring Designs and Practical Projects, by Gordon Hayward (VT: Camden House, 1993), is clear, well-written, and a grand book for both ideas and how-to information.

DESIGN

Backyard Design, by Jean Spiro Breskend, with photographs by Karen Bussolini (Boston: Little, Brown, 1991), is full of useful ideas for dividing and making the best use of outdoor space. Look for pictures of Ragna Goddard's garden, with its handsome rose-covered trellis walls.

GARDENING THEORY AND PRACTICE

I don't know what heading describes Hugh Johnson's book *The Principles of Gardening* (New York: Simon and Schuster, 1979). The line of text beneath the title is probably the most accurate summary: "A guide to the art, history, science, and practice of gardening." If you read, mark, learn, and inwardly digest this book, you will know a great deal about gardens and gardening.

AUTHOR'S FAVORITE

The Country Garden, by Josephine Nuese (New York: Charles Scribner's Sons, 1970). To me, Josephine Nuese is one of the unsung heroines of American gardening. When did you last read a gardening book that made you laugh until you cried? For many years, Mrs. Nuese wrote a weekly gardening column for a paper in northwest Connecticut. Her columns covered every event, dilemma, joy, and experience that a home gardener meets, and she wrote about them with wit, intelligence, understanding, and modesty. The best of these wonderful gardening essays are gathered in this book.

Index

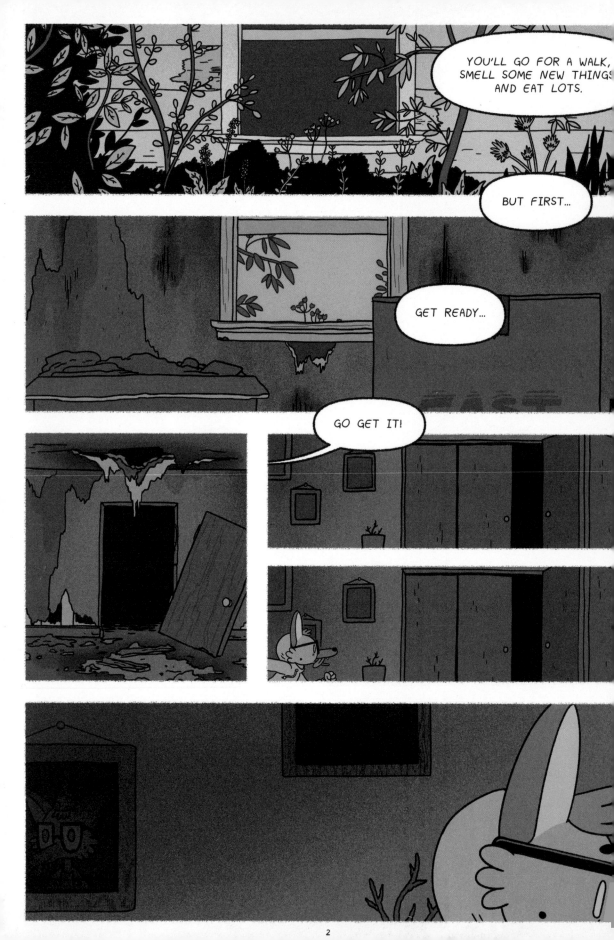

GARBAGE NiGHT

NiGHT BY JEN LEE

NOBROW

LONDON | NEW YORK

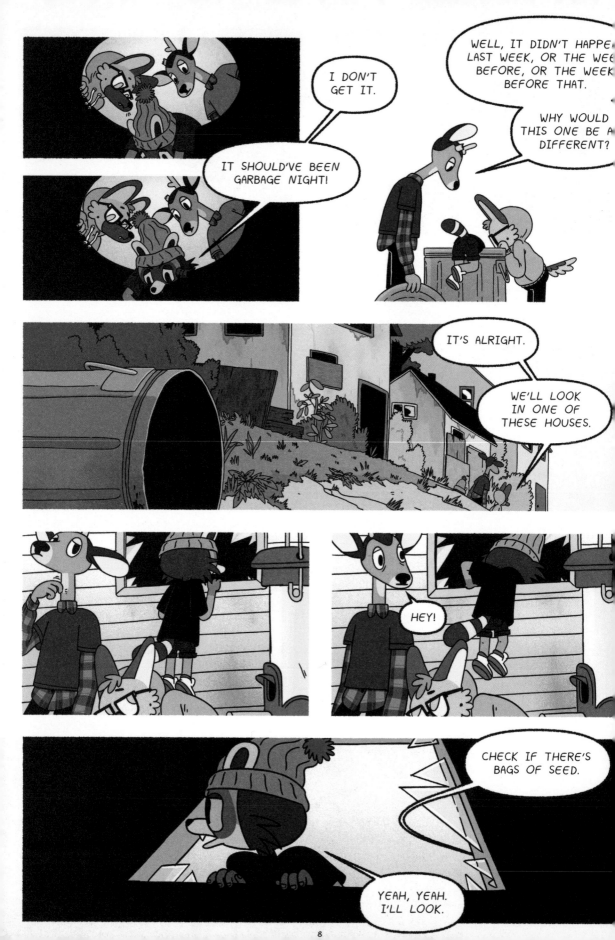

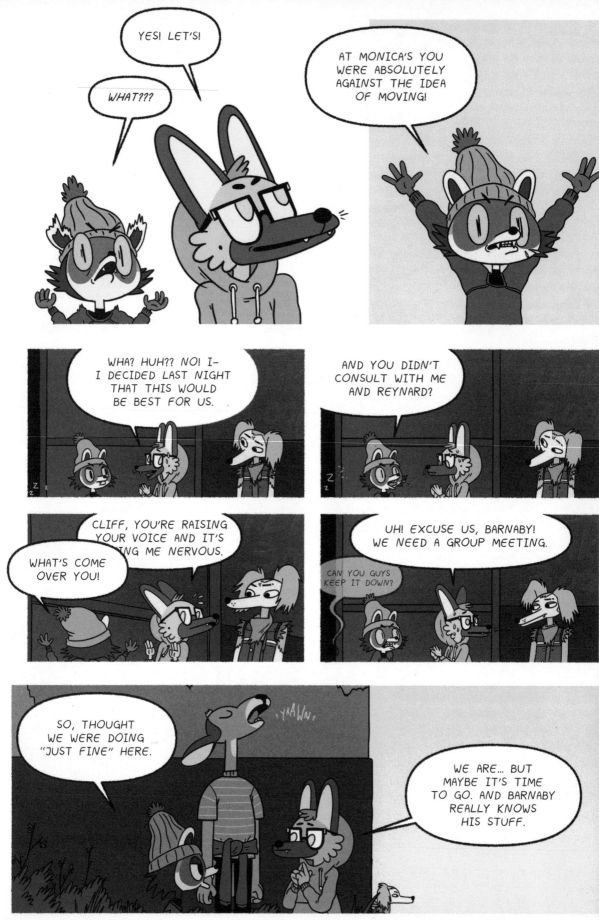

HA! A STREAM.

IT MIGHT LEAD TO A...

LISTEN, I'M JUST SAYIN' HE'S KIND OF A JERK TO ME AND REYNARD.

HE'S NOT TRYING TO BE. HE LIKES TO GET THINGS DONE, THAT'S ALL.

IT'S REALLY NICE OF BARNABY TO BE HELPING US. I'D SAY THAT'S THE OPPOSITE OF A JERK.

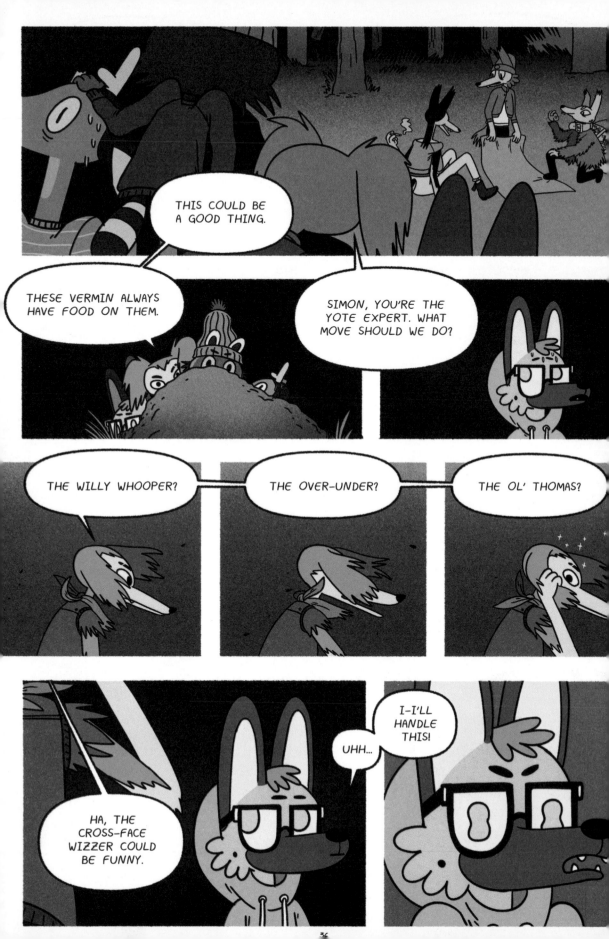

AGH!

WHOA!

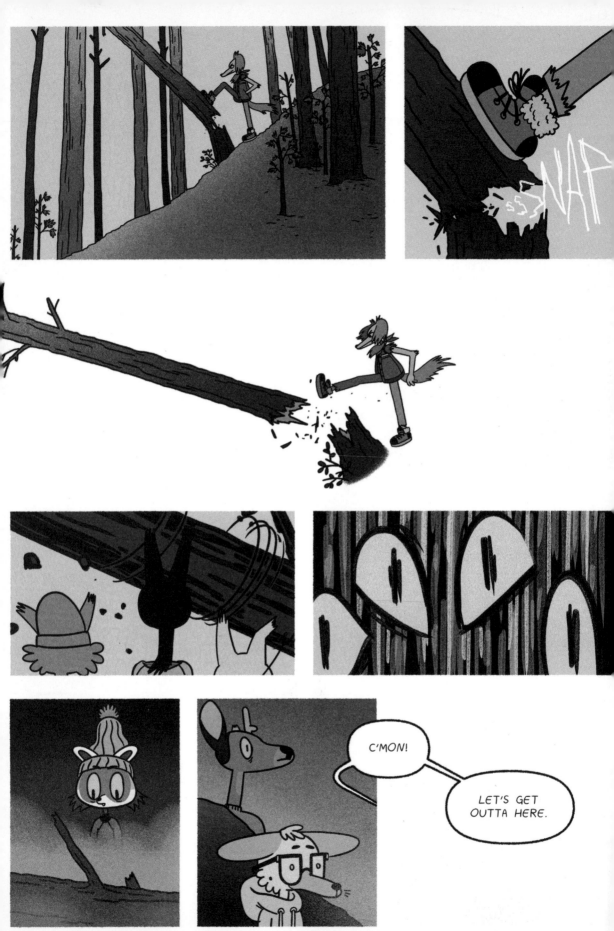

WEATHER'S NOT LOOKING SO HOT. WE'LL STAY HERE FOR THE NIGHT.

I LOVE GOING TO BED ON AN EMPTY STOMACH, DUNNO ABOUT YOU GUYS.

ALSO LOVE IT WHEN OTHERS DON'T PULL THEIR WEIGHT AND EXPECT FOOD TO JUST FALL INTO THEIR SCRAGGLY PAWS.

GUESS YOU CAN'T BLAME THOSE WHO GREW UP LOITERING IN THE DARK, EATING TRASH.

I'M SORRY MY PLAN WITH THE COYOTES DIDN'T WORK. I SHOULD'VE BEEN BRAVER.

YOU ARE NOT THE PROBLEM.

WHAT'S YOUR PROBLEM. I DIDN'T DO ANYTHING.
YEAH, EXACTLY! YOU DO ABSOLUTELY NOTHING.
OU MAKE NO EFFORT TO FIND ANY FOOD.
WE WOULDA BEEN TO THE NEW TOWN BY NOW. I'VE LOST COUNT HOW MANY DAYS BEHIND WE ARE.
I CAN'T EVEN EAT THE FOOD YOU FIND.
I BET I'M MORE STARVING THAN YOU.
JUST EAT A LEAF OR SOME TWIGS, I DON'T KNOW! I'M NOT YOUR MOM!
THIS ISN'T JUST ABOUT YOU. ME AND SIMON DO ALL THE WORK AND GET CRUMBS FOR IT.

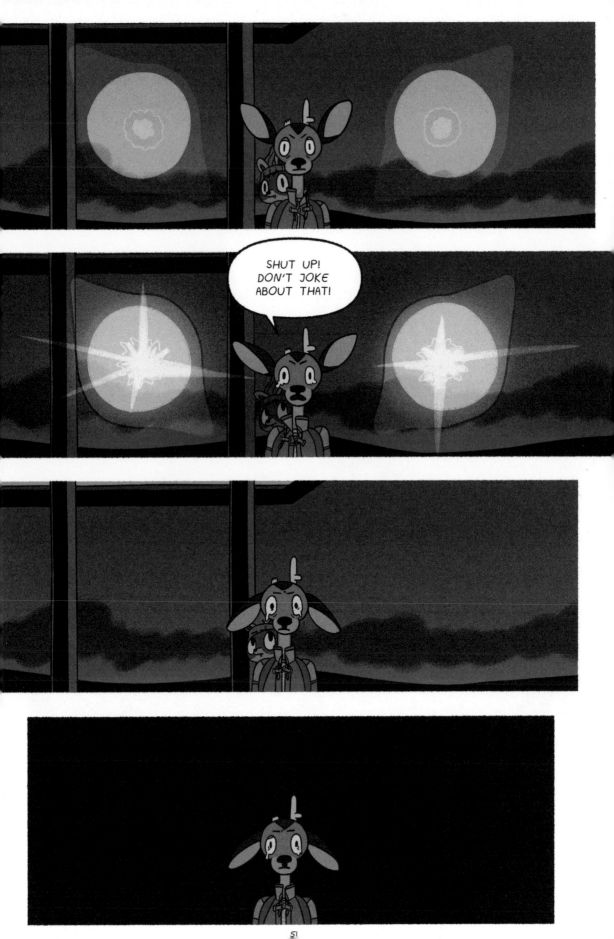

WELL, YOU'LL PROBABLY GET THAT CHANCE. I'M SURE WE'LL BUMP INTO HIM IN FALLBRIDGE.

HERE HE COMES, SWINGING OUTTA THE GATE, LIGHTENING UP THE MOOD AS USUAL.

HE'LL MOVE ON. HE SEEMS TO BE SEARCHING FOR MORE THAN JUST A NEW TOWN.

HOPEFULLY A BATH.

WHOA. HE MADE A JOKE!

I HOPE THERE'S A GOOD CAT POPULATION DOWN THERE. WHERE THERE'S CATS, THERE'S BANQUETS.

OH MAN! TO CELEBRATE GARBAGE NIGHT AGAIN.

WHAT'RE YOU GONNA DO WHEN WE GET THERE, SIMON?

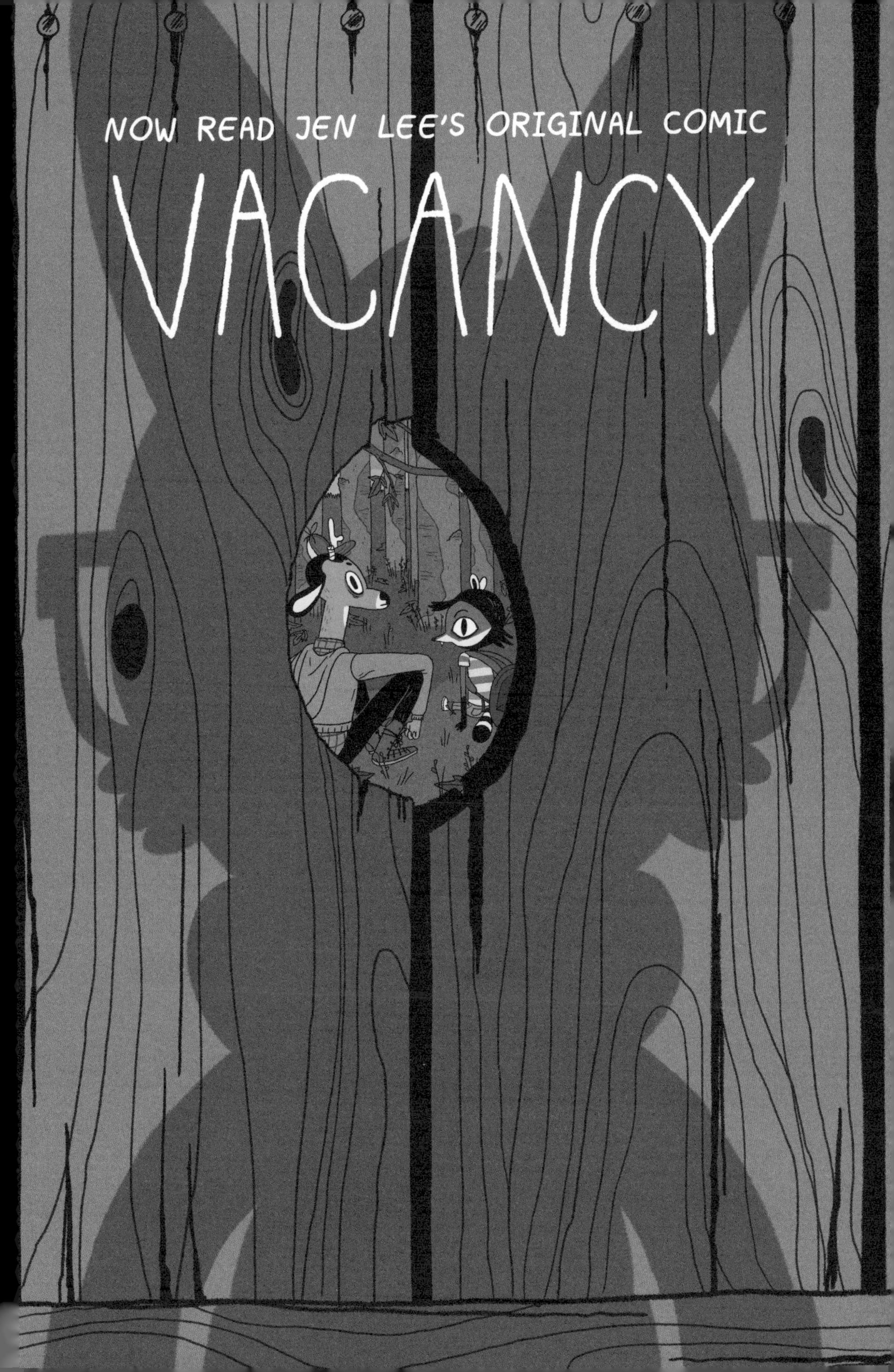
NOW READ JEN LEE'S ORIGINAL COMIC
VACANCY

A YEAR AGO...

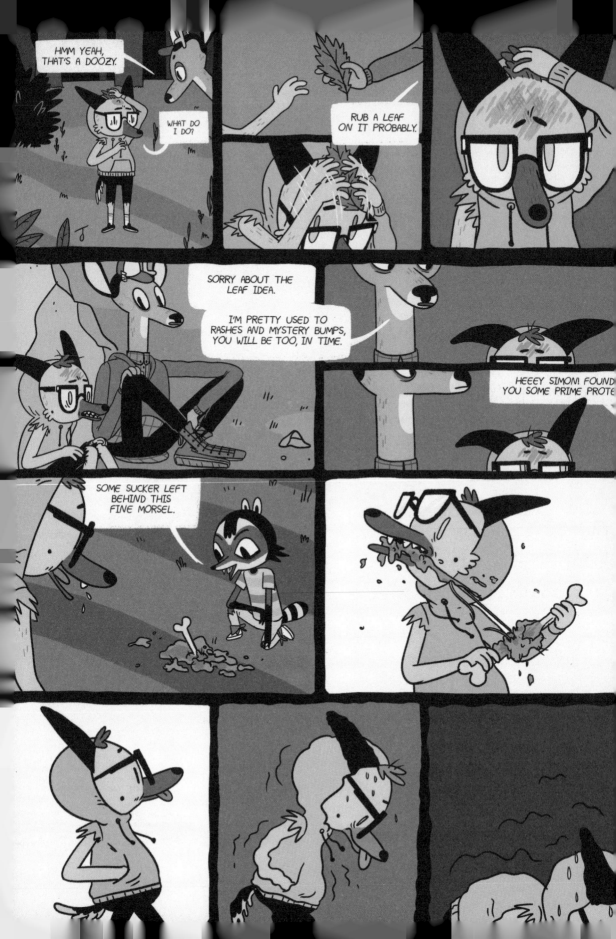

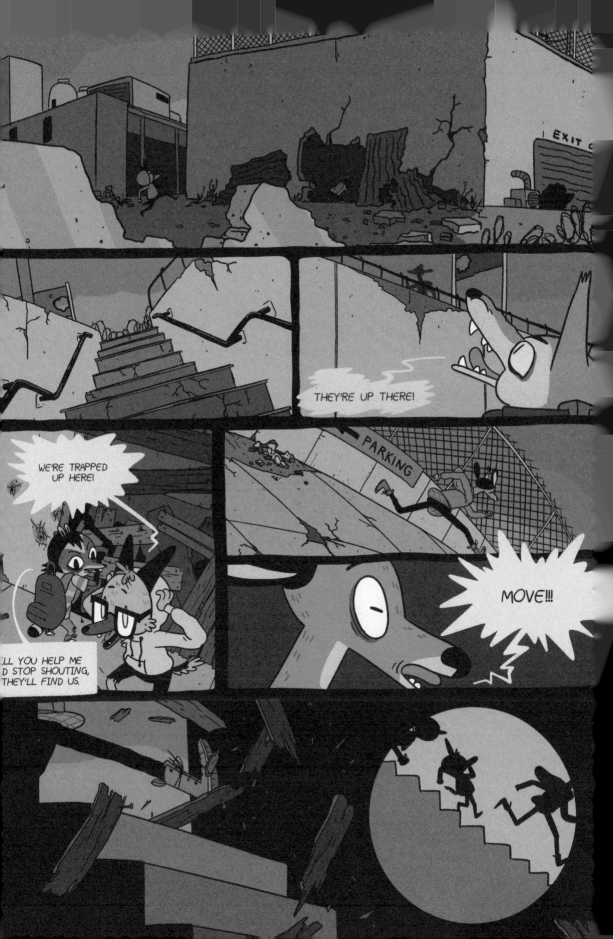

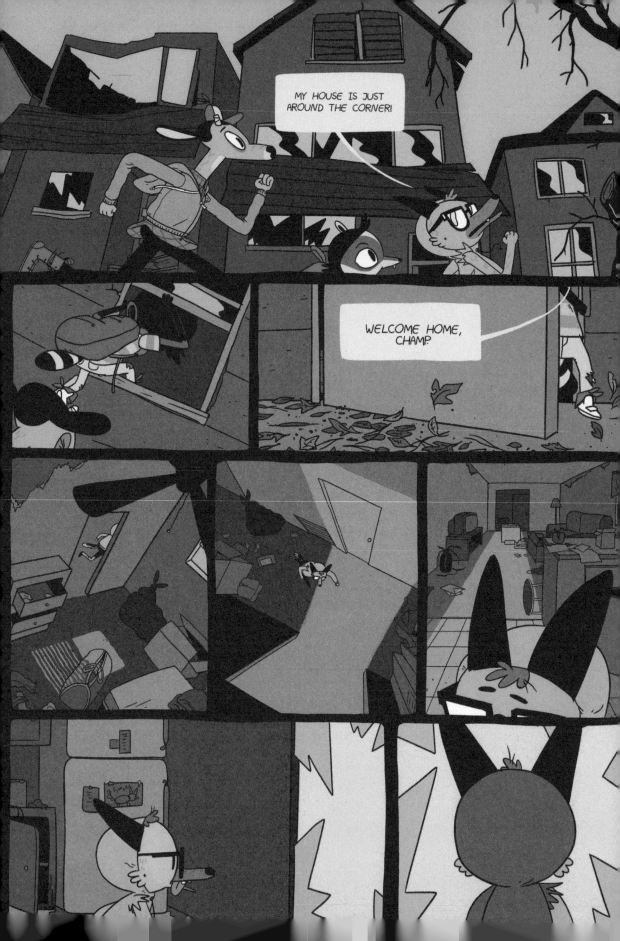